THREE FRIENDS

Roy Bedichek, J. Frank Dobie, Walter Prescott Webb

THREE FRIENDS

Roy Bedichek

     J. Frank Dobie

          Walter Prescott Webb

by WILLIAM A. OWENS

UNIVERSITY OF TEXAS PRESS

AUSTIN AND LONDON

International Standard Book Number 0-292-78012-5 (paper)
Library of Congress Catalog Card Number 70-82957

CONTENTS

I. A Truckload of Living

The letter was dated September 2, 1952, and was addressed to me. It was signed by Roy Bedichek, who drove his pickup truck to the door of the Archives Library of the University of Texas, to bring me the letter and a load of the correspondence that had been piling up on closet shelves, in paper cartons under beds, and, after his retirement, in a frame garage where there was constant danger from fire and termites. It was a relief to him to see the transfer cases disappear into fireproof vaults; it was a satisfaction to his friends to know that this record of living would not be lost.

In his letter to me he said, ". . . I have gone through at a hop, skip and jump the correspondence of fifty years. This accumulation that I could never keep with comfort nor throw away without misgivings is now cleared out and I have you to thank for the suggestion of entrusting it to the Archives. . . ."

Some of the letters may have been selected "at a hop, skip and jump," but not those of his two closest friends, J. Frank Dobie and Walter Prescott Webb. He apparently kept everything they wrote, including scraps and scribbles. In this one truckload he placed in the Archives Library for posterity the correspondence of a quarter of a century between himself and the other two, his highly intellectual, deeply trusting, fiercely competitive friends.

These are not random exchanges. They are the letters of three friends who lived near each other in the same town, worked for the same university, belonged to the same Town and Gown Club—who, in short, saw each other routinely. Letters were not necessary for exchanges of information except on the occasions when one or the other left Austin for a spell. They were intensely necessary for communication. The three talked endlessly, but talk was rarely finally satisfying. They would go home late at night after hours of wrangling over a point, and then be at the typewriter early the next morning putting into letters the clinchers overlooked or not sufficiently underlined in the discussions of the night before. Both Bedichek and Webb confessed that they looked upon letter writing as a literary art. Dobie seemed to regard it less highly, but some of his letters contain literary passages of high quality, as good as anything he wrote.

For Bedichek and Webb, publication of their letters was at least a hope, if the manner of publication could be suitable. After Bedichek had turned down one would-be editor of his letters, Webb wrote him:

I have read the enclosed correspondence with great interest. While I sympathize with your refusal to permit X[1] to make capital of your letters (and that in my opinion is his high secondary purpose if not his primary), I do not feel so sympathetic with your general attitude in reference to the publication of your letters. I have concluded that the time has come for us here in the South and the Southwest to have our say, through publication of letters, diaries, and autobiographies. The New Englanders never suffered under the inhibitions of false modesty which stops the Southerner dead in his tracks. What is the result? They have dominated for more than a century the literary scene, and made New England until recently almost synonymous with American literature. . . .

My associations with these three men began one at a time, and as much by chance as by design. Dobie came first. In 1933, I had completed a Master's Degree in English at Southern Methodist University. We were deep in the Depression and there were no jobs; I was trying to find out what to do next. Henry Nash Smith, with whom I had studied writing, suggested that I go to see J. Frank Dobie at the University of Texas and ask his advice. Smith had already encouraged me in my interest in collecting Texas folklore and writing fiction about Texas life. He had also assigned me to read *Coronado's Children,* Dobie's best-known book at the time. After reading the book, I needed no urging to go see Dobie.

Austin is two hundred miles from Dallas and I had no money for a fare. With no other way to go, I hitched a ride on a freight truck, with a driver who went down one night and returned the next. We left Dallas at dusk and arrived in Austin after daylight. About eight o'clock I found Dobie's office at the university on the ground floor of Breckenridge Hall. The door was open and I could see him at his desk, writing. I had not warned him that I was coming, and as I saw him there I knew I should have. He was then past forty, with a wide reputation as teacher and as editor for the Texas Folklore Society. He would not have time for every student that came by.

I was there and I waited for him to look up. When I told him that Henry Nash Smith had sent me, he asked me to come in and sit down.

I sat on a wooden bench and leaned against the hairy side of a tanned cowhide. He faced me, his arms on the desk, his shoulders broad, his eyes blue and sharp, his

face round and friendly. He asked me why I had come
and I began telling him: I wanted to study more and
Southern Methodist University had no more to offer me.
I wanted to come to the university, but I would have to
work. Of the next three hours I know nothing, for I leaned
over on the bench and went to sleep while I was talking.

When I woke up, Dobie was still sitting at his desk,
working at his papers. I wanted to sidle out the door and
get back to the freight station. He did not let me. As if
nothing unusual had happened, he took up the conversation again and we talked until he had to leave the office,
mostly about the folk songs and games I knew, a little
about what I could expect if I came to the university.

I asked about jobs at the university; I asked at stores
along Congress Avenue. No luck. Then I walked to the
freight terminal for my ride back to Dallas. Nothing about
my future had been resolved, though Dobie had been as
helpful as he knew how to be. Over the long miles,
stretched out on boxes of freight, I had plenty of time to
think over the meeting. It was easy to know that something
of Dobie had stayed with me; it took me years to find out
how much.

Eight years later Dobie sent me to Bedichek. In the
meantime, I had been teaching, studying, and collecting
Texas ballads and songs on aluminum recording discs.
Dobie had convinced Homer Price Rainey, President of
the University of Texas, that the folklore of Texas should
be collected. At the same time he envisioned a series of
folk festivals as free and easy as old fiddlers' reunions.
On Dobie's recommendation, I was hired to record the
folklore and aid communities interested in running folk
festivals.

As there was no office on campus to manage such a
project, I was attached to the staff of Roy Bedichek, who

was then Director of the Interscholastic League, in the Division of University Extension.

On January 2, 1941, I reported to a dun-colored building in what is called "The Little Campus," early enough to find Roy Bedichek alone in his office. Through the open door I could see him bent over his typewriter, intent on whatever he was putting down on yellow copy paper. He stood up, a tall man, and leaned forward to shake hands with me. His face and hands had the brown-burned look of a farmer; his voice and manner were friendly. There was something hawklike in the tilt of his beak, the purse of his lips, the rising inflection of his laugh.

Details of my job had to be worked out, but they had to wait while we talked folklore and books, birds and the Interscholastic League. Our conversation got interrupted from time to time, but it went on most of the morning. At times I felt he was testing me for the job; more often he was talking because he loved to talk, not in chitchat but in wide gleanings from history, philosophy, and literature; not in pretentiousness—his words and anecdotes were too earthy for that.

Our talk went on as long as I was with him, and he never ran out of anything to say, though there were times of silence because he also appreciated silence. He also listened when he knew it was time to listen, as I soon came to know.

One of the early collecting trips he sent me on took me to the state prison farm near Sugar Land, to a field where white guards with shotguns and on horseback watched over Negro convicts hoeing. I went out to hear work songs of prisoners at work, but there was no singing. Their downcast faces, their sullen eyes showed there could be no singing in those fields. There was too much fear. Too upset by what I had seen to wait for night, when the convicts might feel free enough to sing, I headed for Austin, driving faster than the law allowed. I had to talk about what I had seen.

It was dark when I reached the edge of town. Bedichek would be in bed or on his way to bed. I telephoned him anyway and he met me outside his office. I told him what I had seen and felt, and apologized for my failure to get into what we both knew was one of the richest areas of Texas folklore. Except for details, I did not have to tell him. He knew enough of Texas prison life in general; he knew that the will to keep the Negro in his place was stronger in prison than out. I had never heard anyone so sympathetic to the Negro, or so concerned over the Negro question. He helped me understand a lesson I had begun to learn that day: To a collector, people must be more important than their folklore.

Bedichek's work with the Interscholastic League required him to travel all over Texas. At times I went with him. The trips I remember best were those that took us hundreds of miles into west Texas, where roads stretched ahead over flat, sparsely covered earth. New words like "pencil bush," "greasewood," and "caliche" came into my vocabulary; into my consciousness, the cadences of English poetry sounded above the hum of tires on concrete.

On the highways, we belonged to the out-of-doors; in the towns, we took part in the entertainment provided for us. After one of those trips he wrote me:

The day we had together during your last trip left me on a considerably higher level of spiritual well-being than I had been on in months, and I have always found you with that curious power. I think it is the depth and drive of your emotional make-up, your humor which is one phase of the emotions, and a keen intellect, and the instincts of a good healthy animal. Of this last, I shall never forget your dancing folk dances on the platform of the country club at Odessa. You seemed a kind of incarnation of Pan, not wicked, or wilful, but in fun-loving mood, and not in lust, but more as a mere joke, "ready to twitch the nymph's last garment off."

It took me less than a month to regard him not as boss but as friend.

My job with Bedichek lasted only from January to September. The work was not finished, and I was still as interested in folklore as on the day I started. Bedichek wanted me to continue; so did the university. But times were against the project. The war was close upon us, and communities that in normal times would have been interested in their folklore and culture were already embarking on projects related to war and defense. The German armies rolled east and west; Churchill's voice rolled across Texas, with every radio turned on. Bedichek understood that it was impossible for me to go on at that time.

My work yielded for the University of Texas some recordings of rare Texas songs, including a new one made up by "The Gray Ghost" and called "De Hitler Blues." For me, it yielded a great deal more, especially in the close association it brought me with Bedichek, Dobie, and Webb.

It was Bedichek who arranged my meeting with Webb. There was to be a meeting of junior historians at Hillsboro and Bedichek wanted me to attend. He called Webb and got him to take me up and back in his old coupé. It was more than a hundred miles each way, on a rainy night. At first I wondered why Bedichek had stuck me with Webb. He sat hunched over the wheel, his roundish face under the wide brim of a Stetson, his roundish eyes following the road through roundish glasses. He seemed to lack entirely the easy conversational manner of Bedichek and Dobie; at the time I would have described him as taciturn, a quality I would not have expected in a man who had expressed himself so well in *The Great Plains* and *The Texas Rangers.*

The trip up was not a total loss, but almost, from my point of view. The return was much better. He had the same rough exterior I had come to know in Bedichek and Dobie, but he was much shyer; talk did not come easy to him, with strangers or in groups. On the way back, when we were shut in by a wet night, he opened up a little, enough for me to see why Bedichek had sent me.

Webb talked about Texas history in a way I had not encountered before. In sixth grade I had been forced to memorize names of men and battles and important dates. They remained in my mind as that and little more. With Webb, the history of Texas was the history of people opening new frontiers, bringing a part of their past with them, acquiring a different character through the kind of living they met. Consciously or not, he was opening to me new ways of thinking about folklore and the people from whom I collected it, and clearer understanding of overlappings from people to people as well as from past to present.

I knew that Texas had attracted many nationalities, many cultures, to a land that went from timbered in the east to desert in the west. I knew the people of the timbered east: Anglo-Saxon, Cajun French, Negro. He knew the people from east to west, and how and when they got there, the ones I knew and others: Germans, Swedes, French, Englishmen direct from England. All were shaped in some way by what we called Texas, from cotton farmers in the river bottoms to nesters living in dugouts on the plains before barbed wire was invented.

I left Austin in September 1941. For the next ten years I saw these three friends with some frequency, except when I was a soldier overseas. With Bedichek I maintained correspondence, but irregularly, as his chidings often show. Then in 1952 I was on the university staff

for the summer as Director of the Oral History of Texas
Oil Pioneers, and we spent much time together, some of
it looking at the papers in his garage.

At the end of that summer, as I indicated earlier, Bedichek began transferring his papers to the Archives. Fortunately, Dobie and Webb also made gifts of their correspondence to the university.

One stipulation in Bedichek's letter of gift to the Archives Library is explicit: "The editing of my letters and
documents will be assigned to William A. Owens." In this
one sentence he opened to me intimately these three
minds. The gift given, they became even more generous:
They taped several hours of personal history, in a kind of
record that both identifies and illuminates them. Of the
strictly autobiographical, Dobie recorded little; from time
to time, however, he was writing the essays published post-
humously as *Some Part of Myself*. Bedichek and Webb,
as if they could see this book taking shape, taped the
stories that might be most useful to me.

Editing these letters was not an easy task. They represent the continuity of friendship for a quarter of a century,
but they come in sporadic outbursts and the subjects range
far afield. Dobie wrote, "Bedichek was a kind of peg on
which my happiest associations with Webb hung."[2] He
must perforce be the peg on which this book is hung. In
other words, the letters are between Bedichek and Dobie, or
Bedichek and Webb, but not between Dobie and Webb.
Bedichek was also often the spark that set the others off. In
the years before he became a writer of books, he read the
other two, appreciatively, and then wrote letters that
evoked further thought, additional arguments.

Their letters number in the hundreds, and selection became a problem. I chose to exclude from this book those
that do not in themselves have intrinsic value or do not

open avenues of thought, and those that seem to belong to another kind of publication.

The three men are rapidly becoming a Texas myth. My purpose is not to add to the myth—impossible, given some of their personal stories—but to present them in their real dimensions in the best way possible, through the letters they wrote to an intimate friend. Not one of the three needs more than that.

At first I tried to organize the letters according to subject matter. Such a unity might have been satisfactory, but it was impossible. So was a chronological order. Their minds were too encompassing, too full of lightning flash; their syntheses achieve full impact when come upon unaware by the reader.

Not laziness but a recognition of his basic rightness in a solution of the problem caused me to accept Dobie's advice to Bedichek, in a letter dated April 11, 1946, as the only unity possible in shaping this book:

. . . You are concerned with finding "a tough enough string to bind what I say into some sort of unity." Damn it, I gave you one sermon on the unnecessity of coherence, or of mechanical unity. The rhetoric teachers have probably stifled more vigor and reality than they have constructed style. The most delightful and meaty book of natural history I have ever read is W. H. Hudson's *Naturalist of La Plata.* The only strings that bind the parts of it together are geographical and personal. I have read other books by Hudson that were not even bound by geography. Writing of Hampshire, or of Cornwall, he is apt to be his best when he is reminded of something on the Pampas. Or take his *Hind in Richmond Park.* He lets his mind flow. What binds together Gilbert White's *Selborne?* It is bound together by the only binding that binds any book—the eager intelligence of the man, his powers of observation, his curiosity and thought.

I left some excellent things out of the last book I wrote, *A Texan in England,* because they seemed extraneous, and now with rue my heart is laden because I succumbed to the old rhetorical superstition. An auditor of one of Emerson's lectures tells how after Emerson started he dropped his manuscript and the sheets of paper fell into disorder. He picked them up as they were and went on reading his lecture, coming to the last paragraphs first. It did not make any difference. It is said that the way he composed was to write down thoughts as they came to him, put the sheets into a compartment, and then when the compartment was full, stick them neatly together.

As I told Tom Lea,[3] you write with more power, vigor, wisdom, freedom of mind, readability, and a lot of other virtues than any man I have ever met who had not written a book; for that matter, than any man I have ever met who *has* written a book. Bedi, you don't realize how good you are. Hell, go ahead and write as you please; let your wind blow you where it listeth. I'll guarantee to get you a publisher for the book. Of course it is natural for a writing man to be up and down on his own production. He puts all his energy into something; then he is drained and it seems to him that everything he has said or is capable of saying is ashes. The important thing is that he feels fire glowing in his belly while he writes. If he is one who has, as you have eminently, a sense of values, the virtue that has both consciously and unconsciously gone out of himself into the writing will be there, waiting for *virtus* to enjoy and feed upon.

You are incapable of writing thin, pavid stuff. Be of good cheer, my friend. Turn yourself loose on any item that you are engaged upon. The *unum necessarium* that Matthew Arnold was always talking about is, in writing, vitality. Everybody who has anything to say has a chemical mixture peculiar to himself in his own vitality. It is that unique mixture that will make everything in any book adhere into unity and coherence.

This is not to say that transpositions, excisions, braddings, solderings, rivetings are not practiced by the craftsman in the art of writing; but mechanical hinges to make one chapter open into another are extraneous, redundant, and damnable. A man of eager interests lives a lifetime in a house; he has good taste; he gathers pictures and hangs them on his walls; they talk to him; they interest and delight others who are capable of enjoying pictures. They have no art museum unity as respects schools and periods. Read the first paragraph in William Hazlitt's great essay on "The Feelings of Immortality in Youth" and you will get a microcosm of the essential unity that comes from vitality. . . .

The "mechanical hinges" in this book are, by design, kept to a minimum. Perhaps the most difficult problem in editing this correspondence arose from my own personal involvement with the writers. Letter after letter brings back experiences shared; voices on tape take me back in time and space. If objectivity appears at times to have been lost, it was lost because I feel the lasting effects of debts owed, of friendship unstinted.

II. Pioneers of Brush and Plain

These were remarkable men. It is fully as remarkable that they should have been at the same place at the same time, that their lives should have followed parallel courses for so many years, that their commingling should have so enriched and strengthened all three.

Together, they recorded a Texas era that, like them, will not appear again. The frontier, one of the chief shaping influences on their lives, is gone. With them, it was a constant element, not as an obsession but as an energizing force in their personal attitudes and the books they wrote. Naturalist, folklorist, historian—they all saw whatever they were writing through eyes farsighted from a lifetime of looking at unscarred horizons.

All three were from pioneer families; all three spent their childhood on the frontier. They never lost the effect of farm work on their rugged bodies, or the leathering of sun and wind on their faces. Outwardly they maintained the look of pioneers; inwardly, as urban and professional men, they were able in varying degrees to free themselves from the frontier sufficiently to become faithful recorders and severe critics of frontier life. The hold was never entirely broken, however: Sentimentality at times pervades their work, a sentimentality that may be ascribed to the experiences of their childhood, their closeness to the land, their love of life close to the land.

Their complete stories must and should be told by their official biographers, as evaluation of their works must be left to the critics. This is a collection of their letters, with only enough biographical detail to let the reader know who they were, where they came from, and the wanderings of their people. These are necessary if one is to appreciate fully the letters they wrote.

The "westerings" of their families are part of the frontier saga, different in detail but not in purpose. They all wanted land, better land from which to make a better living. For over a century the pioneer movement had flowed west, so that by the time Texas opened up, three streams of migration were discernible: from the East through northern Virginia into the Middle West and down; through the Southern mountain states from the Carolinas; and across the "Old Southwest," the lowlands of Georgia, Alabama, and Mississippi. The Civil War interrupted, delayed, but did not stay the flow. Indeed, many who did not want to fight escaped to Texas; many who stayed and were left in starvation by the war moved on as soon as they could.

Roy Bedichek was born in 1878 in a log cabin about fifty miles west of Springfield, Illinois, in the Sangamon Valley, the third generation on the northern migration route. His grandfather, Frederick Bedichek, had come to America from Czechoslovakia in 1819, by way of Switzerland. He settled first in New York, and then in northern Virginia, at what is now Buffalo, West Virginia. He married into a Virginia family, and, to make a living, built a furniture factory on the banks of the Great Kanawha River. In 1857, after the death of his wife and the loss of his factory in a fire, he took his three children and moved to western Missouri, where he settled at Columbus in Johnson County near the Kansas line, an area already torn apart over the slavery question.

Roy Bedichek's father, James Madison Bedichek, was seventeen years old when the Civil War began. In Missouri, loyalties were about equally divided between the North and the South. The Bedicheks chose the cause of the South, and Bedichek's father joined General Price's army. Wounded in battle, he returned home to recuperate, only to find himself caught in the guerrilla warfare between the Kansas Jayhawkers and the Missouri Bushwhackers. With a Minié ball lodged against the bone in his thigh, he had to be hidden under the floor to escape the Jayhawkers. Unable to get medical aid, he cut down to the bone with a razor and extracted the ball with a hook he had fashioned from a knitting needle.

When Bedichek's father was well again, he had to make a choice: return to Price's army or join a guerrilla band of Bushwhackers. He decided on the latter, and joined the group led by William Clarke Quantrill, a border hero at the time. He remained with Quantrill long enough to take part in the raid on Lawrence, Kansas, a center of abolitionists and Unionists. When he was past seventy Bedichek searched back through memory and recorded his father's story of the raid on tape:

I've heard him tell of the raid on Lawrence, Kansas. He rode down the street side by side with their horses breast to breast into Lawrence, Kansas, at the beginning of the raid. Of course it was Quantrill's strategy just as guerrillas usually do to make a sudden raid somewhere and then disperse and go underground for a while and then they would come together again and make another raid.

My father said that Quantrill was a blue-eyed fellow, light

hair, rather thin—that is, he was a rather lean fellow, medium-sized, and was very quick and active every way. He said that while they were riding down the streets of Lawrence, Kansas, Quantrill reached over behind his back and shot a fellow out of a window who had a shotgun or some kind of a rifle aimed at them as they were galloping down. Says he just reached over behind him—behind my father—and shot. My father said he saw him tumble with his gun out the window. Oh, it was fierce business. They didn't rob. They didn't rob to amount to anything.

They would take horses and my father had gotten hold of one horse—he'd had one horse killed—and he'd gotten hold of another horse. They had rounded up some horses and were there in a little open place close to the city, close to the town, and were getting on their new horses and taking instructions. My father said that this horse he'd gotten was an enormously tall horse, seventeen hands high, and he couldn't possibly get on it. The Quantrill band had all gotten mounted and were getting away. He said he was just fatigued. He'd been going the whole day long and it was a very exciting occupation and he tried to get on that horse and he couldn't. It wasn't saddled and he tried and tried. Presently he looked around and found that all of them were gone and he was there with this great big horse. There was a band of outraged citizens forming up there, of course, to take revenge on any laggards in the band, and he just saw himself being lynched right there on the spot. Presently he saw a fellow streaking back at a dead run towards him and he didn't know whether it was friend or foe. He just waited and it turned out to be one of the boys who at full speed went down under his arm—never got off his horse—just went down under his arm and gave him a boost and he got on his old horse and they rode off together.

Bedichek's father, only twenty-one when the war ended, had served in the regular Confederate Army and in border warfare, where conflicts were bitter, though usually small, and personal enough to be a kind of feuding. He was taken prisoner and spent time in a Yankee prison camp. By the time he was free again he had enough stories to last a lifetime.

The war over, Bedichek's father attended a normal school in Illinois, where he qualified for a teacher's certificate, and married another student at the school. They both became teachers and taught in frontier schools in Wisconsin and Iowa.

In 1884, Bedichek's father left his family in Iowa and went to Falls County, Texas, where he homesteaded a quarter of a section of land and established the Eddy Institute of Literature and Science. Bedichek's first letter was written to his father at Eddy, Texas: "Dear Father, Our pig is growing very fast and Cleveland is elected."

Nearly a year later Bedichek was brought to the Texas frontier:

I remember that it was just a bald prairie. We came in the heat of August just like it is now—drouth, drouth. It was the most dismal-looking place that I ever saw in my life coming right out of the cornfields of Iowa. My mother, who had been accustomed to pioneer conditions, she—it was just something so terrible to her that she—I remember she cried all the way from the train clear to the place six miles away that we went to. We were in an old wagon—an old farm wagon—in chairs, and it was bumpy and the road was rough and there were no fences and there was just dry grass as far as you could see. Oh, it was just a terribly dismal prospect.

When we got there my father had built a very nice little cottage and on the door of that cottage there was a design— an arched design made out of green broomweed that the neighbors—the neighbors had done this and it said "Welcome to Texas" spelled out in great big letters by wisps or rolls of this green broomweed. We found out later this old German lady by the name of Benedict had had the idea and she had come over as soon as she saw our father had left to go get his wife and children. She knew he'd be gone practically all day. She got the neighbors and they gathered the broomweed and made this welcome sign. You know it just helped my mother. There was no end. She'd been crying all the way. She was just as joyful when she saw that thing and she said, "Well, we're in just a fine place." Everything was all right after that.

By frontier standards everything may have been all right, but there were still many problems. It was farming country, thinly settled, and children of school age had to work on the farms. There were not enough students in the Institute to provide either enough work or income for Bedichek's father and mother. His mother bought a little mustang pony and got a school to teach about five miles away. Every morning she galloped off across the trackless prairie, as he said "going by directions, by guess, and by God." At night she came home to cook supper and mother her family. With their combined salaries and what they raised on the land, they got by.

Settlers were beginning to use barbed wire to fence their land, and Bedichek's father was caught in the fight between the farmers and free-range cattlemen. Bedichek remembered how the fight entered their own home:

As a matter of fact he had to defend the schoolhouse he had just built down there in Falls County with his pistol at night several times because they were determined—he was right in the middle of one of these fence-cutting feuds there and he had to defend his property and then the people on one side of the community didn't want any schoolhouse. The schoolhouse belonged to the settler class, the nester class, and they wanted to run the nesters out of the country. So they didn't want him to build a schoolhouse. So they tried to burn his schoolhouse

down. He slept with a pistol at his head and defended it on
several occasions when people were trying to get in there.

As a boy, Bedichek worked on the land and knew what
the ownership of land meant, and the hungering for it.
From Eddy, Texas, when he was thirty years old and still
a bachelor, he went pioneering himself, to take up land at
Deming, New Mexico, traveling not in the traditional
covered wagon but, as he tells us, on a bicycle:

> Then I made a visit home as I hadn't seen the home folks
> in a good while and I stayed there about three or four months
> and then I got a bicycle and I rode to Deming, New Mexico.
> Nine hundred and eighty-three miles or something like that
> with the roads like they were. Well, I done it. Yeah, I got
> tired of staying around home there and didn't want to teach
> any more. I was searching for land. I wanted land. I wanted
> to make me—I wanted to be a—I was just like Shakespeare
> in that respect. I wanted me a homestead, a place that I could
> be kind of a squire-like person. So I went out there. I got on
> the bicycle at Eddy, Texas, and I got off it at Deming, New
> Mexico, and I sold it to the barber who shaved me for twenty-
> three dollars and I'd given Montgomery Ward twenty-three
> dollars for it. So I got free transportation, and I had my
> camping outfit. I didn't sleep in a house but once during the
> whole trip. . . . I think it took me about three weeks but
> stopped several places longer than I needed to stop . . . and
> it was a terrible trip between El Paso and Deming. Oh, ter-
> rific. But I got there and then I fell in with some land pro-
> moters—people who were selling land, who were selling this
> desert land to good old Indiana farmers.

There was plenty of land to be taken up. Bedichek
filed on a tract eight miles southeast of Deming in the
shadow of the Florida Mountains. With the help of a jack-

leg carpenter he built a shack and then dug a well. He worked at improving the land, but he found he had to earn his living working in town, as secretary to the Chamber of Commerce.

At first he batched and then he married Lillian Greer, whom he had known at the University of Texas. They continued to live in the shack till their first child was born. Then they moved to town and became weekend pioneers. With this pretense of living on the land, a common practice at the time, they proved up on the claim and then on an additional tract of desert land.

Bedichek had the land but he did not become a "squire-like" person. He was one of the first to admit that as a farmer he was a failure:

I had built my dreams on that land. I thought that the country would develop and that the land would become more and more valuable, and I could sell off a little piece of my land that I proved up and develop the rest of it. Many farmers did make it that way—make it economically profitable—but it had to be under peculiar circumstances. A person had to be a real farmer to do it. It was a technique I didn't understand. I could write about it and tell about how this man made lots of money and that man made lots of money out of that land, but I couldn't do it myself. You know, as Bernard Shaw says, "Those who can, do it. Those who can't, teach." Well, that's the way I was. I was teaching them how but I couldn't do it myself.

Finally Bedichek was relieved of the burden of the land by his father, who had retired from teaching at seventy. With a new dream of pioneering in New Mexico, Bedichek's father and mother took over the land he had homesteaded. They put up a windmill and, by pouring water on the dry earth, raised all kinds of crops, and made the desert bloom.

Bedichek's father died at Deming, at the end of a long pioneer trail that took him from West Virginia to Missouri, Illinois, Wisconsin, Iowa, Texas, and, at the last, New Mexico. The character of the man shows clearly in Bedichek's account of his funeral:

They brought his body back to the family burial ground at Eddy, Texas, where he had spent much of his life in Texas, right there in that neighborhood, and they had the funeral there in the country church. I had heard of my father's death. They advised me about it and I hadn't shed a tear. I was sad, of course, but I knew that man is mortal. I wasn't touched so much by it, as I had been expecting it.

Well, we got into that little old church and something about the simplicity of the service and the rather natural eloquence of the preacher who preached the sermon wrought me up somewhat. Then something occurred that was a unique experience so far as I am concerned. That is, it shows the power of memory. In the old schoolhouse where I went to school as a boy and my father taught—it was a two-story affair—boys and girls would all line up and come into the schoolhouse and as they went up the stairs you could hear the tread of their feet. Three or four times a day I heard it. I didn't remember it. It didn't make much impression. It was just the tread of many feet on stairsteps or on the floor getting the school started again after an intermission of some sort—in the morning or at the noon intermission. They had arranged a section of the church for the seating of these school children that had gone to school to my father. They hadn't gone to school to my father perhaps, but it was the school they attended. The whole school attended because he was an old schoolteacher and he'd taught the fathers and grandfathers of some of these children. When these children came into that church and I

heard the tread of those feet with my father lying there in a
coffin, why, this old memory that had been buried—this tread
of feet—had been buried in my mind for forty years, it just
surged up in me and I saw the whole picture and I burst into
tears and I just wept like a baby. I couldn't resist it.

Then they had a very simple ceremony at the grave. It was
a country funeral and there were no morticians around. They
did it all. Friends would go and dig your grave and they'd
carry your coffin, and the preacher says a few words and they
put the dirt in the grave and cover you up. I've always liked
that kind of a funeral. It's so much more homely and people
have so much more heart in it.

Well, my father was very fond of wildflowers and it was a
season there where they'd had some rain and the wildflowers
were just abundant all over the country. Each child had gotten
a flower to put in the grave and the last thing they did after
they lowered my father's coffin, this school went by. Hundreds
of children went by, each with a bouquet of wildflowers to
throw into the grave, and they practically filled that grave up
with flowers and it was very beautiful and I was very much
affected by it, knowing the fondness of my father for the wildflowers that grew in that area.

Some time before his father's death, Bedichek had given
up pioneering and turned to newspaper work as a career,
to city dwelling, and to the ways of city men.

Live Oak County, Dobie's birthplace, is some two hundred air miles from Falls County, south and west, and on
a direct line between San Antonio and Corpus Christi. In
terrain, people, culture, the distance is much greater.

Falls County, in the black waxy belt that extends down
through the center of Texas, is bald prairie, with rich,
well-watered land, good for raising corn and cotton. Bedi-

chek described his neighbors as "the nester type"—farmers living fairly close together on small farms. They were chiefly of English origin; their culture was largely English.

Live Oak County, on the other hand, is in the brush country of southwest Texas—a sand and caliche land covered mostly with dust-gray thorny brush marked here and there by groves of gray-green live oak trees—a dry land, sparsely settled, good mostly for cattle ranching, and only when it is not overstocked, overgrazed. Nearer the Mexican border, it is a land of two cultures. Mexicans live on the ranches; Mexicans work the cattle. English is the language of the Anglo owner; border Spanish the language of the Mexican workers. Each has to learn a little of the other's language and ways.

James Frank Dobie was born in a three-room rock ranch house September 26, 1888, the son of Richard J. and Ella Byler Dobie.[1] A fourth-generation Texan, Dobie was able to listen with sympathy to the voices of both the Anglos and Mexicans.

Dobie's great-grandfather migrated from Virginia to Texas in 1830, while it was still Mexican territory. His three sons soon followed him. In the 1840s one son had died; the other two were ranching as partners in Harris County, in the Republic of Texas. Dobie's grandfather drowned there in a stream in 1857. In 1858, the remaining son moved west to Live Oak County. Dobie's grandmother followed there with her family in the 1870s. By then, though they were still on a frontier, the Dobie family had lived in Texas under four flags.

Dobie's father, not an educated man, turned to ranching—horses first and then cattle. In 1887 he married Ella Byler, a teacher in what was called Lagarto College, an elementary school in Live Oak County. She had attended a Catholic convent for a term and then a "female college" at Chapel Hill, Texas. As the years passed they added to their family, the rock house, and the ranch, till they owned seven thousand acres. The house was set in a grove of live oaks, in a bare yard swept clean to keep snakes from coming in. Barns and stables were so close that the house was never out of sound of a whinnying horse or a bawling cow.

Dobie grew up knowing horses and cattle. He absorbed early the pioneer's feeling for the land. Later he was to write, "I did not know it at the time, but I began listening to this piece of land talk while I was the merest child."[2] This land was fifty miles from the Gulf of Mexico. Gulf winds brought clouds but rarely rain. In spite of the dryness it was, for him, a land of rugged beauty. There were the large green live oaks near the house, and a view across the sandy stretches of Long Hollow, where they raised corn and vegetables. There were rough hills covered with mesquite and brush and prickly pear. When spring rains came, there were flowers, the yellows of prickly pear, the pink of primroses, the white of the guajillo bush.

From the time he was big enough to straddle a horse Dobie was out riding the brush, with Mexican cowhands, *vaqueros,* hearing the sound of their language, learning the stories they had to tell. The language of work was unwritten; so were the stories and songs. So the Mexican side of Dobie's culture was largely oral.

The Anglo was different. At home, there were books to be read. At night his father, a deeply religious man, read from the Bible and sang the hymns pioneers had carried westward with them.

Dobie listened to these voices, and his own voice is a mingling of the two.

Stephens County is between Fort Worth and Abilene, three hundred miles to the north of Live Oak County, half that distance to the northwest of Falls County. It is in the West Cross-Timbers, a strip of forest that extends from the Arkansas River in Oklahoma some four hundred miles south to the Brazos. This strip, from five to thirty miles wide, separates the east and west along its length; on one side the thick vegetation ends, on the other the barren wastes begin. For a period of time it served as a natural barrier between white men and Indians. The land, red clay under deep sand, was originally covered with scrub oak and blackjack. It could be farmed with the tools and methods brought by the settlers from back east. From here on west, new ways of farming had to be developed.

Webb's father and mother moved to Stephens County in 1892, on the last leg of a journey that began in Mississippi in the 1880s. Webb himself said, "My parents migrated from Mississippi to Texas about 1884, destitute products of the Civil War in search of new opportunity."[3] They stopped first in Panola County in east Texas, where the land was timbered and the people, like themselves, mostly from the Deep South, mostly still suffering from the wounds of the Civil War. Webb was born in Panola County April 3, 1888. Four years later his family gave up the familiar land of east Texas for the strange land of west Texas, in a move that was later to symbolize for him the emergence of the settlers from the timbered east to the treeless plains of the west, a move that forced adaptation to a new and forbidding environment.

Life was not easy for them in the Cross-Timbers. Webb said of his father: "My father was a country schoolteacher, self-educated, and he never had more than a second-grade certificate. He was one of the last fighting teachers, employed to 'hold school' in the country schools where the big boys had run the teacher off the year before. It was a rough life in a rough country. My father was paid a premium of $10 a month to teach these outlaw schools. He got $50 or $60 a month for a five-month term—an annual income of $250 or $300, supplemented by what he earned in the summer farming or working at anything that came up, at about seventy-five cents or a dollar a day."[4]

"Self-educated" implied a great deal in those days before there were normal schools in the area for teacher training. Webb's father had to study on his own at home and then take examinations at the county seat to qualify for a teaching certificate. The fact that he progressed from third-grade to second-grade certificate says a great deal for him, especially in view of statements like the following from Webb: "He also farmed a little on the side and we hadn't been out there very long before we hit the drouth of 1893 and 1895, and at that time there was no such thing as relief, and I think that in that drouth I saw examples of about everything that I wrote about later in *The Great Plains*."[5]

When Webb was twelve or thirteen his father homesteaded a quarter of a section of land in Stephens County. The land had been homesteaded before and deserted by the owner. According to Texas law, Webb's father had to pay the back taxes and live on the land ten years before it became his own. The burden of fear that they would lose the land drove them to work early and late. Webb's father built a plank house and they began clearing and plowing the stumpy new ground. For at least two years Webb did not go to school at all because his father was away teaching and he had to be responsible for planting and gathering crops, and all the other jobs a man had to do on a farm. He could later say with feeling: "From the time I was thirteen until I was seventeen seems an eternity."[6]

They succeeded in proving ownership to the land, and Webb's father returned to it after his teaching days were over. Webb escaped it, but not until it had left a mark that shows in everything he did.

III. School Bells and the Varmint's Cry

Schooling for these three friends came at the end of the nineteenth century, fifty years after education for all had become a part of the American dream, twenty-five years before the first compulsory school law in Texas attempted to make the dream real even to the dullards. Their personal stories of school days are more dramatic perhaps than the usual, but they illustrate clearly the formula of the times —work and study, study and work—a formula that had taken men of humble origins to the White House.

From the beginning, work held an important place in the morality of the American frontier. In church, boys and girls sang "Work, for the night is coming, When man's work is done"; in school, they recited Longfellow's "Let us, then, be up and doing, With a heart for any fate; Still achieving, still pursuing, Learn to labor and to wait." After Andrew Jackson, education became almost as much a part of the morality as work, and the two were inseparably linked.

To give every child a chance at education, public schools were to be located close enough to each other for every child to be able to walk to school, a plan not achieved in Texas until the twentieth century, and even then many a child went on horseback across land uninhabited except by the wild animals. Provisions had to be made for work as well as for study. Boys and girls set out for school after the morning's work was done; they hurried home to get the night's work done before dark. In either direction, they might be hastened by a wolf howl or a bobcat cry. At night, they read by firelight or candlelight, till coal oil out of Pennsylvania put lamps and lanterns in the reach of all. Schools opened late in the fall so that children could pick cotton or help with other kinds of harvest. They closed in the spring at crop-planting time. Three months. Four months. Five months. Country schools rarely ran longer any year.

Bedichek, Dobie, and Webb were more fortunate than most country boys and girls in Texas at the time. They were all sons of teachers. Under the influence of their parents, they all became readers at an early age, in regions where libraries were rare and where few families owned any books except the Bible. All three were brought up under the formula: work and study. For them another command was added: observe. Work, study, observe. The patterns of youth became the practice of maturity.

Bedichek was doubly fortunate. His father and mother were both teachers; they had attended normal school in Illinois; they had prepared for certification in a formal teacher training program. By the time Bedichek was old enough to go to school, his father was principal and, at times, the only teacher in the Eddy Academy of Literature and Science. Bedichek lived at the school and went to school to his father, of whom he said:

My father was a very original schoolteacher. He didn't believe in corporal punishment even in those days. The first thing he always said to the school was "Now, boys—" He would always have some great big old boys, big as he was. "Now, boys, nobody's going to get whipped here." He says, "We don't believe in punishing people by whipping them or anything like that." He put everybody on their honor and said, "We conduct the school as it should be conducted and, of course, if anybody gets so unruly that they can't get along as citizens of the school, they're just asked to get out and that's all." He taught them from the lowest grade on up through high school. I don't know how in the world he ever did but he did. They'd ride in sometimes from a distance of eight or ten miles. They all had horses, you know.

Bedichek's study habits, as he recalled them sixty years later, were not too different from those of other boys his age:

We had an enormous geography that I used principally to shield the book that I was reading from the teacher. I was a great reader and loved to read but I just despised this old geography, so I would just prop it up on the seat in front of me on my desk and I would have a book that I wanted to read right there and if the teacher's attention—that was usually my father—was turned in my direction I could ease the book I was reading down and stick it under the shelf where they held the books and be studying my geography lesson with a great deal of industry. I can't remember the name of that old geography though to save my life.

Other books he could remember:

We studied Mrs. Pennybacker's Texas history.[1] That's the first thing that I was introduced to. I learned it by heart. I could say it from the beginning to the end before I got through it. Mrs. Pennybacker's *History of Texas*. I can repeat some of it even yet. For instance, the massacre at Goliad. "The next day was Palm Sunday. What a day to choose for such a deed!" And then she goes on, you know. A few years ago I tried to repeat the Battle of San Jacinto and almost got through it. I don't think I could do it now though.

There were also the McGuffey readers:

The standard reader was the McGuffey series, and I think that I've gotten more inspiration out of the McGuffey series of readers than I got out of any other reading that I did during those years. I can tell you a great many of the stories that are in the old McGuffey readers and they just simply made a tremendous impression on me. One that I needed and needed very badly was the story of the farmer and the larks. The moral sunk into me, and I've needed it all my life because I was always so derned lazy trying to get somebody else to do something for me and finally I wake up some morning and I can't get it done any other way, by gosh, I'll do it myself.

These were the books required of most school children at the time. Bedichek had access to many more:

My father sent to England for a box of books and he had them there when we arrived. That was one of the things he equipped us with—books. And it was a good big box of books. In that box of books were Plutarch's *Lives* and, oh, I loved Plutarch's *Lives*. And a poem by Moore entitled *Lalla Rookh* which had a beautiful lilt to it and I soon got to where I could say a good many of those lyrics and I just loved to say them. I believe there were some novels. I don't know whether *Thaddeus of Warsaw* was in that bunch or not but very soon after that we got *Thaddeus of Warsaw*. That's a novel detailing the experiences of Thaddeus. He was a Polish soldier that came over to America and helped with the Revolution—the American Revolution.

And then *Children of the Abbey*. I think that was a little later, too. I can't be sure about that but I read *Children of the Abbey* and cried over the woes of Amanda.

In that box of books there was a thin volume that was a classic of some kind but I can't remember the name of it. I can't remember what classic it was. Oh, I'll tell you. I don't know the author of it but it was a collection of tales of Greece and Rome and that's where I got my first contact with the ancient civilizations. I've had an interest in it ever since, by the way—still read the tales of Greece and Rome.

Bedichek had as much education as his father could give him, but at the end he was still a farm boy, not educated enough even for teaching in a country school, unskilled for anything but farm labor. He knew enough to chop and pick cotton for the farmers around Eddy, a way of life that soon went against the grain:

A very definite influence entered my life when I left home to make my own way. That was when I was—let's see—that was in 1896. I was still in my teens. I had been farming myself out to farmers, working on farms, chopping cotton and picking cotton, and things of that kind, when the school was not in session. Fifteen dollars a month and my board. That was fifty cents a day. I remember very well the place I was in the field when I came to the conclusion that I simply could not stand that kind of thing all my life. I decided that I was ready to branch out into something else besides farm work. So I quit right in the middle of a row, chopping cotton. And I told the farmer that I was going back home. So I walked back home—must have been five or six miles—and told my mother that I'd come in, that I'd worked the last time that I'd ever work in the field, that I just didn't like it. So she asked what

I wanted to do and I said, "Well, I'll tell you. I want to get a job that I can make my way through the university."

Dobie had his first schooling from his mother, before he was of school age. The first year he could have gone to school there was no school near enough, so he was taught by a governess who lived in the Dobie home. In 1896, Dobie's father and two others built a schoolhouse on the Dobie ranch "on a patch of open land against black-brush and guajillo hills," overlooking live-oak slopes to the south and east. Even he and the other children thought the country wild. Wild turkeys fed on the school ground, deer jumped fences along the road, a coyote followed them. These are the things he appears to have remembered most clearly from this first school.

He went to other country schools, walking or riding horseback. Once the teacher in a one-room school drama-tized Caesar's crossing of the Rubicon. Many years later he wrote, "After that day ancient history was something else to me than it had been."[2] Not all of his school ex-perience was so successful, as he confesses in the following: "So far as book education is concerned, the only specific pieces of learning I can recall from ranch schooling are how to spell the word *irksome,* on which I was turned down in a spelling match, and knowledge that a branch of science called physical geography existed."[3]

There were other forms of education, however. The teacher always boarded in the Dobie home. Both his father and mother provided books. There were also maga-zines and newspapers. While he was still a child his mother found a list of ten best books for children under sixteen, a list that would be approved by educators today. She got the books and Dobie was introduced to such classics as *Robinson Crusoe,* Plutarch's *Lives,* and *David Copperfield.*

When he was sixteen, Dobie went to high school in Alice, some forty miles from the ranch. There he lived with his mother's mother and stepfather, a man who sometimes sang cowboy songs. Later, Dobie could recall little of the school or his schooling, but he could recall vividly the characters and scenes of Alice, a town from which live cattle and whitened bones gathered on the range were shipped to northern markets.

American biographies are full of stories of how great and famous men were helped to education by others. None is more unlikely than Webb's, told in his own words in a taped interview:

My father had a lot of books on the place, many of them textbooks, but others, and I grew to about the age of ten and I discovered reading and I became a very wide reader and very early my ambition was stirred to move out into this world that was described so erroneously in these books that I read about. And for that purpose I don't think I ever fitted in very well to the society that was about me. The boys were interested in horse racing and parties, and this desire to get an education was just simply a consuming desire which I never lost sight of.

I think the turning point—well, it's difficult to say just where the turning point was. I remember the first book I ever owned was a little book called *Jack the Giant Killer,* published in very black heavy type on very slick white paper with blood-red illustrations of Jack and the giant and the mighty club. I got it in exchange for ten signatures from Arbuckle's 4X coffee. It came addressed to me in the post office. It was the first piece of mail I ever got. I've always been a fool about my mail. I've always had a post-office box wherever I live. I never wanted anybody to handle my mail first. I don't want it discredited by any clerks or anybody else.

When I was about twelve years old my father settled on raw land. We took up one of the last sections of the open range and I had to fence it and two or three years I didn't go to school but I continued to read and the less I went to school the more I wanted to go to school.

During that time I went into Ranger with my father. When I was quite small my father said that he wanted me to be a newspaper editor. Well, I didn't know what a newspaper editor was, but I got the idea that the publisher of the paper was an editor. So I wandered around to the office of this little Ranger *Record,* and I remember the editor had an Oliver typewriter—first typewriter I'd ever seen. Also, over in the corner he had a stack of dust-covered exchanges: papers that had been sent in to him by an exchange from all over the country. Well, I looked at that and that was reading matter to satisfy the most ambitious. So I finally got my courage up to ask him if I could have some of those newspapers. I remember they were piled up until they just slipped down kinda like a haystack the way O. Henry described it—described the editor's office—by saying that he had no earthly use for a wastebasket because he simply threw stuff in the corner. Well, he gave me permission and I went in and took out all that I thought I could get away with. I wanted more but I took a good big armful and I decided that I'd better not rob him completely.

Among those papers I took were several copies of a weekly paper published at Atlanta, Georgia, called *The Sunny South.* It was devoted to the glory of the Confederacy, and some of the best writers in the land were contributors to it. Such men as Frank G. Carpenter, Frederick G. Haskins, A. Conan Doyle, and Uncle Remus. Joel Chandler Harris was connected with the paper, I believe. At any rate his Uncle Remus stories were running in there all the time. And in reading that paper I saw a statement that they would send it three months for ten cents.

Only trouble was that I didn't have ten cents and they were pretty hard to come by in those days. But I put the matter up to my mother and she dug around somewhere and came up with a very thin dime, and I sent that dime to *The Sunny South* for a three months' subscription. By the end of that three months the family—they were all readers, and we were all in love with that newspaper-magazine, so we took it continually from that time on.

That dime was well spent, as Webb's continuation of the story shows:

In the meantime, this desire to get an education grew, and there was a letter column in *The Sunny South* where readers —subscribers—wrote in to express their views. I wrote a very short letter in which I mentioned my desire for an education, and I don't know what there was about it that had any appeal. It was published in *The Sunny South* in the spring. I know it was in the spring because I was plowing corn, and I remember the corn was about ankle to knee high, and I was sitting on a damned old Georgia stock resting. My sister had been to the mailbox and she came back with a letter bearing a New York postmark: 489 Classon Avenue, Brooklyn, New York, written in a very bold hand. It had a red seal on the back where wax—hot wax—had been dropped on the seal with the writer's initials stamped in it. I had signed my middle name to this letter and had mentioned that my father was a teacher. This letter was addressed to "J. Prescott" in care of "Lame Teacher," Ranger, Texas.

That goes back again to *The Sunny South*. There was an old man by the name of Griffith who was the postmaster at Ranger and he got interested in me because I took *The Sunny South,* and it came through the post office and he read it as it came through. So he knew me, and he knew I was interested in books, so he'd sent this letter.

The letter read something like this:

Dear Prescott:

I have seen your letter in *The Sunny South* and have been interested in what you have to say and especially in your desire for an education. I would like for you to remember that in the bright lexicon of youth there is no such word as fail. With your permission I'd like to send you some books. In fact, I'm sending them anyway.

It was signed William E. Hinds, 489 Classon Avenue, Brooklyn, New York. I, of course, answered the letter and the books came and among them were Sherwin Cody's five little red books. Four or five little red books on English. And then other books came and then a series of magazine subscriptions came. It started out with *The American Boy,* which would indicate my age level at that time. And then he sent *The National Magazine* and he sent *Success Magazine* published by Orison Swett Marden. That magazine had a great deal to do with inflaming this desire. It was the story of how men by working hard and not watching the clock would succeed. It was very popular at that time.

Webb's father, by this time convinced of his son's eagerness to get an education, moved his family to Ranger for a year in order that Webb might take the last year of high school and earn a teaching certificate. Webb did go a year and did get a second-grade certificate. The next year he taught successively in three schools at forty-two dollars and fifty cents a month. The next year he went to Ranger again and got a first-grade certificate. He got a good country school for that year and might have remained a country schoolteacher had it not been for William E. Hinds, with another of his letters:

I think it was in February—maybe January—I went down to the mailbox, got the mail, and there was a long official-sized letter from Mr. Hinds, and he started in by asking me if I had thought of going to college. . . . He said he wanted to know how much money I'd saved—how much money would it take to get through the university, for one year at the university. Then he said that he would, if I wanted, if I wanted to go to school, if I wanted to go to college, that he would be glad to help me. I remember he said that he would consider it—that one would consider it a very fine thing if he had helped someone. I think he mentioned the name of Abraham Lincoln, and he said, "Someday I may be able to take pride in the fact that I helped Walter Prescott Webb."

I answered the letter immediately, and I had saved money and I told him it would cost about three hundred dollars a year to go to the university, and by accident I chose the university instead of some college. Everybody around there went to other places, but, for some reason—I think on account of a remark the superintendent made—I chose the university.

That was in the year of 1908 and 1909 that I got this letter, and so in the fall of 1909 I entered the university.

Webb was then twenty-one years old.

IV. Up to the University

Bedichek was three years old when the University of Texas was founded, on a forty-acre plot north of the state capital in Austin. The university was seven years old when Dobie and Webb were born. By the time they came to it, all as grown men, it had become the leading educational institution in Texas.

It was not easy to get to the university in those days; each had his own struggle. Yet they got there, by various routes and with experiences that made the university seem home to them but at the same time set them outside the academic community.

When Bedichek left the cotton patch he had in mind making his way to the university by working at typing and shorthand, as a male stenographer. How he learned is part of his own story:

My father had an old Caligraph machine—it didn't even have a universal keyboard—with the capitals on one side and the small letters in the middle. I unearthed that from somewhere and started practicing writing on that Caligraph. Of course, it wasn't doing me any good—really doing me harm— because it was not a universal keyboard. But I worked at it and worked at it till I kind of worked up a pretty good speed on that Caligraph.

Someone told me that a law firm in Waco—we were living then only about twenty miles from Waco—Boynton and Boynton, wanted a stenographer. So I went up to Waco and had a talk with Mr. J. E. Boynton. He asked me if I was a stenographer, and I told him no, that I was not a stenographer— that was along in July—but I could be one by September the first. He kind of opened his eyes. He says, "You don't think you can be a stenographer in a month or two?" Well, I tell him that I've done considerably better than that at some things; it didn't take me long to learn anything. He said, "All right, we'll give you a trial. We're not giving you a job, but we'll give you a trial. On September the first you come up."

I went down the street and went into a secondhand bookstore and looked around there and finally found a shorthand book. It was Longley's revision of the Pitmanic system. . . . I saw that it had all the characters and all that kind of thing, with many practice sheets and all that, so I bought that copy for fifteen cents and I went home and went to work on it.

My mother said that I filled not only our pasture, which was a small pasture, but a big sheep pasture full of notes, shorthand notes, practicing making these shorthand characters. I had just unlimited paper and I'd just go to work in the morning and practice on these characters and then get my mother to dictate to me, and I would take them down. I put in a tremendous amount of intensive work, working fourteen hours a day every day, not missing Sunday or anything else, until the first of September.

I went up with considerable confidence in my shorthand ability but not much in my typing ability because I didn't have a typewriter to practice on. I found out in the meantime what the universal keyboard was. I explained this to Mr. Boynton and told him that I'd be very slow to start with on the typewriter but that I'd practice on it, but I could take dictation. . . . He was willing to give me a try, so he employed me at I think twenty dollars a month.

Boynton started Bedichek reading Blackstone, but instead of talking law they talked literature.

At times Bedichek did some stenographic work for W. C. Brann, who published *The Iconoclast* in the same building on the same floor. Brann was a different kind of education, as Bedichek's account shows:

I could see him come in. I could see old Brann come in, and take off his hat. Boy, he dressed like a perfect gentleman. He was a dandy in his dress and everything had to be spotlessly clean about him. I'd see him come into his office and I'd often wonder, oh, what a wonderful thing it would be to be able to write a magazine. He wrote the whole magazine himself, every month, and he sold it for a dollar a year subscription. I've seen him go down to the bank with a wastebasket full of checks and small change—dollars and pennies. He never would let anybody deposit it except himself. . . .

Occasionally I was called across to take some dictation from him . . . so I got in closer touch with him, but he never limbered up to me. He never treated me as anything except just help around the office, but no personal interest. I admired him very much on account of his ability to write.

I remember that on one occasion he got into a quarrel with Baylor University and had accused Baylor of being just, oh, there being sexual irregularities out there at that time. One of the professors or somebody connected with the institution had an illegitimate birth. It occurred in his home and he was taxed with being the father of the child. . . . Brann was a regular muckraker and he made a great to-do about it and it incensed Baylor tremendously. Some boys came and they kidnapped him one afternoon—university boys. And they took him out there to the Baylor campus and they put a rope around his neck.

They were going to hang him, and they led him around for a while. . . . Professor Greer[1] talked the boys out of it and got Brann free.

Brann came back to his office and he was infuriated. He called me over there and I don't think he recognized me at all. He never looked at me at all. He had a big box of cigars on the table. He started dictating an interview for the *Evening Telephone*—that was the evening paper in Waco—telling about his experience. He would take a cigar out of that box as he was talking and put it in his mouth and strike a match, and bring the match to within about a couple of inches of the end of the cigar and puff, getting no smoke at all. Not lighting the cigar, but just holding it there until he nearly burned his fingers, then throwing it down. He would chew the cigar—just chew, chew, chew, and then he'd take another match and hold it out there about two inches from the end of the cigar and suck but get no smoke. I suppose he must have consumed a half a dozen cigars while he was dictating that interview. That interview appeared as he entitled it: "Ropes, Revolvers, and Religion." He just excoriated the mob spirit at Baylor University—just what he wanted—and he later worked that up into a leading article for his *Iconoclast*.

That was the most memorable contact that I had with W. C. Brann, although I've seen him drunk and I've seen him knocked down. . . . He was eventually killed. I had already gone when he was killed.

In Waco, Bedichek heard a promotional speech for the university and decided to go, though he knew he would have to work to pay his way. He worked for a boarding house, meeting trains and persuading students to become boarders; then for the registrar, who was John Avery Lomax, before he became famous as a collector of American ballads and songs; and finally as a tutor in the Department of Philosophy.

No doubt Bedichek could have stayed at the university after he finished his degree, but he wanted to try other things. For about ten years he was away from Austin, reporting for a newspaper in Fort Worth, teaching English in high school in Houston and San Angelo, and then homesteading in New Mexico, where he also tried his hand as a newspaper reformer.

His account of that experience is full of the wry humor with which he could look at himself and some of his less successful performances:

I quit my job as secretary of the Chamber of Commerce at that time and took over a paper that I bought. I remember there was a seven hundred and fifty dollar mortgage on it, which I assumed. . . . I had had no experience whatever in running a paper in those days. I don't think a student in journalism, as far as I can say, would make the same mistakes I made, because they are taught that the business end of a newspaper is the vital end of it. If you kill the business end of it, why, you haven't got a newspaper. I had read the traditions of great reformers and people who had really done something with newspapers and so I became too much of a reformer for the good of the business end of my paper.

I had a good following for perhaps a year but then the prohibition campaign came up and I was a violent prohibitionist, although I took a drink occasionally. I was one of these what Jim Ferguson[2] used to call a "drinking pro" and not to a great extent, however. Well, we had that campaign there—prohibition campaign—in Luna County and Deming was the county seat of Luna County and had sixteen saloons run by very important people. The saloonkeeper was really quite a substantial citizen of the community and had many lines out. He had a great deal of influence.

As I developed the campaign I guess I must have gotten pretty vicious because I commenced to find the saloonkeepers rather cool to me even personally when they met me. For illustration, an old friend of mine and I used to go to Tony Irwin's saloon for lunch—had free lunch over there with beans. They would serve you a stein of beer and a dish of beans and there was considerable nourishment in those beans. So when I got to writing so viciously about the saloons, why it kind of hurt my conscience to go over there and get a glass of beer even. I began calling for buttermilk. . . . Old Tony didn't make the profit on buttermilk that he made on beer, so the dish of beans commenced to getting smaller and smaller and smaller and he was grouchy because he didn't like me. I was right across the street from him. Finally one day John McTeer said, "Tony, we've been patronizing this place a long time, but now this dish of beans that you gave yesterday was certainly insufficient. We feel like we're entitled to more beans with our buttermilk." Old Tony reared back and said, "One buttermilk, one bean. One buttermilk, one bean." He looked positively aggressive and didn't smile at all.

The trouble was that the man that owned the beer license for the city—that is, he sold all the beer—he got a profit off of every glass of beer that was sold in the town. He also owned that mortgage for seven hundred and fifty dollars on my plant and I wasn't making much of a profit. I'd married in the meantime and had some expenses—a child was coming on and all that sort of thing—so he began to be very insistent about the payment of this mortgage. He just squeezed down on me until finally, why, he just closed me out. That was the end of my reforming in the city of Deming with sixteen saloons and quite a number of bawdyhouses.

After quitting Deming, Bedichek worked for a time as city editor of the San Antonio *Express,* and then as secretary of the Young Business Men's Club at Austin. In

1918, when he was forty years old, he came home to the university as athletic director for the Interscholastic League. He then became director, a post he held until his retirement.

Dobie's parents were active Methodists, and there was some hope on his mother's part that he would be a preacher. When he was ready for college, they sent him to Southwestern University at Georgetown, the leading Methodist college in Texas at the time, and a center for training divinity students in the Methodist church. Dobie entered Southwestern in the fall of 1906, at the age of eighteen.

Fortunately for him, on the first day he met Robert Stewart Hyer, the President of Southwestern. They talked about books, and Dr. Hyer invited Dobie to come to the sermon on opening Sunday, to hear him preach on James Parton's *Life of Thomas Jefferson*. Later Dobie wrote: "That essay-sermon, which ranged over the great literature of the world and its influence on the mind and spirit of man, elated me with ambition to know."[3]

I share his appreciation of Dr. Hyer. When I was a boy trying to make my way in Dallas a cousin took me to Dr. Hyer's Sunday school class. I do not remember the lesson, but I do remember how I was stirred by his wide knowledge of books—the Bible and others. He was then retired as President of Southern Methodist University, but with such an active mind that I wished for a chance to study under him. On a Sunday afternoon I went out to the campus and walked around the closed buildings, wondering what it would be like to be a student there—to be able to say, "I am in college."

During four years at Southern Dobie learned a great deal about English literature and something about writing. His best compositions were about ranch life in Live Oak

County. At the end of college he took a job as principal and teacher of English at Alpine, Texas. In the summer between he worked for the San Antonio *Express,* reporting fires and funerals.

The year Dobie spent at Alpine was good for him. The land was higher and drier than Live Oak County, but it was cattle country. There were trail drivers to talk to, and Mexicans to revive old sounds and rhythms of speech. In Alpine, Dobie got the material for his first book, *A Vaquero of the Brush Country,* and some of the chapters for *Coronado's Children.*

After a period of less rewarding work in Georgetown, Dobie went on to Columbia University, where he took a Master's Degree in English literature in 1914. The subject of his master's essay was *Thomas Heywood: The Golden Age.* His analysis of this Elizabethan play is probably no better, no worse than the average master's essay; it does not, however, reveal the earthy quality or the romantic sweep of the mature Dobie. One would have difficulty recognizing Dobie in this statement of his method:

If it be urged that I might better have the essay in two divisions, devoting one to *The Golden Age,* the play proper, and the other to Heywood, the author, I can only answer that, while such a division would seem easier, to me it has seemed artificial, and, though neat, not capable of allowing the relations I have endeavored to demonstrate.

This experience was apparently enough to make Dobie forsake both the subjunctive and the academic.

After spending the summer as a reporter for the Galveston *Daily Tribune,* Dobie became an instructor in English at the university, at a salary of twelve hundred dollars a year. Two years later he married Bertha McKee, whom he had known at Southwestern.

After two years in the field artillery in World War I and another year of teaching, Dobie resigned to manage the Olmos Ranch in La Salle County. Later he wrote: "It was certainly lucky for me that I left the university in 1920 and learned something."[4] What he gained in that year was a new perspective on the legends and ballads of the brush country. He decided to collect the legends as John Avery Lomax had collected the ballads.

Soon he was at the university again, teaching, writing, and editing the publications of the Texas Folklore Society. The brush country was in his system as much as ever. He had learned to turn it to the uses of a writer.

Webb's first years as a student at the University of Texas were in a continuing partnership with William E. Hinds, as Webb reported in an interview:

In the fall of 1909 I entered the university, and I went through about half of the year. My money ran out along in about the middle of the year—a little after—and I wrote him and the first of every month I got a check for thirty dollars, and I went two years. By that time I owed him five hundred dollars and he wrote and said that he thought I'd better not go any deeper in debt. He suggested that I go out and go to work a year. So I did. I worked in the summer and I would make money in the summer, enough to get started and I'd always keep him informed about that. And so I'd come out to Throckmorton County and got a school out there—a six-month school, very good salary, ninety dollars a month. And again I saved my money and I came back. I paid him back in part— two or three hundred dollars—and told him, though, I wanted to come back, and so he said, "All right, go ahead." And I went another year and I was back about five hundred dollars in debt. Then I went to Beeville as principal, to teach history in the high school. One hundred dollars a month. And again I saved my money, and I had got a fellowship from Lindley Miller Keasbey in Institutional History, and so I came back in 1914–1915.

The year I was at Cuero he died, and I had been paying him back. I knew nothing about it. Hinds died. And I had a letter from his lawyers saying that they had this note. I gave a note, without interest, for what I owed him, and I'd always pay on it. They wanted it settled and in a little while I had a letter from his sister and she said that she had taken over the note and that she didn't want any bother about it.

Well, in the meantime I married[5] and I went to San Antonio as history teacher in the San Antonio High School. Miss Ida Hinds came to San Antonio that year and spent the winter with us. She stayed at one of the hotels—the Menger or the Gunter Hotel. We were with her a great deal. She told me a good deal about this man. He was a bachelor. He was a small importer. He told me one time that he wasn't a rich man, although I think he did have a pretty good income. She said that he helped a great many boys. I have often thought that I'd like to get in touch with them and see what happened to them—what the result of his investment was.

In my own case, it was unfortunate—in a manner I have always regretted that as far as I could see he never got any return on his money while he lived, because I don't think that I showed any promise at all of doing anything that would justify him in the trouble and the risk that he took. All the things that I was able to do came after, and I wasn't very much promise.

One thing he did was to encourage me to write letters, long letters, letters of description. He said that was one of the best trainings that you could get to be a writer. He even took the trouble to consult some writer in New York, and I remember he said that I should read the Old Testament for loftiness of style and read the New Testament for simplicity and directness.

Let's come back to Miss Hinds, Miss Ida Hinds. She left San Antonio and went to California. By that time I had paid this note down to about one hundred and seventy-five dollars. One day I got a letter addressed in her handwriting with a note inside saying:

> When you receive this you will know that I have passed away and the money that you owe, I want nothing done about it. There is nobody that would be interested and I don't want you to attempt to pay it to anybody.

There was nobody that I could pay it to. There was no attorney, so I never did hear from anybody. But I think that I felt the obligation, and I think that I have done what I feel is most appreciated and that is to do something for somebody else. You know, to pass along this. In fact, he said that one time. He said, "There is nothing that what I do for you, you can't do for somebody else." That experience is to me— it's something like a miracle.

It had this effect. In this effort to get along I would see my friends and companions go out on the wild path and do things that they knew and I knew weren't exactly right. There'd be a certain amount of envy. I'd think it would be nice to do those things, too. But all the time—every time I would veer off or think of quitting—why, the memory that this man expected things of me—he never seemed to doubt. When I first came to the university I sent him my grades but they finally got so bad that I quit. I also sent him some itemized accounts. He never raised any question. He never showed the least impatience. Anything I did was all right. I still don't understand it. He made it absolutely impossible for me to go wrong, without just being a complete traitor.

Webb completed his A.B. at the university in 1915, his A.M. in 1920. Once in between he had a bout with the fever of journalism. Bedichek recorded the incident:

Webb tells this story of our acquaintanceship. He tells it always with a kind of a smile on his face that indicates I didn't know much about writers because one day when I was at my desk down there—this is the way he tells it—down there in the editorial rooms of the San Antonio *Express* he came in and wanted a job. He wanted to be employed as a reporter and I talked to him awhile and I found out that he was a young teacher, that he had a college education, and was teaching in one of the high schools there in San Antonio. And I thought of the damnable way in which the management of the *Express* treated their employees and I simply could not encourage him to give up his job and come and be a writer on the *Express*. So I discouraged him in every way that I possibly could and turned him down as a writer. He retails that in my presence every time the subject comes up that I certainly turned down a writer.

In 1918, Webb was appointed instructor in history at the university, at an annual salary of twelve hundred and sixty dollars.

V. Mavericks Roam the Forty Acres

During the tenure of these three friends, approximately forty years, the University of Texas developed from a small college to one of the great state universities. Of the many reasons for this growth, two are outstanding: money and dedicated professors. From 1923 on, the date of the discovery of the Santa Rita oil well on university lands, there was a great deal of money for putting up new buildings and buying books and collections for the library. Within twenty-five years the campus took on its look of red tile roofs and fossil-flecked limestone walls; scholars traveled great distances to use rare books and manuscripts in the various libraries.

By act of the state legislature, however, oil money was not to be used for faculty salaries. For these, the university administration had to go hat in hand to the state legislature. Money was provided, but not enough. Professors had to be dedicated to remain at the university year after year at salaries of four thousand dollars annually, or less. Many men did, men whose names today are legend in the development of higher education in Texas: H. Y. Benedict, T. U. Taylor, W. J. Battle, Leonidas W. Payne, and many others. They were willing to exist on low pay and high resolve, themselves a subsidy in order that their students might have a better chance.

Brains and spirit were there, enough to nurture and stimulate men like Bedichek, Dobie, and Webb, each of whom had seen enough of intellectual barrenness in his own region of Texas. Bedichek and Webb studied under them; Dobie met them in other ways. Webb's statement about Lindley Miller Keasbey indicates something of the quality of the men and the problems they faced at the university:

I think that to me Keasbey was the greatest teacher I ever had and I got more from Keasbey than I ever got from one teacher or any group of teachers. I say that because of the fact that Keasbey is a man that a great many people didn't like very much. He was an intellectual aristocrat. He came to the university, I believe, to teach economics but he was so unorthodox that he didn't get along very well with the classical economists and I suppose they shelved him. They gave him a department of his own called Institutional History, maybe thinking that he'd wither up, but instead of his withering up he made it one of the most distinguished departments—sought-after departments—in the university. Students flocked to him. The thing that I got from Keasbey was an appreciation of the relationship between a society and its environment. And the second thing which I got from him, which is very important, was the process of rational thinking—of putting two and two together and always getting four—of consecutive reasoning, building up from a solid foundation a process of thought. I took everything Keasbey gave.

I was one of the younger members in the department, and it was necessary for me to teach. When I got out and was ready to go into the high school I had to say what I was going to teach. Then I discovered that there was no such thing as institutional history anywhere else in the world. It was only at the

University of Texas. I had had very little history. In fact, I had had only two courses. When I had to say what I would teach I said, "Well, I'll teach history," and then listed these courses in institutional history. I carried this method of teaching into the high school.

Like Keasbey, the three were too individualistic to fit into the usual academic patterns. Also, their goals were different from those of most of their colleagues. At the time when professors in the Department of English were stressing Shakespeare, Chaucer, and Anglo-Saxon, when some were insisting that nothing of value had been written since 1800, Dobie, without denigrating the study of these, proposed that the students learn something about their own environment. When the professors in the Department of English told him there was not enough Southwestern literature for a course, Dobie retorted that he would then teach a course in the *life* and literature of the Southwest. When the professors in the Department of Education were concerned with what they considered the ill effects of educational competition or competition as a device for education, Bedichek was running the Interscholastic League, a statewide organization devoted to competition in athletics and also in art, literature, and music. Webb was challenging both the professors and the politicians with a book like *Divided We Stand: The Crisis of Frontierless Democracy*.

Professors, regents, buildings, beliefs—everything about the university came under their scrutiny and often their criticism. Unroped, unbranded, they spoke what they felt, privately, publicly, with words incisive enough to bring anger to the attacked, laughter to the unscathed.

Dobie's criticisms made the newspapers regularly. When the university tower was built, with its Spanish red tile at the lower level, its Grecian columns twenty-seven stories up, Dobie suggested that it should be laid on its side. He described the Coppini[1] fountain at the entrance to the campus as "a conglomerate of a woman standing up, with arms and hands that look like stalks of Spanish dagger; of horses with wings on their feet, aimlessly ridden by some sad figures of the male sex, and various other inane paraphernalia. What it symbolizes probably neither God nor Coppini knows."

The Ph.D. became for Dobie a major target for criticism and ridicule. He said of it: "Ph.D. worship in American universities and even in jerkwater colleges has destroyed casualness and substituted Ph.D. theses of Germanic methodicalness and pedestrian turgidity for books of brightness. The average Ph.D. thesis is nothing but a transference of bones from one graveyard to another."[2]

Dobie decided early that he would not go beyond the M.A., a decision that created problems for him at the University of Texas, where the Ph.D. had become accepted as the badge of academic excellence and the first requirement for promotion. He was forty-five before he became a professor.

Bedichek never progressed beyond a few graduate courses at the University of Chicago. As he was administrative rather than academic at the university, the Ph.D. was not so necessary to his promotion. Lacking the Ph.D., he was never invited to join the Department of English, where his wide knowledge of literature and his enthusiasm for knowledge would have made him especially stimulating to students.

Webb's struggle for the Ph.D. is now part of academic folklore. His own account is fully as interesting as the legend:

I am constitutionally unable to work on anything that doesn't interest me. Therefore, I haven't had the kind of plastic nature that made me ideal for professors who wanted to stamp out a Ph.D. I didn't get into the university until I was twenty-one, and I didn't have any credits when I came except a first-grade certificate. I skipped more grades than I made, and it all showed up by the end of the university. I had things to overcome all of my life. If I had a subject I didn't like, I would read something else.

I went up to the University of Chicago. I was there in summer school. I went up there, I think it was in the year 1922. Wife and baby. Saved up about twenty-eight hundred dollars, in cash, and had a fellowship. I'd just had an article accepted by *Scribner's* magazine, the six-shooter article, and so my prestige was pretty high. I was about as far along as some of the people that were teaching so far as achievement is concerned. I had a job. I guess my prestige was too high, especially with this inability to remember everything somebody says.

My professor suggested that I come up for the preliminary examination. Well, I thought the thing to do was to do it—do what the professor suggested. And so I did that after I'd been up there only three months, which is something I wouldn't let a student of mine do at all, under the present setup here at the university. Naturally I was not acquainted with these men. I didn't know their philosophy of history.

This examination was held on the twentieth of February, and there was snow on the ground about six inches deep, and very bright. I remember how it glinted in the starlight as I walked home that night. Well, I did miserably. I think I would do miserably today. I don't think there's ever been a time when I could pass a decent oral examination. So they sent me out of the room after this torture had gone on, oh, for quite a long time. They said that they thought that I wasn't prepared, that I ought to take more time. Old Dr. Andrew McLaughlin came out and he was a very kind old Scotch gentleman. I said, "Well, I'd like to make a statement to this committee." And that's where this legend about my doctorate came from. He was a little reluctant about that, but I didn't put it to him in a way that they could refuse. So I went back in there and I said, "Well, the only thing that I regret is that I came up." I said I was encouraged to come up. And I said, "My program is laid out. I know what I want to do, and what this does will make it difficult for me in the job that I have. It's the humiliation. I shouldn't have come up. I don't know the men, I should have known that, but I was encouraged to come up." And I said, "My program is laid out for ten years. I know what I want to do for ten years ahead." I saw *The Great Plains.* I knew I had something pretty big.

McLaughlin told me the next day that if I'd made the speech before the decision instead of after the results would have been different. "Well, then," I said, "I'm going to stay here. I'm going on because I need the training. But I can never pass the kind of examination that you men gave. I just don't have that type mind. I never could do well on it."

Well, I came back there. To climax that—that was on the twentieth of February—we all came down with the flu about two weeks later, and I think I came as near to going over the brink as I ever did in my life. I'd had this flu and I—well, I wouldn't go into detail as to my feeling, but it's a feeling of resentment against having gotten myself into this situation. I'd find my mind just racing on it and I remember that I wrote to Barker[3] and told him I was coming home, and he said no, not to do that. So I did stay through until the end of the summer. I remember walking along Sixty-third Street one day and I said to myself, "Well, here, can't you control your own mind? You're letting your own mind get away from you. Just by an act of will you've got to take it in hand and do something with it."

So I came back here. I was thirty-five years old; I was three hundred dollars in debt. And I said, "I'll be damned if I'm not through. From now on I'm working for myself, and doings things the way I want to do."

So I started writing, and they began to write me letters to come back. Well, I never did say categorically that I wouldn't go back. I just said, "Well, I'm busy. I'm doing things. I'm not coming now." *The Great Plains* came out and made the front page of both the *Times* and the *Herald Tribune*. And finally Dr. Barker said this—he said, "You'd better listen. Take your degree here." I said, "I haven't finished the thesis." He said, "You can use *The Great Plains* for a thesis." I said, "I don't want to use that book for a thesis." He said, "I think you'd better do it." So they just gave me the degree.

That's that story, but it's grown into quite a legend in Chicago, I understand. They told me later that my name was taken more in consideration with graduate work there—and these students have built up the legend that I bawled them out and walked out on them. It's known in the historical fraternity and, well, I never said anything about it for years— any more than I did about my experience with Mr. Hinds, but I forget that damned machine's there—

Bedichek, Dobie, and Webb were outspoken in their criticism of political intervention in the affairs of the university. Academic independence was difficult to achieve in a system in which the regents were politically appointed, and in which money for salaries had to be appropriated by the state legislature. Professors who were non-conformists, or who made themselves heard outside the Forty Acres, came under the surveillance of both regents and legislators. Members of either group could demand the dismissal of any professor who roused their ire. Too often, administrators yielded to these pressures instead of standing up for the professors and the university; indeed, at times they led in harrying out the dissidents.

Webb's story of Lindley Miller Keasbey may not be typical but it is indicative: "I think that to me Keasbey was the greatest teacher I ever had and I got more from Keasbey than I ever got from one teacher or any group of teachers." But Keasbey did not fit into the accepted pattern. "Keasbey violated every rule of procedure laid down by the officials of the university. . . . He was the despair of the administration." During the early years of World War I Keasbey took the German side, along with about half the members of the faculty. When America became more involved, the others recanted when told to do so. Keasbey did not. For making a pro-German speech, he was ordered to stand trial. When he refused to appear, he was fired.

Others took themselves away or were let go. Bedichek had his own opinion: "I've noticed that when the matter of academic freedom comes up, that it's always the brilliant men who are fired first. You can see it right in the history of the university."[4] He cited the case of Hermann J. Muller, the first Nobel prize winner who had had any connection with the university. A group of students at the university organized what they called a Communist cell and published a paper, for which Professor Muller wrote an article. The president of the university wrote him that he would have to stand trial for making this contribution to a Communist paper. A liberal but not a Communist, Muller resigned rather than go through the indignity of the trial.

In time, each of the three men came under fire from members of the Board of Regents.

Bedichek was first. In June 1940, Regent Lutcher Stark presented a motion for the dismissal of Roy Bedichek and others for their support of a change in eligibility rules for students in interscholastic athletics. Stark disapproved the change. Bedichek testified in the hearing that Stark's son would have been ineligible to play had the proposed change been put into effect. It was voted down by member high schools.

Bedichek was not fired, but his case served to heighten the conflict that was beginning to grow between President Homer Price Rainey and the regents.

This conflict, too long-drawn-out and involved for recounting here, was enough to test any professor's loyalty to the university. Several basic principles were involved: academic freedom, rights of tenure, outside control of assigned readings, the case in point being *U.S.A.* by John Dos Passos. On November 1, 1943, the regents dismissed Dr. Rainey. At the same meeting they appointed Dr. T. S. Painter Acting President. Later he was appointed President.

Letters among the three friends during this period are not numerous. They do, however, show considerable activity on their part in faculty and committee meetings. They saw the point of the conflict, and had the courage to fight for academic freedom, as it is embodied in this statement prepared by a faculty committee:

Any competent president understands the principle of academic freedom and he knows how imperative it is for him to defend it in the larger interest of the institution. He must, if compelled to do so, defend it against the board, and even against the public, because he realizes that he is adhering to a principle on which the success of the university and the morale of the faculty rest. Any president who retreats before the attack on this principle immediately forfeits the respect of every scholar in the land. . . .

Bedichek and Webb remained with the university until they reached the age of retirement. Dobie was let go, after forty years of service, after his name was a household word in Texas and beyond. His highest academic honor came not from the University of Texas but from Cambridge University in England, where he was given an honorary M.A., with a citation which reads in part: *"De bobus longicornibus quod ille non cognivit, inutile est allis cognoscere* (What he does not know about longhorns is not worth knowing)."[5]

His separation from the university came *after* this honor, and with none of the drama of his earlier conflicts. He had been absent on leave one year teaching at Cambridge, and then a second year lecturing at the Shrivenham American School in England and to American troops in Germany. In April 1947, he applied for an extension of his leave through the fall semester, on the grounds that he had a manuscript to complete and also that cedar fever, from which he had long suffered, could be alleviated only by absence from the juniper hills around Austin during the fall. In September, when Dobie had not returned, President Painter had his name removed from the budget. The regents approved the deletion. So ended Dobie's distinguished career at the university, but not his devotion, or his criticism of what he considered the follies of the administration.

Webb paid for his freedom of criticism by having his promotion to professor held up year after year. He received his Ph.D. in 1932. Not until another twenty years had passed, when he was sixty-four, was he made a professor, and only then after the administration of the university had conducted a hard fight with certain regents.

On February 20, 1951, Webb addressed a letter "To the Honorable Members of the House and Senate" of the 52nd Legislature. It may not have helped his case for promotion; it did provide a definition of the purposes of a university, and especially his plea that the University of Texas be made first class. The last two paragraphs represent Webb at his best:

I have taken the liberty of presenting this matter to you in in this way because I know that you are torn in many directions, and perhaps lack the time to think out in detail all of the problems put before you. Also, I know, as you do, that there are many cross-currents in political life, and that many persuasive arguments are presented to you from sundry sources, some of them presented in a manner far more skillful than I could hope to master. Still, I think I have pointed out something fundamental, namely, the fact that each legislature, and each member, has the privilege of deciding what sort of institution of higher learning the people of Texas deserve to have. If you keep that responsibility in mind, it may help in steering your course through all the cross-currents and coming out with the feeling that you have had some part in carrying out the original intent of the men who created the University 75 years ago.

Though I am addressing you in my role as a citizen, I do want to say a word on behalf of the University faculty. It ranks pretty high in the nation and is spoken of with some respect wherever scholars gather on this continent. You might be surprised to know how human most of us are, and that we are as shy of you as you sometimes seem to be of us. In our business of dealing with ideas, we sometimes come on dangerous ones which have to be studied and understood in order that they may be coped with intelligently. It is the business of some members of a University faculty to deal with the venom of rattlesnakes, the deadly effects of drugs, the diseases of smallpox and cancer, and the destructive power of the atom; it is the business of others to deal with ideas, ideologies, and all sorts of theories about human relationships as they exist in the world. This does not mean that the first group are advocates of venom, strychnine, smallpox, or atom bombs, nor does it mean that the second group are advocates of comparably destructive but more elusive forces operating in society. Taking a university as a whole, its function is to survey the whole world of facts and ideas, and if a university could speak, it might well say with John Wesley, "The world is my parish." It would seem that the state of Texas would be fully justified in making it possible for one institution with such a broad purpose to exist; whether it does depends on the quality of the faculty and on the legislative body which holds a mandate from the people to provide for the support of a university of the first class.

Bedichek retired in 1948, Webb in 1958. Not before had the university contained three such men. Not again will it have their mixture of intellect, ruggedness of spirit, and appreciation for the land, the people, the lore, and the culture that made their Texas.

Correspondence among the three friends about the crisis at the university is limited in scope and sketchy in detail. At times it appears cryptic, chiefly because they were writing a kind of shorthand about certain particulars of a large problem they discussed often and at length in faculty and committee meetings. Though the following letters indicate only a small amount of their involvement, they show strongly the depth of their personal feelings. October 15, 1943, Webb wrote Bedichek: "The thing I like about the institution I work for is that it is filled with pure-hearted, high-minded people who always keep their eyes on a lofty star."

> Austin, Texas
> April 27, 1942

Dear Bedi,

Saturday night I attended a song-fest at the faculty club, the last place you would ever expect to see people be spontaneous, at which Zanzig[6] led in singing. It was the most unusual performance that I have ever seen in twenty years of attendance at that dreary place. At first, books were handed out and the people sang under Zanzig's leadership. Then came refreshments, after which Zanzig sat down at the piano and began to play with tunes. Some half dozen filled in when the music could hardly be heard above the chatter. I got interested in what he might accomplish and suggested that he play "Dixie" and one or two other Southern favorites. The result of this was that people from all over the room began to move towards the piano like range cows to salt, and in fifteen or twenty minutes everybody in the house was singing, except myself and the club cat. . . .

Sincerely yours,
Webb

Austin, Texas
January 7, 1944

Dear Webb:

It ain't a gonna hurt you a goddamn bit to go with me some evening over to Taylor and conduct a forum on English universities, or England at war, or England and anything you goddamn please, and I'm not a gonna phenagle or impress you into this service but am simply scheduling you under the impression that you are a gentleman. Enclosed is a date-sheet. Simply write your name opposite the date that suits you best. If you want to escape my company, put it in early May, as I shall then be taken up with the State Meet and can't go.

And don't wait any longer on this as I am tired of putting up with your dilatory tactics—by return faculty mail, please.

You should have heard Rainey last night. He was at his best. The more the opposition, the better he is. There was poor reaction to Whitman, but a fine reaction to Rainey. He quoted you quite flatteringly on corporations and drew down condemnation of a judge or two. You should have been there to carry your flag into the breach, like a true hero, which you are not.

Yours,

Bedi

Austin, Texas

Dear Webb:

Since reading the statement last night, I find one phrase sticking in my craw and it won't go down, and that is the one which disclaims any interest on the part of the faculty in which side of this controversy wins. It seems to me that punches a hole in the bottom of the vessel and lets all the contents drain out. Nothing is left but a shell. What then are we protesting about? This quarrel between regents and presidents is not made out of thin air. It has a substantial foundation. Are we indifferent as to which side wins? It is hypocrisy to say that we do not want the president's point of view to win out. Tudey Thornton[7] wrote a piece for the Dallas *News* in which this point of view was taken: "just bickering between the president and regents which should be composed." Certainly it should be composed, but on what terms? It isn't necessary to say that we are not concerned with which side wins. As a matter of fact the statement declares very definitely which side we think is right, and then follows with the statement that we are so neutral that we do not care particularly for the right to prevail. Just leave that out, that neutrality clause, and let the reader determine for himself whether or not we are neutral. It might be OK to say that we are not defending any one point of view, except that we defend its right to be heard, its right to have its day in court. Research is by definition concerned with the unknown, and as the results of research become apparent it is often forced into defending the unacceptable. We might say with candor that the partisanship we have is not personal (except incidentally), but it is a partisanship for the moral and intellectual life of the institution, which is the only life which an institution of learning has.

I am writing this out because I may fail to see you today. I am going out in the woods as soon as it gets daylight, and if I have good luck, I shall spend most of the morning there.

Bedi

Austin, Texas
December 13, 1944

Dear Dobie:

In reply to your question, I take pleasure in explaining and documenting my protest against the translation from the Latin of the motto on the university seal made by Regent Bullington[8] during the recent Senate hearing.

I first recalled to the committee that Regent Bullington quoted in a sneering tone the motto which is carved across the front of the Main Building: "Ye shall know the truth and the truth shall make you free." I declared that I could not at first make out whether he was sneering at the sentiment of the quotation, or was merely contemptuous of a student body and faculty which didn't know its own motto.

I was therefore enlightened when he declared that "Ye shall know," etc., is not the motto of the university, but that "Disciplina Praesidium Civitatis" is the motto inscribed in the seal of the university.

So far so good, and I thought that he had scored a point. But when he gave his surprising translation, I was again taken aback. "Being freely translated," he said, "it means *discipline* is the protection of the state." Really, that is not freedom, but license in translation. I declared to the committee that *disciplina,* according to information furnished me by competent Latinists, never stands alone in Latin for any kind of discipline imposed from without; but that, standing alone, unmodified, as it does in the motto, it always means mental training, or education, which, of course, always involves a kind of self-discipline. It was obvious that Regent Bullington was assuming that *disciplina* might be used to indicate "control gained by enforcing obedience or order, as in a school or army; strict government," which, of course, is one of half a dozen senses in which our English word "discipline" may be used.

After giving this exceedingly "free" translation of the motto, he pointed an accusing finger from the table at former President Rainey, and asked why he hadn't used this discipline of the motto to quell or control the students and faculty, or words to that effect. I do not have the record before me, so must quote from memory; but that is the sense of his objurgatory remark. This was charging in on the faculty's own sacred ground (that of linguistic interpretation), where even "angels fear to tread."

I proceeded to point out to the committee that these three Latin words were a direct translation from the English by either Dr. Fay or Dr. Battle of Mirabeau B. Lamar's famous and oft-repeated saying: "Cultivated mind is the guardian genius of democracy." Simply that and nothing more. One or the other of these scholars had translated "cultivated mind" into the Latin *disciplina*.

I further said that it was an error of the German fascists to substitute discipline (in the sense of imposing a regime by force) for education in their dealings with German universities and with their school system generally.

The documentation for my position in this matter is to be found in *The University of Texas Record,* Volume VIII, January to December 1908, pages 110–15, in an article written by no less an authority than Dr. William J. Battle, then and since professor of Greek in the university. It is recorded there that a new seal was adopted for the university by the regents on October 31, 1905, on recommendation of the president and the faculty. The agitation for a new seal was started by Dr. Battle himself three years prior to its adoption. Writing in 1902 with considerable eloquence, Dr. Battle called attention to the beneficent influence of certain historic seals and their mottoes, notably that of Harvard and that of Oxford. He expressed dissatisfaction with the state seal which was then used by the university.

He said that The University Act of the Legislature of 1881, Section 7 (Revised Statutes Art. 3845), provides "The Regents and their successors in office shall have the right of making and using a common seal and altering the same at pleasure."

It may be pointed out in passing that no authority is given, however, for mistranslating a motto on said seal by any regent, or by action of the whole board, for that matter.

On November 15, 1881, according to Dr. Battle's article in the *Record,* a committee composed of Ashbel Smith,[9] Thomas J. Devine,[10] and Smith Ragsdale[11] was appointed to "devise a seal." The following day the committee reported, recommending "a Texas Star inscribed in a circle, a second circumference being circumscribed, leaving a narrow space between the two circumferences on which shall be engraved the Latin words 'Universitas Texanus' . . . and the Latin motto: *'Non Sine Pulvere Palma.'* "

Dr. Battle's acid criticism of this seal was, "except for the word 'Universitas' it might just as well be the emblem of the state penitentiary." He also objected to the design as incorrect heraldry. Then he submitted a design himself, drawn by Charles Young of Bailey, Banks & Biddle of Philadelphia. This is described in heraldic language as follows: "Within a circle gules bearing the legend *Sigillum Universitatis Texanae,* a disk of azure with motto *Disciplina Praesidium Civitatis.* Surrounding a shield tenné bearing a mullet within a wreath of olive and live-oak branches argent on the chief of the last of an open book proper."

Explaining the division of the shield, etc., he concludes:

"Disciplina Praesidium Civitatis . . . is Professor Edwin W. Fay's terse Latin rendering of the apothegm of President Mirabeau B. Lamar . . . 'Cultivated mind is the guardian genius of democracy.' "

"Surely we have here a truth," says Dr. Battle, quite prophetically, "that the American people have need to learn. Could a truer and more timely watchword be found for the institution which stands at the head of the educational system of the State? It is at once the justification of the University's existence and the ideal of its future. By the side of this ringing battle cry, the old *Non Sine Pulvere Palma* seems feeble and spiritless."

President Prather put this, Dr. Battle's proposal, to the faculty on November 3, 1903, and, on their recommendation, took it to the Board of Regents. The regents acted on it October 31, 1905, and at that meeting adopted the design with the substitution of the English "Seal of the University of Texas" instead of the Latin *Sigillum Universitatis Texanae*. The substitution of English took more room and demanded a new drawing and hence more delay. The artist, Mr. Harry Eldridge Goodhue, of Cambridge, Massachusetts, drew the design of the bookplate for the university library including the new seal. From the seal of this bookplate a separate electrotype was made for the catalogue and other official publications. "Oddly enough," says Dr. Battle, "it is the first drawing of the 'olive and liveoak branches' prescribed by the Constitution. . . . In every form of the state seal so far found, even in the Great Seal itself in the Secretary of State's office, the oak branch is that of a deciduous, not an evergreen oak."

Yours truly,
Roy Bedichek

Port Isabel, Texas
January 7, 1945

Dear Bedi:

. . . Well, we came down here to get sunshine, freedom from cedar pollen, and I hope peace for some creative writing. Damn it, I can't find what it takes to unlock me. Yesterday I spouted again on the Rainey university business to the diminutive Port Isabel Rotary Club. My piece was printed in valley newspapers this morning. I sent Rainey my copy. Papers are rationed down here, strictly. I hope the Brownsville boys sent the article all over the state. I put a cocklebur under Strickland's tail right here in his own pigpen. This Board of Regents won't fire anybody that stands up and fights them. It looks to me as if Coke[12] might find a lot of blocks on his skidway. I hope so. Good luck.

Your friend,
Frank Dobie

March 13, 1945

Dear Webb:

The whole point is not the virtue of Rainey but the evil purpose of the gang that has captured the university.

Are we going to let the pirates, numbering only 10 per cent of voters of Texas, capture the ship and dispose us around in positions of absolute subservience to their purposes, which is chiefly to act for *their* masters in the exploitation of this state?

Rainey's[13] virtue (you may say it is his sole virtue) is that he sees the point and has enough courage to fight the issue out —and that's enough virtue for me.

Bedi

For Bedichek and Webb in particular, the crisis at the university reached a peak May 29, 1946. Homer Price Rainey had been ousted as President. Theophilus Schickel Painter had succeeded him as Acting President. A faculty meeting was called for May 29 to endorse the appointment of Painter as President. Bedichek had led the opposition to the appointment of Painter as Acting President; Webb led the opposition to his appointment as President.

Two letters exchanged between them and Webb's resolution to the faculty indicate how heated the argument had become.

Austin, Texas
May 27, 1946

PERSONAL AND PAINFUL

Dear Bedi:

I want you to come in and be present at the called meeting of the faculty on Wednesday where Duncalf[14] is going to present a report of the Committee to Help Choose a President.

Tonight I attended a caucus in Garrison Hall, and made the mistake of saying something. Result: I was appointed one of a Committee of Five to draw a resolution of no confidence in Painter.[15] The large committee waited, and instead of going with the small committee, I went to my office and wrote out what I would say, sketching the history of Painter's perfidy. The Committee immediately adopted it in lieu of what they had, and the whole Committee accepted it and turned their guns on me to present it. Finally, I consented, although had I known the turn events took, I would have remained away.

You are a good part of the reason I accepted it, unwittingly, no doubt, and I would therefore like very much for you to be present. You recall when Painter was appointed, you stood up in faculty, puzzled and confused by the fact that those who you thought should support you were throwing their influence in favor of endorsing Painter. I made the only speech I have made on that occasion. Here is the situation: Duncalf, Stayton,[16] Parten,[17] and Bobbitt[18] came from Houston urging that we accept Painter as A.P. In my speech I reminded the faculty that all concerned were urging acceptance as the lesser of evils. Moreover, we had Painter's word for it that he would take the job temporarily, would not accept it permanently if elected; he even said some uncomplimentary things about the regents who had appointed him.

You, knowing all this, stood up in lone protest, hardly knowing what to do, and I argued back at you, as I recall.

So, my dear Bedi, I have an unpleasant task, but it will be a little less unpleasant if you will come and sit where I can see you. Really, I'd appreciate it. The fireworks are going to be good.

God knows I'll never whitewash a painter. Well, that's bad, but I can do worse in the pun line if I really try.

Yours,
Webb

Cedar Valley
Travis County, Texas
May 30, 1946

Dear Webb:

How important is leadership since the greater number of men are merely corporals. You appeared before the faculty yesterday with the impassiveness and reserve power of an Avenger, the Nemesis figure in Greek tragedy, although one in your audience, reputed to be the greatest classical scholar of the lot, failed to see the resemblance and himself descended to a quite minor role.

The language of truth is simple, and I felt a kind of sympathetic shame at seeing a number of my old-time friends writhe under the lashes of your sentences.

Pittenger[19] appeared to best advantage in the opposition since, like any first-rate or even third-rate lawyer, he acknowledged the disagreeable truth to begin with and proceeded to put the best possible face on it. It was a rather poor face after he had done, but it was a face. Calhoun,[20] Barker,[21] and Battle[22] by resorting to what I must consider (with great regret) a disgraceful demagogy, failed to construct any kind of a face. To say in defense of your charge of broken faith that any man has a right to change his mind is merely to repudiate all pledges by putting them in a class with the whim of a dyspeptic who changes his order from fried to boiled eggs for breakfast. Thus the most solemn compacts become false as dicers' oaths.

I didn't believe these men could take such a stand. I know that not one of them would put himself in a position to require the defense he is making for another.

I was surprised at Battle's reiteration of the term "honorable man" as it was a mistake in connotation which no literary man should have made. Says he, "Dr. Painter is an honorable man" and repeats, and every literate person in his audience (and there were many) completed the sentence under his breath, "So are they all, all honorable men."

I say nothing of Fitzgerald[23] because I have come to expect nothing. He reminded me yesterday of a spoiled and boisterous child of four protesting in a falsetto rage the action of a nurse who has deprived him of an all-day sucker.

Painter's defense was pitiable: The faculty had broken faith with him and therefore he was going to break faith with it. His decision was unilateral. Dolley[24] threatened dire disaster: little more. I should have liked to hear a word or two from Burdine,[25] and many others were listening for Burdine, too.

Your resolution and supporting statement endows the whole

episode with a museum permanence. You caught the action of this man in the clear amber of a purely factual account in which it will be preserved for those students of a later generation who happen to become interested in studying the nazification of (or the attempt to nazify) the university. I am hoping that the present effort will prove to be only an attempt, and that you yourself (I can think of no one worthier of the honor) will write its epitaph in the same triumphant tone which Dr. R. D. Kollewijn uses in concluding his description of the Dutch universities under Nazi domination:

> So ended the struggle of the German occupant against the universities of the Netherlands, with its material victory but with its moral defeat. What could be done by force and violence, he accomplished. He could drive out, imprison and kill students and professors. But he did not succeed in enslaving the free Dutch universities or in turning them into centers for the preaching of his own abject National Socialist ideas.
>
> With a resurrected Netherlands the universities and colleges, independent of earthly powers, take up once more in concert their historic task of searching for truth and fighting for justice.

If our own scientists could only understand that it is just as much the historic function of a university to fight for justice as it is to search for truth! Unless to their "research, research, research," we add "fight, fight, fight," human gains are lost.

Yours,

Bedi

At the meeting of the General Faculty of the University of Texas on Wednesday, May 29, the undersigned voting members of that body will present the following resolution:—

Whereas in October, 1944, Dr. T. S. Painter was appointed by a Special Committee, of which he was a member, to go to

Houston with two other faculty members and cooperate with the Ex-Students' Committee in ironing out the differences between the Regents and the President, and

Whereas, he returned on November 2 with the appointment of Acting President, and

Whereas, it was his desire that the faculty approve by vote his acceptance of the position temporarily, and

Whereas, he gave the following pledge to the faculty, to wit: "I want it definitely understood that I am not a candidate for the position of permanent president, and I will not accept it if it were offered to me," and

Whereas, on the basis of this promise, the faculty did on November 3 give him a unanimous vote of support and confidence, and

Whereas, Dr. Painter has on later occasions stated or implied that he would not consider permanent appointment, and

Whereas, the Faculty Committee on the Selection of a President spent many months canvassing the field to find a suitable president and failed to recommend Dr. Painter, and

Whereas, despite the facts recited, the Regents did on May 24, 1946, elect Dr. Painter Permanent President and he did on the following day accept the position without consulting the faculty:

Therefore, the faculty by this resolution expresses deep regret that Dr. Painter has not reciprocated the trust the faculty reposed in him, but has, on the contrary, broken faith and violated his pledge. Despite this regret we will give our support to all measures conducive to the success and progress of the institution we serve.

Walter P. Webb	C. M. Montgomery
Frederic Duncalf	Clarence Morris
C. E. Ayres	Aaron Schaffer
J. M. Kuehne	Robert C. Stephenson
Robert H. Williams	Kenneth C. Davis

Dr. Painter became Permanent President. However, the "era of tranquillity" proclaimed by the Regents continued in many ways to an "era of hostility." Dobie left the university. Bedichek and Webb fumed in letters to each other.

Austin, Texas
September 11, 1951

Dear Webb:

I was first astounded and then benumbed by the length of the list of subversive organizations the faculty is being required to swear no connection with, now or in the indefinite past.

Many of these organizations put out journals of one sort or another, but include "membership" with subscription. You may have a curiosity concerning what such an organization puts out in the way of propaganda and send in a "trial" subscription for a short period, and the organization then lists you automatically as a member. How the hell am I to know that I am not a "member" of one or the other of these organizations in the sense that I subscribed to its periodical to see what they were putting out, and in the hope (always proved vain) of getting the low-down of Things-as-They-Are? I know that I once subscribed for *The Living Age,* and that it later turned out to be subsidized by Japan. I don't know whether or not the subscription included some membership in something or other. Knowing that faculty members are prone to do the same kind of thing I have done, that is, subscribe for periodicals, I'm afraid many an innocent party will suffer from this outrageous requirement.

Is this thing bothering you?

Why don't you "appear" sometime?

Bedi

Austin Texas
September 17, 1951

Dear Bedi:

No, the oath is not bothering me at all. The first one did, but after it my pride was gone, and maybe my virtue too. A combination of poverty and a general reluctance to "belong" to anything probably offers me a protection which I haven't earned. If by chance I got on the mailing list of some questionable outfit, the burden of proof with my signature will rest on the prosecution. In the meantime I shall blithely assume that I am as pure as the regents or the members of the legislature. You know, of course, that the attorney general has declared the retroactive clause—the ten-year thing—unconstitutional. Surely, you, I, and all the rest have not joined the YMCA since learning how dangerous joining is. What the hell difference does it make at our age anyway?

Now that cool weather has come at last, I'll be able to see you without our growling at each other with mutual incivility. Every bit of energy available has gone into the manuscript. How fortunate that I did not teach this summer. Had I done so, the book would have been delayed at least a year. Now, it seems that I may get it to the publishers in time for a fall publication for 1952.

The grind is opening here with young-men-in-a-hurry, middle-aged men in suspense, and old ones in resignation.

In reading the last sentence of your letter, I see that you are concerned about the faculty in general. Some are going to be embarrassed, but I doubt that any action will be taken if they hold still. If specific cases arise, there is sure to be some cooperative effort made to see that they have all the protection to which they are entitled. Our democracy has come to a new position when it has to make laws to protect itself. Heretofore it has been like a healthy body, able to throw off bad germs, to keep its doors open with the feeling it can take care of anything that enters. What did Walt Whitman mean when he said that democracy would need strong compellers?

Yours,

W. P. Webb

Webb was thirty-four years climbing the academic ladder from instructor to professor, and his last promotion, to "distinguished professor," came only after a battle between the regents and the administration. Webb was then sixty-four, approaching retirement, and widely accepted for his studies of the frontier. He was also weary of paying year after year for the luxury of individuality, and ready to fight. Fortunately others carried the fight for him, but they could not make up for the outrage he felt.

Austin, Texas
June 8, 1952

Dear Bedi:

I enjoyed your letter very much, and in response to your vivid account of Utopia, I, like the readers of Moore, Bacon, and St. Pierre, shared your pleasure vicariously. I could for a time smell the desert flowers after rain, view the sunset and sunrise across the dimples of the limitless landscape, and fill my lungs with the nipping western winds that always remind me of a frolicsome colt.

Your comments on the late-blooming flowers are most appropriate in my case. I have always been late, in getting to the university, in finishing, in graduate study, in taking the Ph.D. degree. I could have got through the university earlier had I been willing to drudge at such jobs as I might have got. I was too old, too independent, and too mean—perhaps too

lazy—to follow that program. It would not have been good
for me.

It seems that my appointment involved a real issue between the administration, including deans, president, and chancellor, on the one hand, and the regents, specifically Mr.
Woodward,[26] on the other. Jim Hart[27] had made up his mind,
worked very hard on the business, and was resolved to win the
principle involved. I can tell you more about this when I see
you. The fact that Jim was apparently determined to fight the
thing out makes me a little uncomfortable over what might
have resulted had he not had his way. As for my part, I had
made up my mind to make an issue after I was turned down
by the regents. I wasn't clear on procedure, but had in mind
an open letter with a direct charge of interference in the details of university administration. That would have barred me
for all time from further recognition, but at my age recognition
is not important. Of course I could not have made the issue
without having definite proof that the whole administration
had acted favorably. This information would have been in
hand. As it turned out, the vote in the board was unanimous,
though I have learned that the discussion extended over the
two days. I like to think that Jim Hart has won on a principle
far more important than any individual concerned. Of course,
he will have to win it over and over with each new board, but
the fact that he understands its importance, and is determined
to be firm, is of great importance. I think he has won a victory
and I wish that all the faculty could know the extent to which
(in my opinion) he was willing to go in order to win. I don't
know how far, but I suspect the limit! What a man!

Gutsch[28] last year promised me a stag dinner if the appointment came through, and I was to invite my close friends.
You were naturally on the list, and I regret that you will not
be here on Thursday night. I know you are having a fine time
in the Far West. Friday I leave for two weeks in the East,
ten days as the guest of the Du Pont Corporation in an

indoctrination program being conducted for the "benefit" of educators from over the nation. It will be an interesting experiment, one that is being carried on by several of the great corporations. If you want to communicate with me from June 16 to June 26, inclusive, address me at Hotel Dupont, Wilmington, Delaware. I shall go on to New York, and may go to Boston if the publishers have any reason for my doing so.

You no doubt know that we are having rains, and the country looks good. Rodney has a camp full of boys, and is feeling fine—most of the time.

For *you* to say that I am "in company with Thoreau" is the accolade. Did you know that Gandhi got his inspiration from Thoreau, and that he developed his whole philosophy on the frontier of South Africa when he went there as attorney, a very prosperous one, and got involved in a fight on behalf of Indian laborers—any Indians—who were being penalized by the British and Boers? This came out in a report by one of my graduate students in the frontier seminar. It is certain that had he not gone to this frontier, he would have remained a rather successful Indian lawyer with an Oxford degree. With his philosophy and technique fully developed in South Africa, he returned to India to work for the freedom of his whole people. How far this frontier influence is going to go, I have no idea, but it extends itself with understanding.

Sincerely yours,
W. P. Webb

VI. Friday Mountain Boys

Pioneer men, when they wanted to talk, went to the barn or field or woods. For them, man talk was different from woman talk, in the words they used, the things they talked about. This distinction persisted in rural America. At church meetings, the chief social event in most country communities, men and women came together during preaching and the search for salvation. Before and after, the women were likely to gather inside the church or under the brush arbor, while the men hung on wagon beds or hunkered in groups beyond earshot of the women. At country stores, men gathered Saturday evenings to talk dirt and politics; women who came to the store at all on Saturday did not linger.

Bedichek, Dobie, and Webb grew up in homes where a wider range of interests than usual prevailed, but they were still homes pervaded by Victorian morality, with only "nice" subjects permitted for discussion, with the language cleaned up to the extent, as Dobie reported, that a bull was called "a gentleman cow." In their own homes they overcame this attitude toward "niceness" to a certain extent, but most of their best talk with each other occurred outside their homes.

All three were brought up close to nature; they were all naturalists in outlook and, when women were not around, in language, kept less natural by the distinctions between barnyard and parlor. All three escaped the land as a way of making a living, but they returned to it every chance they got, and their work made the chances frequent. Bedichek camped out to watch birds and study their habits; Dobie packed by mule through Mexico in search of songs and legends; Webb found that he could see the frontier more clearly through the smoke of a campfire. For the most part, their wives stayed at home on these trips, as well as on the picnics the three arranged when they felt the need to talk over what they had learned.

In a way, they were all looking toward something like Friday Mountain Ranch, which Webb bought in 1942, when he was fifty-four years old, and of which he later said: "In 1942 I did what turned out to be a wise thing. I bought the old Johnson Institute in the hills southwest of Austin and changed its name to Friday Mountain Ranch because a hill there is named Friday Mountain and I liked the name." It was more than a ranch; it was a retreat.

It is sixteen miles from Austin, in a region where there are juniper-covered hills and valleys, and creeks that run when the rains come. The main building is a two-story rock house, built as a part of the Johnson Institute about the time of the Civil War. Bear Creek runs a few hundred yards away. Friday Mountain is to the south. It is a place of beauty and quiet, a haven of peace where men of like mind and like spirit could drink and eat and talk.

These were no ordinary picnics. The preparations were simple but careful, the company limited to the few who could talk their language. Wives would have inhibited talk. As a matter of fact, these men and their wives rarely got together as two or three couples. There was friendship, but at a distance. Each, when speaking of his wife to another, more often called her not by her first name but by "Mrs." This practice was left over somewhat from the manners of the Old South, a practice they were free to discard but did not. The laughter that echoed from Friday Mountain would have been more restrained with women present. Many of the stories would never have been told at all.

The preferred time for these meetings was after the heat of the day but in time for the clear blue of the sky to redden with sunset. They stayed until darkness had spread over the hills—not blackness but darkness made luminous by stars shining through unmisted air. Light from a low-glowing fire tinged their faces. Night sounds mingled with their talk.

In one evening their talk might range from the dialogues of Plato to the wisdom of a cowboy; the expression from the literary and sophisticated to the bawdy of the outhouse. Their talk, surprisingly like their letters, was often lightened by an anecdote. A Dobie favorite shows his love of irony: A cowboy named Smith, fed up with the boredom of riding the range, took his pay, told his wife goodbye, and rode into town for a spree. After drinking too much he got into a shooting scrape and was killed. Someone had to tell the widow and a cowboy was given the job. It took him all the way to the house to figure out how to break the news. He rode up to the door and yelled, "Does Smith live here?" A woman came to the door and said, "Yes." The cowboy said, "I bet he don't," and rode off.

Theirs was genuine male friendship, and their letters remain as an unusual manifestation. Like Walt Whitman, whom they admired and quoted often, they were unashamed in their expressions of affection. In their most intimate relationships, they were simple, direct, honest.

Theirs was a remarkable three-way friendship, filled with sentiment but sparse in sentimentality.

Austin, Texas
October 21, 1941

Dear Webb:

Enclosed is the Garza bill on Leon Green[1] party. On reverse side you will see note of expenditures which brought total up to $2.71. If you did not spend this much, you owe me half the difference between this amount and the amount you spent. It couldn't be enough to bother with so let's forget it.

Enclosed also is check for three dollars on rent of hideout from October 15 to December 15. Of course, this is experimental, just as you are experimenting. The danger I see is visitors as our mutual and respective friends discover the place. I am not naturally inhospitable, but only reason I want this place is for some retreat where I can go and be either alone or with company of my own choosing. My friend, Kidd,[2] has a place up on the lake. Shelby[3] has a place next his. Seyers[4] has a place on other side. Nearby is Painter's,[5] and near that Mrs. Benedict.[6] All these people have many friends. It's just a nice Sunday afternoon drive, and so—you know what. Being social and friendly and normal human beings, Kidd, Shelby, Painter, et al. all like this, but I wouldn't. You may be a human being for all I know.

Yours,
Bedi

Austin, Texas
October 22, 1941

Dear Bedi:

I must owe you about $1.25 or thereabout. I'll settle in cash, or forget it.

I understand about the camp. Certainly no one will go to that camp without our permission, and it will not be run as an open house. I may occasionally take a party out for an evening, but will notify you well in advance. The situation is such that people will not drop in as at the Country Club on the river. The setup just does not invite that sort of thing. I took one of my card gang out, and he *did not* like it. Another can't go because he must be available by telephone. The one who does not like it is the only one who would, or could, show up there. Unless the whole gang goes, none will go. So there you are. Minatra[7] has some claim on my hospitality, but he has many rural interests, and is the last one who would intrude himself.

It is my intention to keep the place for at least a year. I understand that you are experimenting and I promise that there will be no supersensitiveness here should you decide to hunt a deeper hole in the mountain.

As ever your friendly enemy,
W. P. Webb

The Log Cabin
Willie-Walker, Texas
November 9, 1941

Dear Bedi:

"Memory, a pensive Ruth, went gleaning the silent fields of childhood and found the scattered grain still golden and the morning sunlight fresh and fair."[8]

I have just learned that the guy who wrote that was past fifty and that he spent the night before in a log cabin out in the woods, so far that he could barely hear the anguished wail of a game rooster proclaiming his inadequacy for the coming day.

You remember how in the Big Bend small things took on importance. For example, there was the morning headline in

Jack Wise's camp of the return of the cat. Well, so it is here; I'm learning some things and remembering others that were well-nigh forgotten. And these things are important, about wasps in the house and why a country coffeepot is big at the bottom and has to be.

Last Wednesday Mildred and I came out and spent the night and would have spent Thursday had it not been for a funeral. She cooked on a wood stove for the first time, and learned that it has points, that it will bake without burning, and that it gives you time to get things done. We brought horseshoes (in a keg in the shed room) and set some pegs. The cows and horses had been around, and while I drove the pins, I suggested that she take the shovel and clear up in the immediate vicinity of the horseshoe track. Well, she had never used a shovel and only made matters worse. I finished with the pins, took the shovel, and with a few "deft strokes" soon had the way cleared. Mildred, without any thought of being humorous, said: "It's all in knowing how." It's not often these days that a father gets a word of appreciation out of a grown daughter. Mildred likes it here, and will come back, and maybe learn about some other paternal accomplishments.

I came alone yesterday (Sunday) and arrived about 11 A.M. Had worked late the night before, and after setting up camp and walking to the back of the field to see what our armadillo had done, I decided to postpone a meal and combine two. So I promptly went to bed, read with interest an old *Time,* and went to sleep. When I woke it was 4:30, time to cook supper. Before going to sleep I discovered several wasps in the room, got some out, and then decided to kill them. When I got rid of one, here came another. Bang! Right against the screen. When I got up and built up a fire in the fireplace, I discovered that about fifty had collected on the screen of the front door. My first impulse was to use *Time* on them, and then I remembered that a burning newspaper was the thing for angry wasps. These were big as Spitfires and just about as mean.

I forgot to relate that shortly after I arrived the bay pony signaled with his bell that company was coming. I looked down the valley and saw a woman coming. I took it to be Mrs. Walker and went out to exchange greetings. It was Miss Willie, who was going to pass me up. We talked over the fence and I invited her to come by and see what sort of housekeepers we are. She went back to the gate and came up the green way, her face lined with the marks of more than 18,000 monotonous days. She made an inspection, told me the cabin was plastered in 1925, and that Mrs. Allday had fixed it up real nice. I called her attention to the leaks, and explained that they were due to the insufficient overlap of the sheet iron. She looked at the sheet iron and said:

"Yes, that brother-in-law of mine. That's what you call stretching sheet iron—making it go further." There was a whole volume of personal relationship and a commentary with footnotes on parsimonious rural economy in the subtle irony. The late Mr. Walker was no extravagant man! That's what she told me.

Then she began to inspect the openings under the house, and to hunt for rocks with which to plug them. She said she had stopped most of them, and with some pride, that she had boarded up the shed room herself. She confirmed our suspicion that rattlesnakes den up under these old houses in winter, but she thought they would not be out until spring. I told her that you and I thought only little rattlesnakes could get in or under the house. She studied about this, and after stopping some of the bigger openings, expressed the view that we were probably right. The last rattlesnake fatality here was a dog.

Now this is news which I believe should be broken to the womenfolks gently—say one snake at a time!

Cooked supper at 5:30. Not much fun to eat by yourself. Eating is a social affair.

Worked until 10:30. Actually got something done. May do some decent writing if the snakes will just sleep. Woke at 4

A.M. Enjoyed a little misery in bed by thinking of all the things
I had done that I shouldn't and of those I should have done
and haven't. Up at 5; coffee, toast, eggs, and bacon just as day
was breaking. Am beginning to think: "Town boys sit up a
good part of the day waiting for night; country boys sit up a
good part of the night waiting for day." Walked to the back
of the field in the dawn. What a lift to the coming of day.
Your birds were calling their notes while the crows beat the
drum. I could hear the near ones flutter, but it was not light
enough to see them. On the return, what with the grass soft
to the feet and memory of horse hunting, I had a momentary
recurrence of the feeling of youth. How fast these hours of
silence move!

And now it's eight o'clock and I've got to read a goddamned
Ph.D. thesis and go to town and hold a seminar and sit on a
goddamned faculty club council. It makes me want to stretch
sheet iron.

Yours,
Walter Prescott Webb

Better take out a gallon of kerosene. That lamp really uses
oil. There is a gallon here, but I fear it may not be clean—
good for fires.

Austin, Texas
November 12, 1941

Dear Webb:

It seems to me that you have struck a new vein in your old
age. This "adventure in contentment" of yours appeals to me
greatly.

It has, of course, its pathetic side. I think I could write a
witty and very sad poem about a henpecked father of distinction in whose heart world-praise had soured, leaving such

empty yearning for the more intimate approbation of his family that (on one occasion) his daughter's casual praise of his efficiency in S***S*** warmed the cockles of his heart to such temperature that he glowed like a lightning bug for a week. Against the gray cyclorama of the lives of sad-eyed and far-gazing Mrs. Walker and of wee-willie-winkie, I think you can build a stage piece of great artistic merit, and at the same time let off a dangerous accumulation of emotional steam. Maybe the old Antaeus in you is touching earth again?

Yours,

Bedi

Austin, Texas
August 21, 1942

Dear Webb:

. . . Once or twice in the last few days, suffering with a burning thirst, I have tried to reach you, but without success. In all probability, if I can dodge this Pre-flight School business tomorrow, and disentangle myself from one or two tentative engagements, I shall load up with water and provisions for "over Sunday" and with Pop, take to the woods. Glad to have you go with me, if you will. I may go to Friday Mountain Ranch—certainly will, if you can accompany me.

Yours,

Bedi

Austin, Texas
February 13, 1943

Dear friend Bedi:

I received a letter mailed on January 9 from Colonel Webb and cutting out the Association-business details, I am sure that you will be interested in the following paragraphs:

. . . "Just after Christmas I developed a cold, and I want to tell you about the remedy so that you can use it if you need. I had secured from one source or another a can of dried milk by the curious trade name of Klem and a can of Cocomalt. I had also a bottle of Scotch whiskey. Now it seems that my system requires milk, more than we get at table, and it is not averse on occasions to either Cocomalt or Scotch whiskey, though it may have a little leaning one way or tother. The Egyptologist had lent me a little pan to heat things over the coal fire, and so I decided to make a brew of dried milk, Cocomalt, and Scotch whiskey, supplemented by hot water until it had reached the right consistency. O. Henry wrote a swell story about the Lost Blend, but if he could have known of this, his story need not have ended so tragically. I took a generous portion of this divine concoction and went to bed with a pig (a 'pig' is a hot-water bottle) and dreamed that the white rocks on Friday Mountain are dried milk, the brown loam in the valley Cocomalt, and that Bear Creek is running bank full of Scotch whiskey. I haven't been the same since, and as I know you have colds in Texas, I just wanted to pass the information on to you. Of course you may not be able to get the ingredients. I am getting low on dried milk and especially Cocomalt, but I have plenty of Scotch whiskey, which is not so bad just by itself. Bedi suffers with colds and I hope you will explain this remedy in full to him."

I think you will appreciate the last paragraph even more when you note that the English censor will not allow a letter to come through requesting any specific commodity to be sent over by international parcel post. We had sent over several cans of Klem and some Cocomalt. Shakespeare never concealed something more cleverly in a play than did the Colonel in telling that he was running low on Klem and that his system required more milk than he got at the table. You see he says he can get the Scotch whiskey. I think his cold enriched both

English and Texas literature even though it might not do for general publication.

Come by to see us.

Yours,
H. Bailey Carroll[9]

Austin, Texas
May 19, 1944

Dear Webb:

This month's *Harper's* (I mean the current *Harper's*—don't know whether it's May or June) has an article in it on the American's way of fighting by a man named Brogan, Scotch, Cambridge professor. You should read it to find quite a lot of thunder for your particular thesis. He shows how the frontier has fashioned the military psychology of the American military, and how they are fighting now in the way they have learned so well in conquering the continent. It's principally logistics—I had never thought of it, and maybe you haven't. He makes a strong—and humorous—case. And like all the damned English he writes well.

Yours,
Bedi

P.S. also read in same issue *Harper's* reason for not publishing a critical article on MacArthur.

P.P.S. When are we going out in the country? When are we going to drink a bottle of beer? When are we going to do some wild irrational thing, such as we promised each other we would do, every so often, like, say, hitchhiking to Fredericksburg, or selling souvenirs on a street corner in Dallas?

P.P.P.S. L. J. Ireland,[10] telephone 2-9194, 4907 Avenue G

has a good story in him. He has a method of reconditioning lubricating oil, but the big boys won't let him use his invention.

                                                    Austin, Texas
                                                    May 20, 1944

Dear Bedi:

Your note of yesterday hurts a conscience already sensitive over my comment on your former invitation. I am really tired and long to get away from audiences—never liked them or the experience of amusing them by personal appearance. It ain't my *forte*. Besides, I want time for what I can do, if not well, at least better.

If we have not done something irrational *together,* it is your fault. I do it constantly on my own hook. I've bought a truck—a dump truck, at that, and it won't dump—yet.

Are you willing to set up camp on creek for a week in June or July? We can get a tent and live well on little.

I knew Brogan, visited in his home—Irish, not English, taught at Minnesota. Versatile, encyclopedic, industrious—and ambitious. Have *Harper's* but have not read that article.

Let's go see this Ireland—maybe he is the cue for something irrational and foolish. There are so many fool things I'd like to do, and I was proper for so long. How I envy you, who did them when young. There are so many things that I can now do only through imagination! Too many.

                                                    Yours,
                                                    Webb

                                                    June 23, 1944

Dear Webb:

Returning Bartram's under another cover. Thanks. It touched three areas of my interest quite nearly: 1. natural history; 2. romantic revival in English lit.; and 3. Indians. Contrast between Creeks and Seminoles is a revelation.

Was poised for flight to Friday Mountain, but Sarah[11] last night had telephone call from her husband in San Francisco, just landed from 20 months in SW Pacific. She's all in a dither and may leave any moment. He's detained there a week for orders. So I have to stay on deck and see that everything goes according to somebody else's orders and that nobody makes the mistake of following my advice or instructions or suggestions—you know how it is.

So goodbye to this weekend, and to others also since God and his coadjutors have entered a conspiracy to frustrate every timid little hope that buds in my fading brain. I wish I were young again so that I could get drunk.

Yours,

Bedi

Austin, Texas
April 23, 1945

Dear Bedi:

Monday begins right with a salty note from you. R.L.B. sent me a copy of your letter and one of his which I'll enclose if I can find it and don't forget it after I do find it.

Am reading two books, one here and one at the house. Here it is John P. Marquand, *The Late George Apley,* and at the house *Fighting Liberal,* the autobiography of George Norris. George Apley and George Norris represent the poles of nineteenth-century American life. Apley is Bostonian, nurtured on the accumulated wealth of a nation, self-contained, self-assured, yet miserable in the feeling that he has missed the boat. George Norris missed the boat but never knew it because he had no basis of comparison. He lived in reality, poverty, and hardship, and once arrived he had every reason to be a conservative. I am referring only to his schoolteaching days, when he was living in a tool shack in Washington state where he had been lured by stories of the West. What a century the nineteenth was, when any boy who was willing to pay the price could go anyplace he desired. I can lend you the Norris but not the Apley, which is borrowed from Hornberger. I sent you Tony Thomason's[12] *Go Tell Them*. If you like it give him a hand. He is finding himself at last, has talent and promise. I'll send you soon a copy of his poem describing a farmer coming in to pay a hundred-dollar note to the rich man. It is deep east Texas and damned good, in my poor unpoetic opinion. Of course some guy who has corrupted his taste and blurred his vision by reading the classics might not like it at all.

The suggestion of a trip to Friday Mountain Ranch with you opens the valves of my gas tank and my grateful heart. The damned sheep have kept the flowers down there, but the road thither is a blanket of the heavens on a clear dark night, with color effects. A year ago I planted forty dollars worth of mesquite grass seed on a wet day just before a long drought. The grass came up like baby hair, but the sun blasted cracks in the ground that a mouse could wallow in and the baby grasslets passed out in sickly yellow wisps. Yesterday I found forty bunches, more or less, that had survived and are now bearing seeds. It's a new kind of grass, and I am hopeful that it will make my fortune. At a dollar a bunch it ought to be good! Since you are a city gardener, I know you have no background to appreciate such returns on agricultural investment. Of course my grass is perpetual (theoretically) but your garden is an annual transient. My grass will live after me but your produce will furnish stuff in which to bury your bones, if you garden long enough. Moreover, my grass will spread a kindly mantle over my grave, provided it is sufficiently neglected, while your truck will never find in you either substance or sustenance.

Sincerely yours,

W. P. Webb

VII. Talk Swapping

These men learned to take note of things around them; the look of the weather, the call of a bird, the sound of the words of a cowhand or a cedar cutter. They filled their minds with the near and now, as well as with the far away and long ago. Aside from their work as educators, they were naturalist, folklorist, historian. Each, by avocation at least, was intensely interested in the others' areas. They knew what to look for, and their exchanges, written or oral, went beyond mere gossip or tale telling.

In this sense they were all historians of Texas and the Southwest, but not conventional historians. The frontier lingered with them, especially in their appreciation of simple ways and the primitive art of folk telling. They were indefatigable in their search for the fact and how it happened; they were likely to color the fact by what the people said and how they said it. On occasion, they were all tellers of folk tales.

To some extent, their mature works are the result of collaboration. The lore they swapped showed up as a part of the fabric in finished works, sometimes as a detail, more often as a humor.

The kind of talk they got into at times is recorded with fidelity on a tape made by Bedichek and Dobie:

BEDICHEK: Dobie and I one time got into a conversation—or got into a letter-writing exchange—about the earliest birds that sing. He was up at Kerrville and I was here, and we exchanged several letters just detailing the earliest birds and the succession of birds that began to sing in the morning. I had the advantage of the thing because I had a screech owl nesting in my yard, and the screech owl opened up usually about three-thirty every morning. And then came along the dove, I believe. Wasn't it, Dobie? The dove was the next one that made a noise? Anyhow, it came along like this—doves, then cardinals. Cardinal's a very early bird. The mockingbird, in my experience—unless it's a moonlight night—he goes to sleep and he oversleeps himself. He will sing late just like a rounder will. Be out late at night, you know, and then oversleep himself. I've rarely heard a mockingbird sing before sunup in the morning. Oh, he may have been singing at midnight, in the night.

I have a curious situation. I have a martin box where there are sixteen compartments and occupied by a great many martins, but the street lights—the tower lights—here evidently interfere with the martins' sleep and they wake up and give a weak little song, sounds like they're singing in their sleep. Any time of night.

DOBIE: I've heard several birds wake up after midnight and give three or four notes and then go right back to sleep. Go back inside there and go to sleep.

BEDICHEK: The order in which birds sing is very interesting in any locality, and I think it varies a good deal in various localities, of course as the bird population changes.

DOBIE: I wrote Bedi that he should write an essay on who is the early bird.

BEDICHEK: I remember Dobie had called attention to a

thing I had noticed but had been unconscious with me. And that is, if you're camping out west where these ravens live, the white-necked raven. The white-necked raven replaces the crow about fifty miles west of Austin. You find nothing but white-necked ravens on out west. If you're camped along the highway there you'll hear these old ravens croaking up the highway before daylight. Dobie called my attention to that, and I think the reason they do that is that the killings on the highway provide them with early morning breakfast. They're out early before the buzzards, and they've learned to go up that highway and pick up these rabbits and other stuff and get their breakfast before anybody else does.

DOBIE: I told you about that time I saw them. I was coming home from New Mexico—been out in the mountains by myself, camping. About ten o'clock, I guess, I stopped at Van Horn, bought some gasoline, and thought I'd drive on till I got sleepy. Well, I didn't go but eight or ten miles before I got sleepy. I drove my car to a kind of a wagon road off to the right, drove up that wagon road maybe a hundred yards to where it was quiet, got out of my car, pulled out my bedroll, put it on the ground, and was asleep in a minute. Woke up a good while before daylight. Morning star was bright, though. As I started to roll up my bedroll, why, some of these ravens came over my head. They were flying east. Well, before I got the bedroll back to my car, there'd been three or four little bunches of ravens over my head—

BEDICHEK: Were they going in the same direction?

DOBIE: All going east. I guess they'd come miles and miles, because there's no trees in that country. They'd come maybe fifty miles from where there were trees, their roosting place. When I got back on the highway my lights were still burning but the dawn was coming. I hadn't gone any distance till I saw about three or four ravens eating a jack rabbit. Drove on a little farther. There were some more ravens eating another rabbit. It was getting dawn now and I turned my lights off. In twenty miles I came to fifteen dead creatures—most of them rabbits, maybe a skunk or something else—and not all had been killed that night—some of them were a night or two before. When daylight came, other scavengers joined these ravens. One place it was a buzzard. About two places there were hawks, and one place there were two crows and one buzzard and one hawk.

BEDICHEK: Two ravens?

DOBIE: Two ravens, yes, around this jack rabbit.

BEDICHEK: That was in competition—

DOBIE: That was in competition, but no competition before daylight. I know those ravens patrol that highway every morning. That was years ago. I bet you go out there now and you'll find them doing it.

BEDICHEK: That illustrates what I was telling a while ago, that hard times and stiff competition encourages thought and develops intelligence. Now you take the situation that Dobie just described, and it is a new situation comparatively. There weren't any highways there fifty years ago where animals were killed and laid on the side every night. That is a new development. Now what daylight animal takes the first cognizance of that? It's the raven, and the raven is known as being a wise bird. That is, he's smart in many other things. He saw the point and he adjusted his sleeping habits in the morning to getting an early breakfast.

Now you see that they did the same thing out there in west Texas where there's very little nesting material. They can fly for miles, and they'll not find a stick to make a nest with. But when these utility companies, telephone companies, began running through the country and clipping off pieces of wire, the raven was the first bird to utilize the little short pieces of wire to build his nest with. So we find in a great many places they utilize the poles they set up as nesting places. It soon became a very great problem for the utility companies because the wire nest would short out the circuit, and an old raven would

frequently be killed right by his nest when he made a connection between his two feet. They just found him dead. One
utility company told me they had to spend something like
forty-five thousand dollars a year clearing their wires of raven
nests in order to prevent short circuits. So, you see, the raven
there in those two instances shows that he is able to take advantage of situations which other birds don't notice. What's
forced it on him is the fact that he's had hard times.

DOBIE: You can apply hard times to some people. It
wouldn't make them intelligent a-tall. I'll tell you that.

BEDICHEK: No, but you apply hard times to a people,
why, it'll develop intelligence in those people.

Bedichek tells about wild turkeys:

Well, there is only one remark that I want to make about
the wild turkey and that is I admire his treatment of the
female. You know, the wild turkey doesn't pursue the female
at all like the ordinary bird does. He doesn't work around
and give her a whole lot of display and dance and tease, you
know, and all that sort of thing. Not at all. What he does—
I watched him down here on the ranch. This wildlife refuge.
They have put just lots of them down there—hundreds and
hundreds of them. In the spring he selects a little knoll—
a bare knoll that's in sight of a considerable area around there.
He gets up on top of that knoll and he utters a call. He
gobbles, and if nothing shows up, why, he will gobble again.
Then maybe he'll scratch the earth and throw his stiff wing
feathers down there and scratch the earth with them; and his
note gets a little bit tougher, a little bit more commanding
and dominating. Presently there's a nice sweet-looking female
sticks her head out from the brush and looks at him. He calls
once or twice again, and, by gosh, she comes right up there
on top of that knoll.

Well, that female goes on off and then he calls up another and another. Then on another knoll somewhere you'll commence to hear another gobbler gobbling, and these old turkeys —female turkeys—sticking their heads out and looking around and sneaking up there to that knoll. He never moves out of his tracks. He never moves off his knoll at all. He does it all by calling. And I think that domination of the gobbler over the female is something that I would I could live with forever.

Their talks often were enlivened by anecdotes such as this one from Bedichek:

Say, you know we mentioned this man Wilhelm from San Marcos. He told me a story that I believe is the truth, although it sounds like a folk tale, about the poor little girl that never had been bitten by a rattlesnake. He said it actually happened in a family that lived up there near Cedar Valley many years ago. It was a big family of them, and the rattlesnakes were very plentiful around the place. It was a pioneer situation so there was a good deal of running around in the bushes and in the grass and so forth by the children. And every now and then one would get bitten by a snake—a rattlesnake—and they'd apply the remedies. None of these things were fatal, but after three or four of them had been bitten, and some of them had been bitten twice, why, this fellow who was a great joker—this father of the family was a great joker—had one little girl about ten years old that he was always joking. And he said to her one day, he said, "Well, here's poor little Mary, never been bitten by a rattler. Poor little Mary. Rattlesnakes won't bite her. They'll bite everybody else but they won't bite her." Well, little Mary looked kinda cowed about that. She didn't take it the way he thought she would take it, and he sort of teased her a good deal so that the next time anyone was bitten he said, "Well, it wasn't Mary. They won't bite

Mary. She's never been bitten by a rattlesnake. They bite everybody else but they don't bite Mary."

Poor little Mary. She got so that she'd cry every time he did that. Every time he called attention to the fact that she was kinda ostracized by the rattlesnakes, that she just got the feeling of inferiority. And she got paler and paler and her schoolwork went down. And she didn't make good grades and she was just generally—they thought that something serious was really the matter with her. They moved away from there up toward Blanco, I believe. Opened up another farm up there. And this little girl didn't do any better in the Blanco schools. She was just simply stupid, it looked like.

Well, one day, by gosh, she was out in the pasture and a rattlesnake bit her. She got to the house, why, she told them that a rattlesnake had bit her, with a great deal of pride. And they beat it around and put on the proper tourniquet and so forth and scarred the wound and made her awful sick.

She was lying in bed and her father came in, and she said to him with a weak little smile, she said, "Well, one did bite me, too." And the old man says, "Well, well, the rattlesnake bit Mary. Well, well, well." And he talked to her and jollied her up awhile and finally she got better and got out on her feet again and went back to school. And she commenced making better grades. And her health commenced to pick up and, by George, she was a girl among girls.

Their talk and letters indicate how much their minds overlapped in such fields as nature and folklore. All three had interests acquired through years of country living, close to nature and among people who talked but rarely wrote their thoughts. All three had a professional interest in such material: It was good for anecdotes and illustrations. They were remarkably generous in their sharing. For example, Dobie collected a great deal of material but aban-

doned the idea for a book; Bedichek, who had contributed
his material to Dobie, took it up and published it under
the title *The Sense of Smell*. In this respect, their letters
are often notes for some future book by one or another of
the three.

Austin, Texas
August 22, 1937

Dear Dobie:

The story runneth thus—

Once upon a time in the wilds of west Texas, Hank Hotch-
kiss, famous bear hunter, and compadre, pitched camp in a
deep canyon, cached their supplies, except for bag of frijoles
which was overlooked, and made off into the mountains to
find a bear. On their return that afternoon, about three hours
by sun, they found evidence that Bruin had visited their camp.
The bag of beans had been torn open and apparently consumed by the raider, for only a few frijoles were found scattered
around on the ground.

Although very tired, they took up the trail which led towards
the wildest part of the mountains. Snow had fallen and the
animal was easily followed. Presently, Hank began to notice
a very curious mark in the snow between the impressions left
by the hind feet of the animal. This neat little hole in the
snow puzzled these experienced hunters very much. As the
trail got warmer, these marks centering between the tracks
became more frequent and deeper, and still farther on they
began to merge and form a sort of trench, as if the bear were
dragging something. But the marks were too even and uniform for this theory to satisfy.

Very much mystified they went on and on, up one canyon,
over a divide, and into another. Presently they heard a sound,
very peculiar for that region, and certainly not like that of
any animal either had ever heard. It was more like the *tat-tat-*

tat or *put-put-put* of a motorcycle being cranked on a cold morning. The tracks by this time merged with the central mark, and a little later the tracks almost disappeared. It seemed that the bear was dragging his belly along through the snow in an attempt to smear out his own trail, but there were no scattering hairs along to uphold this theory. The sound was now very distinct and sycamore leaves fell about them, seemingly from a great height, although there was no wind, and no sycamore trees in sight.

Finally, rounding an abrupt turn in the canyon, they saw their quarry, a huge bear resting his enormous distended belly on a great granite boulder. A well-placed shot brought peace again in the great solitude.

"Well, where the hell did them sycamore leaves come from?" asked Hank's companion.

For answer, Hank pointed to a clump of sycamore trees immediately to the rear of the bear, stripped clean of their crisping autumn leaves.

R.B.

Dallas, Texas
September 6, 1937

Dear Dobie:

Before I forget it, I want to give you two well-authenticated stories.

1. A. C. Preston, Capulin, N.M., has a cow pony that he uses in connection with a ton Ford truck on his ranch. The Ford truck will go *almost* everywhere, but not quite. The pony goes with him in back of truck, hanging his neck over the cab and thus bracing himself as the truck careens around the rough mountain roads. When they get to a place where there is riding to be done Preston lets down endgate of truck, the pony *dis*mounts and Preston *mounts* him, and away they go.

When work is done they return to truck, the pony climbs in with no prompting whatever, and off they go to another place, and so on.

My friend (and yours) E. E. Davis, of Arlington, was with him this summer and they drove up in this truck to a bunch of apparently wild ponies out on the range. Preston got out, let down the endgate, whistled, and the pony left the herd, came galloping up, and jumped in the truck. Davis was with him for several days on his rounds and actually saw this pony perform numbers of times. And this ain't no folklore.

2. Davis also told me this one. He and Mrs. Davis were in a powerboat on Lake Worth, returning from camping party. Davis, running the boat, saw ahead of him a snake swimming. He speeded up, intending to run him down, but on closer approach, he identified the snake as a huge rattler, swimming along at a leisurely pace with head well out of the water. The lake was clear as crystal and there was no mistaken identity, Davis assured me. He swerved the boat to one side, fearing that he might throw the snake into the boat. He then circled him, trying to hit him with the oar, but the old boy showed fight. He threw himself into a coil to strike, and bluffed Davis out, for he was afraid he might take a wrap on the oar and come right into the boat. He circled him half a dozen times as the snake made for the shore. He got to the shore, and crawled up the bank, his rattles vibrating, which Davis saw plainly but did not *hear* because of the roar of the motor in the boat.

I have had hot arguments with old-timers in west Texas about the aquatic abilities of the rattler. I saw one swim a hole in Spring Creek near San Angelo when I was a boy, and have had story disputed many times. Davis told me this story in presence of his wife, who confirmed it. I have no doubt that it is true.

Maybe you have encountered same skepticism in this matter that I have. You may put this case in the record as an authentic case not only of rattlesnake's ability to swim, but to fight in the water.

Yours,
Bedichek

Austin, Texas
September 19, 1937

Dear Bedi:

I have been gone a month or more—away out in New Mexico. I had a great trip and learned lots. Upon my return, to keep up the atmosphere, I find your stories of the smart cow horse who works from a truck, the bear that ate the beans (who makes me think of the mile-or-mo' bird), and the rattlesnake in the water. Twice in my life I have seen big rattlesnakes swimming, once for fun and once because of a flood. There were two swimming for fun. They kept their rattles dry. Mary Austin in *One Smoke Stories* has a frijole yarn very much on the order of yours. Thank you much for the stories.

Your friend,
Dobie

Austin, Texas
January 7, 1938

Dear Dobie:

Concerning the aromatic virtue of burning mesquite, I have often (in fact, I always do while camping in mesquite country) held my hands in the mesquite smoke every little while during the breakfast period, so that they will smell of burning mesquite all morning. For hours afterward I can smell the odor on my hands, and I enjoy it very much.

Bedi

P.S. Concerning the use of mesquite as an ornamental wood: I was down at Clarkwood near Corpus the other day and found an old gentleman smoothing up and polishing curiously shaped mesquite roots, being careful to preserve the natural contours of the root. He ran a hole from bottom to top to admit an electric connection, topping it off with a little fancy carving and an ornamental electric light globe. He made a number of these "mesquite-root lamps" for presents to his grandchildren. He had seen better days when he could give them all expensive presents, but it seemed to me that this original bit of handicraft work was better perhaps than any of the presents he made in his better days.

R.B.

Kerrville, Texas
November 19, 1938

Dear Bedi:

Thank you sincerely for sending me the essay on Pearce.[1] It is a real interpretation, just, equable, revealing, as usual when you do speak, your power to see into things. I hope you will publish this in the *Alcalde*. I notice not infrequently that academicians in preparing resolutions or essays on the departed become, as soon as they leave chronology, unmodified liars in attempts at an estimate. The resolutions on poor old Campbell, written in part by Griffith, wherein Campbell was called a "Great Thinker," illustrate. You don't eulogize at all. I agree—indeed, I have so expressed myself—on your estimate of Pearce's writing in *Tales That Dead Men Tell*. It is a shame that that book should be buried as a bulletin.

Well, I am not doing as much writing as I could. I am working on *The Longhorns*. This is the only book I have ever blocked out completely before beginning the composition. I am afraid I am withering. Why, I could almost make an outline of the book tonight, before I have started the first chapter.

I had a long talk this week with a man I'll tell you about. His name is Dent,[2] and for years he has been with the Game Department. He has trapped perhaps 20,000 wild turkeys and thousands of deer. He knows the habits, instincts, nature of these animals better than any other man I have ever conversed with, I believe. You have to work to steer him, but he sure knows some things about nature. Now, if ever I get to it, I may write an essay entitled "Love at First Smell." I steered Dent to smell. I told him how the old wolf and bear trapper Nat Straw told me that one winter he paid $5 for a quart of urine from a menstruating woman, used it, mixed with something else, as a lure to his traps, and damned near caught every wolf on the San Augustin Plains of New Mexico.

Dent told me about a pet buck, two years old or maybe three, he was thinking of bringing out of Frio County. The rancher who owned the deer was not at home. The healthy, mature wife went out to the little patch where the deer was confined and turned on a hydrant to let water run in a bucket for the deer to drink. He came up, when he got near the woman smelled her, and tried to mount her. She slapped him off and Dent also shoved him away. He had seen the deer. Twenty-eight or 56 days later—he can't remember which but is positive that the time was one or the other—he was back at the ranch. Two or three men were with him—witnesses, he calls them. He had some deer in the truck and was going to take this young buck this trip. Again the rancher was not in and again the woman went out into the little pasture to toll up the deer. She turned the hydrant on and had something to feed him. She had not been near him for several days, she said. The buck came up, became very much interested in his sniffing, and again tried to mount her.

Slapping him away, the woman said, "I don't know what can be the matter with that deer."

"Lady," Dent sensibly said, "I do. It's your condition, and you should recognize the fact in dealing with these animals."

The high school here has for a mascot a buck deer now two years old. Dent, who lives near the school and takes a great interest in it, raised this deer and takes care of him. He was the mascot last year, when a yearling. Now, a yearling buck will mount a doe, though he does not get many chances. At two years old, when the rutting season starts, he starts too, though he is not so active as a three-year old. Many girls as well as boys come to see Scrappy, as this mascot buck is called. He is kept in a pen fenced with wire netting. Dent says that if fifteen girls line up along the fence to watch him and Scrappy walks along the line, as he habitually does, a man can tell by the actions of the buck if one of the girls is menstruating. He will pause before her, smell in an unusual manner, and otherwise betray his interest.

I have all but lost my own sense of smell, but the manifestations of this sense have become for me the most interesting phenomena of nature. Most of the so-called "mysteries" of nature could, I am sure, be explained through it.

I don't mean for you to answer this letter. I'll be back in Austin about the first. Next weekend I am going up into San Saba County to see if I can circumvent the nose of a buck.

Your friend,
Frank Dobie

Austin, Texas
January 29, 1941

Dear Webb:

Here is an experience of mine for your philosophical mind to chew on: last night I was out around a campfire with three young university instructors of the best class—I say, young—in their thirties. After a feed, we sat around a campfire. Con-

versationally, for some reason, I was entirely passive. I simply
listened. According to my watch, they talked 90 per cent of
the time about sex. Rapes, homosexuality, seductions, mastur-
bation, etc., not stories about but incidents drawn from observation and experience—no personal sexual experiences, however. I could not fail to draw a contrast between this supersexed
conversation and the conversation we heard among the cowboys
down on the ranch. Of course, the latter was likely restrained
and diverted from its usual course by our presence—but still
—isn't there a difference?

Yours,

Bedi

Austin, Texas
July 9, 1941

Dear Dobie:

Here's another one you can put down in favor of your
roadrunner.

I had been struggling through the cedar brake for four
hours a terrifically hot morning and was ready to go back to
camp very tired and sweaty. A paisano came out of a clearing
about twenty steps ahead of me and posed with tail and crest
up. Then he suddenly dived into the bushes. There was something about his motion that made me know he was going for
prey. I could hardly hope, even by scrambling up the ledge,
to see what he caught, but my conscience smote me, when I
had the impulse to turn back to camp without making a try.
Says I, "Dobie would like to know what this bird did, and I
might get an observation for him." So for your sake rather
than for my own, I went back, climbed the ledge, and looked
down through the hole in the bushes through which he had
disappeared. I was rewarded. There within twenty feet of me
was my paisano calmly but with great gusto devouring a

centipede eight inches long. Apparently he had just got him dead enough to eat. He still flopped him down, one side and the other on the rock, to be sure he wouldn't bite, I reckon. Then he began eating him. He tore off section after section of this much sectionized insect, and ate him up. He wiped his bill on a stone, threw up his tail and crest, and, becoming for the first time aware of my presence, darted away.

So he eats centipedes.

Bedi

Austin, Texas
October 3, 1941

Dear Dobie:

Your article is exceedingly interesting. The last sentence in it is quotable as a proverb. I have copied it down for use.

Mrs. Dodson[3] should give us the name of her neighbor-witness and the name of the high school science teacher who didn't notice that the devil's horse had been beheaded and tried to chloroform it.

I have heard these insects called, also, "the Devil's Knitting-needle."

You vouch for the credibility of your witness, but I cannot believe the story. Knowing the muscular power and superior weight of the hummingbird, I cannot believe that the latter could not shake off his comparatively frail antagonist. Dr. Casteel[4] can give us some scientific information on the flesh-tearing mechanism of this insect, if any. So I am in the attitude of attentive skepticism.

Your story is the kind that stimulates people to look about them.

Yours,
Bedi

Austin, Texas
October 8, 1941

Dear Dobie:

Since reading your praying mantis article I have done some diligent research which inclines me to believe that you have something besides folklore or an overimaginative correspondent. Aforesaid "diligent research" means that I have talked two minutes over phone with Dr. Casteel and four minutes over phone with Dr. Breland,[5] and have read almost half a column in the Encyclopaedia Britannica. I have reported to Mrs. Dobie on part of conclusions reached in the course of this laborious research, viz., that Dr. Casteel was inclined to poohpooh idea of mantis killing hummingbird; that Dr. Breland, on the other hand, who is on much more familiar terms with the insect, is not so sure that your informant was dreaming, says it's possible at any rate. Britannica article says large species of mantis in South America kills frogs, lizards, and *birds*. Breland says that in section reported from (near Mathis, I understand) there may be a larger, stronger species of mantis than we have here. South and west of Austin, he says, larger species occur. Britannica article says also that peculiar attitude of mantis and coloration underneath simulates an open flower to attract insects right into his jaws. You know how the hummingbird is always prospecting among flowers. You can deceive one with a paper flower. Well, there you are: hummingbird punches trap. Only problem: can mantis manage this strong, muscular, lively critter? Hummingbirds' wings move 1600 times a minute, counting upstrokes and downstrokes. He can dash across the Gulf of Mexico—flies like a bullet. Whips jay birds off their roost. I suggested to Mrs. Dobie that your informant might have mistaken hummingbirds for hummingbird moth. Of course, mantis would have no trouble with the moth. My researches in the half column of Britannica also reveal the fact that there is more folklore the world over about the mantis than about any other insect. He is worshiped in places, ancient augurs used to use him—you could get a dandy article about him by nosing about. By all means call on Breland. and see his collection. I understand he is studying a parasite with which the mantis is infested.

Yours,

Bedi

April 28, 1942

Dear Dobie:

Thanks for permitting me to see the enclosed letter. I have copied the ornithological part into my notebook. I think it is extremely interesting. I have seen ducks mate, also geese, but never ducks with geese. The trailing member is very obvious, also the rough-and-ready way they go at it. This contrasts strangely with the absolute faithfulness of the goose to his mate. Did I ever tell you of the pair I noticed on the lake one spring? The female was wounded and could not fly north with the flock, so the male stayed with her until he was killed. It was pitiful to see him swoop down over her, begging her apparently to be gone with him to the far northern mating grounds, and to see her make the effort to rise, and fall back every time. Then he would return, day after day to be with her, and so remained with her to the end.

I think there can be no breeding between rusty blackbirds and starlings, although they associate together, migrating here together in the fall and leaving together later. The starling also associates with other Icteridae, as meadow larks and grackles. But after all, they are not of the same genus or even of the same family—starlings belong to the family Sturnidae, while the blackbirds belong to the Icteridae. No case of interbreeding between different families has ever been recorded, so far as I know.

Thanks again.

Bedi

Austin, Texas
May 27, 1942

Dear Dobie:

If you ever happen to be out Menard-way with a little time on your hands, you should take the occasion to look up one Mack Burch and his horse, Redlight. Burch seems to be manager of a ranch about twelve miles from Menard on the Ft. McKavett road.

This man knows horselore and loves the horse with that personal affection which begets understanding. "Unless a man is willin' to give a hoss credit for havin' as much sense as he's got, he's got no business with a hoss," says he, and then qualifies: "Of course, there's some hosses that have to be bossed. I got one you can't ketch to save your life. But I can go in the pen with her and pick up a rock, and she'll come right up and put her nose in my hand. She's just a fool like some people."

What Burch intended to say, I think, was that unless you're willing to give a hoss credit for having as much sense as you have, you've got no business having a horse, that is, a horse worthy of the name "horse." Something like that was in his mind.

But this horse, Redlight, which he showed me with such great pride, was a horse with a soul. He is a powerful animal —larger and better muscled than the ordinary cow pony, deep bay and wide between the eyes and benevolent-looking in the face. When a busted rodeo put its stock up at auction, Burch bought Redlight for $15, for nobody could ride him. When he went out of the chute pitching, a rider might stay with him until he went into reverse, and then he always lost his rider. Burch called him in his pitching aspect "a spinner."

When he first decided to ride Redlight, he told his wife, he said, to git her horse saddled.

"What, do ya think he'll throw ya, Mack?"

"Well, you git yer hoss."

Sure enough, Redlight threw him as soon as he issued from the gate into the pasture. Indeed, the horse is as gentle as a cat in the pen, but the moment his head goes through a gate or narrow passageway of any sort he goes to pitching. This is the result of long rodeo training. The animal is eight years old, and his whole education, rodeo.

But Burch is a real master of the horse. In 18 months he has Redlight so gentled that he can ride him any time, anywhere, and even rope anything from a wildcat to an outlaw steer from him. I wish you might hear Burch's lingo. It is the best cowboy talk I have heard since I used to sit around with the cowboys out in the free range country in southern New Mexico thirty years ago. I had come to believe that cowboys had forgotten their lingo, but Burch has restored my confidence.

He had just been down to an old settlers' reunion at Bandera riding Redlight. He made his expense and better betting ambitious cowboys ten dollars they couldn't ride Redlight. "One hand on the choke and one in the air, and if ya pull leather, yer throwed," were the simple rules he laid down for the contest. Five of 'em tried it. None rode him.

Burch tried to explain to me that there is something about the conformation and toughness of the shoulder muscles of Redlight that prevent a spur from hanging right to steady the rider in a pinch. "It just won't stick," he said, "and he's the only horse I ever rode that didn't give that spur hold." He moved his spur up and down the place, but I don't know enough about such things to quite understand what he was driving at. But doubtless he had something.

He told me about a neighbor coming over to get an outlaw mare he had sold him. He had her in the corral, and told him to go ahead and get her. She chased him out of the corral three times. Finally, the neighbor asked Burch how he was going to catch her.

"If you'll just stand, you'll catch her," Burch replied dryly.

I asked him how he ever gentled Redlight. I wish I could give it to you in his words, but I can't.

"You see, Redlight thought pitching a man off ended the day and he got fed. That's the way they do a rodeo pitchin' hoss. They don't feed 'em before the show. But as soon as he throws his man, he's taken to the stall and fed. You see, Redlight had been doin' this all his life. Well, it was hard to convince him that it was not all over when he throwed me, but when I did get him convinced, he never pitched me no more until I made him. Of course, he can throw me any time he wants to, but he don't. He's the only horse I ever saw that can throw me."

Burch is quite anxious to get into the air service. He's really pining to do some fighting for his country. I suggested that he might be a little overage for the air service.

"I ain't but forty-two."

But I think you said you were married.

"Yes, I'm married."

Any children?

"Only five."

Well, I said, I doubt if you can get in with so many dependents. Any physical defects?

"No, none, natural."

I then asked about artificial defects and found that he had two silver plates in his skull. He had gotten them by "talking back to a policeman when he was a little drunk down in San Antonio."

I then asked him about his eyesight.

"Fine," he said, "out of one eye."

The skull injury had evidently paralyzed a nerve and he was completely blind in one eye.

Further than having a cracked leg from having had it "broke twice," he was in excellent physical condition for an air service examination!

I told him sadly that his function in saving the country was as a producer of good meat, in my opinion. He philosophized about the decline of neighborliness, and believed that the war would restore it somewhat, maybe, he hoped. You must see this cowboy the first time you have a chance.

Bedi

Austin, Texas
October 14, 1943

Dear Webb:

The red flower we found on your creek is, as I told you, *Lobelia,* common name: cardinal flower. Mrs. Schultz[6] says of this flower, "I have found three specimens of it in five years' field work in the San Antonio region." I suggest that you buttress the seepy places along the creek above the flood level somewhat and plant seeds of this flower. You can have a wonderful fall display of this rare plant in a few years.

The dark green-leaved small tree near the cave, spray of which I took containing black drupes, belongs to the buckthorn family, *Rhamnus caroliniana,* common name: Indian cherry. The other cherry belongs, of course, to the rose family, *Prunus serotina,* common name: wild black cherry. As I told you, it is extremely rare here.

Yours,
Bedi

Austin, Texas
December 31, 1943

Dear Webb:

This rare and beautiful species of agarita (*Berberis Swazeyi*) I found on your place not in abundance but rather common. It should be encouraged. Perhaps one of the projects you should have in mind is a nursery for supplying the plant commercially. Ramsey has been selling it for 25 years, but not advertising it as he should. A nursery in its natural habitat should be profitable. It bears a translucent berry, in clusters, which are quite palatable raw when ripe.

Hoping the old wood chopper is enjoying his holiday and getting out plenty of wood with which to hold up the public, I am

Sincerely yours,

R.B.

P.S. Saw your public-spirited wife and more public-spirited daughter at Lyndon Johnson speech last night.

Civic slackers turn such functions over to their womenfolks. I accompanied my daughter there.

R.B.

Austin, Texas
March 14, 1945

Dear Bedi:

Here is *The Hope of the South,* which I'd like back. Also an item on Jesse Jones[7] for your friend Drew Pearson.[8] It came to me from G. B. Foster, Melba Street, Dallas, who has sent several pounds of literature during the past two or three years. He is an inveterate liberal. I have never met him, and don't need to to have an idea of him. I'm going all this week Town-Halling in Houston, Waco, and Forth Worth. I am "all o'er sib" with this business of saving the world. Next week I'm putting on my boots, carrying my spurs and 30-30 and going with Bob Snow[9] to where the panthers curl their tails under the black chaparral in Zapata County. I'd rather do that than sup at the right hand of the Almighty right out on the boulevards of the City of the Blessed. I may bring you back a panther steak. I hope to drink a beer with you before I leave. I have a new brand for you to pronounce upon.

Your friend,
Frank Dobie

Austin, Texas

Dear Dobie:

The lovely baby-blue flower we saw with the sharp pointed petals and sepals and plaited leaves is called, quite appropriately: Celestials. Belongs to iris family, cousin of the blue-eyed grass which we found blooming all about, and scientific name is *Nemastylis acuta.*

The equally interesting yellow-breasted-and-greenish-head-and-back-with-white-wing-bars bird, warbling in the top of the hackberry, echoed clearly from the limestone bluff, turned out to be, as I expected, the pine warbler (rather rare here), *Dendroica vigorsi.*

We shall forget the perch we caught and ate, but not these two beautiful mementos which Nature gives us of our little outing: April 12, 1945, Hearst's Creek. Nor shall we forget the *shock we got when we got home.*

Bedichek

Austin, Texas
November 12, 1945

Webb:

The tree whose vivid green leaves amidst the fall foliage attracted me yesterday in wood at base of Friday Mountain is the yellow buckthorn, *Rhamnus caroliniana,* or Indian cherry. It is not to be confused with the wild black cherry, which belongs to another genus. It is in its native habitat there in rich soil at base of a limestone bluff. It is easily brought into captivity, and grows fairly rapidly from seed, which I am planting in pots and will share with you if I have luck with them. They are highly recommended for ornamental trees in yards or spaces where a single tree is desired. Since the berries are red in late summer, turning black in autumn, and since the leaves are such a beautiful green and the tree is *tardily* deciduous, I think I shall find sites for two or three of them on my lots.

Yrs.

Bedi

The leaves of this tree tend to form a loose rosette around the clusters of berries, giving a pretty effect.

March 12, 1946

[To Webb]

It has rained, O desiccated denizen of a musty classroom, and spring has been born, coming clean like one of your kids I found this morning fresh licked off by a solicitous and suspiciously staring nanny.

A flame is starting here and there on every hillside—not the red flame of destruction but the soft green flame of life.

Your pitiful little dam makes barely a ripple this morning in the dirty flood that is coursing down "Bear" Creek, and the pool by the cave has merged with the falls above so that there is now no pool; and the limestone crags below are shedding torrents of water.

The sod is oozy.

Every leaf is weighted down with a globule of water as big as an individual unit in a pile of goat-droppings. If Elizabeth Barrett Browning can refer in one of her most delicate poems to "droppings of warm tears," I should be permitted the use of "droppings" too.

Not less than three inches.

R.B.

Cedar Valley
Travis County, Texas
March 24, 1946

In re Forestiera pubescens Nutt.
(*Adelia pubescens* [*Nutt*] *Kuntzo*)

Dear Landlord:*

This shrub is multifariously named, having four folk names in addition to its brace of respectable scientific designations (given above), as

1. Elbow Bush, because from its long wandlike stems it thrusts out branches at right angles;
2. Spring Herald, because it comes out early, beating even the deciduous yaupon by a week;
3. Spring Golden Glow, from its early flowering before leafing, giving an old-goldish color;
4. Devil's Elbow, because it's hard as hell to get through.

It resembles yaupon, but it's more of a leaner and bower-down, and its twigs are opposite instead of alternate. It loves ravines and is native all over the seaward side of the Edwards escarpment, of which the Bear Creek valley is an indentation.

* If there ever was one.

In very early spring, goats browse avidly upon it. There's a bunch growing out of the middle of a clump of agarita by the road about halfway from the pasture gate to the house. Every tentative hand it sticks out from the thorny protection of the agarita is closely nibbled by the goats. My friend H. B. Parks, curator of the museum at A. & M. College and in charge of the S. M. Tracy herbarium, says *F. pubescens* grows profusely in Kerr and Kendall Counties, furnishing excellent early browsing for goats there. Ask your friend Calculatin' Coke about this.

I would trust him farther in the field of goat provender than in the field of politics or government, or economics or common honesty.

One curious habit this plant has is leaning over backwards until it touches the ground, and there taking root. Thus it becomes a thick and matted undergrowth with roots tenaciously clutching the soil. And it is this earth-grabbing habit which suggests it as a natural aid and ally in erosion control for certain areas on this place. Wherever, for instance, a wash breaks off the flood plain and pitches into the creek, gouging away some of your good soil in the operation, it would, I believe, do a fine job. The planting should be made for a hundred yards or so from the break over the bank up each one of the gullies that are forming.

F. pubescens grows readily from cuttings, and there is enough growing on the place to furnish an ample supply for the purpose. Get a sack of cuttings on your shoulder and, choosing a wet time, walk up the gullies sticking the cuttings in the ground. If it weren't so much like work, I'd do it myself.

Maybe, however, you with your air of quiet confidence (or confidence man) could easily arrange sticking-parties on the plan of the pioneer cornhusking or house-raising. Bring along a bunch of Ph.D.s each with just enough mechanical sense and executive ability to insert with downward pressure a sharp stick in soft ground. Furnish each victim with a sack of cuttings and head him up a gully. For the price of a few steaks and a little palaver you could get it all done in a jiffy. But please *time* your sticking-parties to correspond to my weekly evacuations, not physiological but vacational, i.e., to be still more explicit, my weekly evacuations *of* not *on* the premises.

The shrub I am recommending also makes a splendid cover for certain birds. If you want to stock up on quail, pheasants, or other ground-seeking game birds, you couldn't provide them with better protection. Incidentally, you would be providing at the same time protection for all the finch tribe, also, which contribute not meat, but songs and color, echoes and intimations of a spiritual world of far greater importance than broiled quail or roasted pheasant. But who would expect a booted and spurred ranchman in a brand-new red truck to be influenced by such transcendental considerations?

So, finally, I return to goat feed, erosion control, and quail-harbor to motivate you in planting *F. pubescens.*

Respectfully submitted,
Roy Bedichek,
Tenant

Cedar Valley
Travis County, Texas
November 8, 1946

Dear Webb:

. . . In first beams of this morning's sun, I saw two flickers and a pair of bluebirds atop the steel tank tower. They flitted about, changing and interchanging positions, restless, dissatisfied, and apparently quarreling.

Remembering the bluebird's fondness as a nesting site for the old diggings of the flicker, I imagined the following colloquy:

"Hurry, hurry up, and drill, *drill, drill."*

"Tut, *tut, tut, tut*—no *tank,* no *tank.*"

"Hurry up, *hurry, hurry!*"

"Shut up, you fool, shut up, shut up! Can I produce a bunghole without a barrel?"

And the realistic flickers flew away to bide their time, while the simple-minded bluebirds stayed there, twittering and fluttering about, little patches of blue, blue sky, symbols of hope, truly romanticists, looking with the faith that passeth understanding for the homey bunghole of an uncreated barrel.

Yours,

Bedi

Austin, Texas

April 29, 1947

Dear Dobie:

Yours is the sort of letter especially soothing to the immured. Listening to the earliest pipe of half-awakened birds and shadowing armadillos brings me intimations of freedom; and before long I shall indulge myself whether or no.

Thanks for the two titles, but you either failed to enclose clipping anent "worm turning" or I lost it out when I opened the letter in the post office to read it then and there without getting back to my office. I have only two or three correspondents whose letters inspire this impatience.

I shall turn out an essay on the "Early Bird," but in the beginning I shall count several birds out. The martin, I believe, sings in his sleep. I hear him almost any time during the night, so it would be unfair to other birds to count him as an early bird when he is probably dreaming.

Also, the mocker should be ruled out because his night singing is erratic and likely to happen any time, moon or no moon. All night birds such as the chuck-will's-widow, the screech and other owls, are out, for although they are often

most active early in the morning just before daybreak they
are likely to be vocal any old time.

The only way to make this study is to go out in the woods
before daylight many, many times, and at different seasons, for
I am sure there will be seasonal variations. It will be well
also to divide the birds into residents and migrants, and one
should have an accurate watch along with him, for I might
hear a Carolina wren awakened by the tower lights in Austin
sing at 5 o'clock while down on Onion Creek the bird might
not utter a peep before 5:30. Thus another division: *city* birds
and *country* birds.

So you see I have been putting my little head to work on
this and I'll send you the result when it is finished.

Enclosed are some clippings I selected with the criterion of
"Probable Dobie Interest," and also a letter to Sam Rayburn,
which will do no one any good except me; and, realizing its
futility, I got little relief from blowing off.

If you're still there when State Meet is over I might run
up there and make you a short visit.

Yours,

Bedi

Kerrville, Texas

May 10, 1947

Dear Bedi:

I am mighty sorry about your laryngitis and mighty sorry
that you are not riding this way. I went to town at noon today, before the post office closed, and got both copies of your
letter. Otherwise, I should by now have had your bed made
up. It is raining here and has been raining off and on for the
last 24 hours. I have just started a fire in the fireplace, not on
account of the cold but for the sake of cheerful company—
and the fire is comfortable. One of the reasons I want to build

a house is to see a quotation from Frederic Remington's *Sundown Laflare* inscribed on the mantel-stone: "They sat down by the fire, the greatest philosopher in the world." Measured by heat units, the British waste a great deal, an enormous amount, of coal by burning it in open fires instead of converting it into heat through pipes, but I feel positive that the loss to poetry, other literature, and to the spiritual content of British lives will be equally enormous when all the urban dwellers are heated through pipes.

I told you I would give you a note for your "Who Is the Early Bird?" You are free to quote or use otherwise.

About 1939 I was driving to Austin from New Mexico, where I had spent several weeks trailing down the Lost Adams Diggings and Nat Straw's grizzly bears. I was alone and had my bedroll and camp outfit in the car. I passed through Van Horn about 10 o'clock at night, drove on east some miles, saw a dim road leading off to the right, and turned on it and drove until I was well away from the highway traffic, which by now was sparse. On a good flat place I stopped, unrolled my bed, and in a few minutes was sound asleep. When I woke up the morning star was about to pale. Without taking time to make coffee, I began rolling up my bed. Before I had tied it into a roll, several ravens flew right over my head, low, going east. While I was putting the bedroll in the car, another small detachment of them flew over, quite low. With lights burning in the growing light, I drove back to the highway; just as I was turning into it, coming east, a third detachment of ravens passed me, going the same direction.

Dawn comes fast in that clear, high country, but my lights were still on, though I could have done without them, when in a mile or so, I saw several ravens on the pavement ahead eating a freshly killed jack rabbit. About this time, some more ravens passed, flying right over the road. I looked at my speedometer. Between that place and the Diablo Mountains,

20 miles, I counted 15 dead rabbits, both jack and cottontail, at which ravens were eating. Some of the rabbits appeared to have been killed a night or two preceding; some were just off the side of the pavement instead of on it. At two or three, as the day got brighter, there was a buzzard or two with the ravens. At one, a hawk, a buzzard, and three or four ravens were all eating.

It was clear that these ravens were making their morning patrol for meat left nightly by man and his machines. Their very early traveling struck me. I don't know how far they had flown when they first came over me. Ravens and crows like to roost in concentrations, and I have been told by a student of their habits that they fly 20, maybe 30, miles for food away from their roosts, coming back in the evening. These I saw were not cawing much, but, as I recall, they were making some sound. I have told this experience to two or three men accustomed to traveling in raven country very early as well as very late, and they have corroborated my deduction that the bird is a predawn patroller after highway leavings. The coyote has this habit in some parts of the country, but he is a nocturnal bird by nature, though diurnal also.

Always now when I am in a crow or raven country I notice for an early voice. In the fall of 1946 I went to Lawrenceville, New Jersey, to talk at the boys' school there. After the talk, I spent the night in the home of the president of the school. It is amid beautiful trees. I woke up a good while before daylight, and just at the first intimation of dawn I heard the crows. A little later I saw them.

My experiences in central Texas is that the canyon wren, in his range, begins singing ahead of any other bird. Within the last six months I have heard the canyon wren first on bluffs of the Colorado River in San Saba County and on Devils River Canyon in Val Verde County. The whole wren family get out early.

I don't know that the canyon wren starts his matins any earlier than the redbird, which sometimes seems to peep out in his hearty way even before he is well awake. I say this because he will sometimes subside a few minutes before giving a full program of song.

When I was at the American Army University at Shrivenham, in Berkshire, England, late in 1945, I had to walk several hundred yards to breakfast through woods, before good daylight. Along in November, perhaps also December, I could hear the song thrush singing—and he has a very beautiful song—as soon as I came outside my house. At this time of year in this vicinity, the song thrush was more of a "herald of the dawn" than the skylark. In *Wild Lone* by "B.B.," a superb nature book written around the life of a fox, the notes of the song thrushes come first to the fox even on summer mornings, in the Midlands of England.

I think I'll be home this coming weekend but will not swear to be. The coyote hath me enthralled.

Your friend,
Dobie

Austin, Texas
May 14, 1947

Dear Dobie:

Your story of the early-rising ravens reminds me that I have lately surprised a mockingbird twice at the corner of Red River and Manor Road, much before sunup when driving lights are not necessary but comfortable, capturing crippled insects in the street. The early bird gets the crippled worm is a revision for the automobile age.

Enclosed is letter and speech from Rayburn.[10] It's about what I expected. After us the deluge, that is, after us who are already along in years, say about threescore and ten. I feel like telling him so, but what use?

Let's go and see the Negro University on East 13th Street, law department of which Regent Woodward[11] and Dean Mc-Cormick[12] testify on oath equals the University of Texas Law School for whites.

Well, I'll be seein' ya this weekend.

Bedi

Austin, Texas
November 3, 1955

Dear Webb:

Maybe vegetative species would suit your purpose better than animal, as reflecting climatic and other environmental conditions. Both, of course, may be used to illustrate your point. But if you took the oaks, familiar to everyone, and followed the genus from east to west Texas, you would find in Houston, for example, live oaks with a circular shadow-casting area in summer at noon of nearly 200 feet diameter. Here in Austin, 150 miles west, the spread and height of the same species is considerably reduced. A hundred-foot spread is a big tree in Austin and the height is reduced proportionately. Another 150 miles west oaks dwindle, except in peculiarly favorable conditions, and some oaks become mere shrubs, mere chaparral or shinnery growths. Go on west to the Monahans sands and you get Havard's oak only eight inches tall, bearing good fat acorns, however, in the top branches.

So with any single feature of the plant world, the leaf, for instance. Note how it dwindles from the spacious magnolia leaf to the skinny leaves of the mimosas. Leaves here in the Austin area begin turning into thorns, or are absorbed into the stems—leafless plants.

Thus climate and soil conditions are reflected much more

spectacularly by plants which travel only by *generations* than by animals equipped with *individual* means of locomotion.

Texas is certainly the ideal *political* unit which illustrates what I take to be your point.

Yrs.

Bedi

VIII. Texans Abroad

I remember distinctly Bedichek's remark when he learned that Dobie had accepted a professorship at Cambridge University: "Dobie may not teach the English much but they'll teach Dobie a lot."

Bedichek knew out of experience. He had been to England in 1907, when he was twenty-nine, when he went more as a taster of English life and thought than as a tourist. The influence on him was profound. He was able to get some perspective on his own provincialism reasonably early in life. Dobie and Webb shared this provincialism with him, but they were middle-aged men before they were able to begin to shed it.

Theirs was a double burden of provincialism and chauvinism: the Confederacy and Texas. It did not matter that both nations had been reabsorbed into the Union before they were born. They, like the people around them, were victims of a chauvinism compounded of the romanticism of Sir Walter Scott that lingered in the Old South and hero worship of the men who died for the "Lost Cause" or at the Alamo.

Bedichek said in a taped interview:

Then we had Barnes's *History of the United States.* I was
such a thoroughgoing Rebel that I learned all the battles in
which the Confederates whipped the Yankees, but I wouldn't
learn any of the battles where the Yankees whipped the Confederates. So I had a one-sided view of the situation and never
could realize why in the dickens it was we didn't have the
South to ourselves since we whipped them every time.

Such deliberate and delusory sentiment was hard to
overcome. As Bedichek said, a broader view was necessary:

I had just been reared in that Confederate atmosphere—and
my father was a Confederate soldier and my uncle was a
Confederate soldier and my mother was sympathetic to the
South—so I couldn't get any other viewpoint at all. But,
of course, I've overcome that many times. I'm very glad the
war turned out just as it did, since I've gotten a larger view
of world history.

Dobie was fully as explicit about his feelings:

I don't recall that Grandpa talked much about the Civil War,
but he must have contributed to my youthful adoration of
General Robert E. Lee and sentimentality over the Lost Cause.
The first picture of any kind that I bought, the year I went
to college, was a colored print of "Lee and His Generals,"
and after I went to Austin to teach in the University of Texas
I used to take off my hat every time I walked past the
Confederate monument on the capitol grounds with its "Died
for States' Rights" inscription defying by half-truth the whole
truth of democracy. My salutes in those days sprang from sentiment alone. Sometimes now when I see the small Confederate
flags people stick on their automobiles—more through hate
than love—I remember how the blood rushed to my head and

tears to my eyes when I heard "Dixie" played in a New York theater while I was attending Columbia University.

Webb came closer to being a victim of the Civil War than either Bedichek or Dobie. His parents, as he himself said, were left destitute by the conflict, and moved to Texas hoping to find new opportunities. They were barely surviving when Webb was born, twenty-three years after the war was over. Even after they moved on to west Texas their lives were a fight for survival. Bedichek and Dobie admitted their romantic feelings about the Confederacy and Texas. Webb was a realist, made so in part at least by the effects of the war and the hardships of life on the Texas frontier. Still, he was emotionally bound to the South and to Texas. The first book he wrote—not the first he published—was a study of the Texas Rangers. First and last, his books show his concern with his own region.

Webb had two teaching assignments in England. In the spring of 1938 he was the Harkness Lecturer in American History at the University of London; during the academic year of 1942–43 he was Harmsworth Professor of American History at Oxford. Dobie was Visiting Professor of American History at Cambridge in 1943–44; in 1945–46 he lectured to American troops at Shrivenham in England and also in Germany. Out of these experiences Dobie wrote one of his most appealing books, *A Texan in England*.

Over the years the three men had come to be regarded as spokesmen for their region. It is true that they had centered their work on a region, but they were regionalists only in their use of subject matter. Their ideas reached beyond any regional boundaries. The time came when they were harshly critical of the attitudes and beliefs of their neighbors.

Webb expressed his disgust in a letter to Bedichek:

Actually, I am beginning to feel twinges of shame over being a Texan—not because of Texas, which I suppose I am very fond of, but because of the blatant yapping about it that goes on in all quarters. There is a vulgarity about this so-called Texas spirit that reminds me of the flashy tie, the "Hot Springs diamonds," and the "refined" manner of a spieler in front of a sideshow exhibiting the headless or tail-less woman.

In a taped interview with Bedichek and Dobie I observed, "Outside Texas, Texans are rather poorly regarded. I don't know whether you hear that or not. I'm amazed at how much criticism there is of Texans in the North and East."

This remark brought forth the following dialogue:

DOBIE: I think it's justified. They make so damn much noise.

BEDICHEK: They brag so much and they're just like the native sons out in California. They think they are the people and wisdom will die with us. That doesn't run through the whole of Texas society by any means. Now the typical Texan in my opinion is not a bragger at all. The typical Texan's a rather silent man. But there's been an influx—sometimes when I want to be funny, but I mean in a joking way, I says, "Before we had this great immigration from Kansas and Oklahoma, why, we weren't such braggers." I mean there's been an influx of people that have crusted over the old pioneer and cowman civilization and they're the ones that really create this racket. Don't you think so, Dobie?

DOBIE: We've been journalesed, too. You know, Oscar Wilde said, "Nature follows art." All the literate people in the country are being subjected to art of a kind. That is, they're subjected to newspapers and television and radio. Why, you can go out there to west Texas where the only occupation is grazing. Go to Fort Davis, say. There's a picture show about twice a week. Not enough population to justify more'n two days a week.

All you'll get at the picture show in Fort Davis is a Western. Now those cowboys, cowmen, ranch women all know that Hollywood's version of ranching is ridiculous, but they want it, and gradually they are molding themselves into the Hollywood form. A great many legitimate Texans—not bastards— listen to and read these Texas bragging things and they get the idea that they've got to brag.

BEDICHEK: That it's Texanese to brag.

DOBIE: That it's Texanese to brag. Why, some jackass of a woman came to me and begged me to reply to a travesty on Texas. It came out in *Esquire* magazine two or three months ago. Well, I told her, I said, "That's absurd." But Texans asked for it. If they're as strong as they say they are, why, let them take it.

Such criticisms of Texas were not well received by Texans, as the following letter to Dobie shows:

Mr. J. Frank Dopey
Austin, Texas

Dear Mr. Dopey,

I would like to inform you that you can go to England any time you wish and I will not cry over it. You have made yourself a nuisance here long enough, so I will appreciate your making a nuisance over there for a change.

Of course everyone knows you are a little crazy and not in your right mind, but if you were sane when you made some statements I have read coming from you I would call you a yellow-bellied bastard. I would also punch your face in if I thought you were in your right mind and if you weren't a decrepit old fool, but since you are a little "tetched in the head" and since you are a decripit, good-for-nothing old fossil and fool, I'll let it go.

Fooey to you from me

Sincerely,

Me

Dobie sent this letter on to Bedichek April 13, 1945, with the following comment:

I got this letter the same day as yours, which did my "tough Texas guts" good and also taught me, by sending me to the dictionary, the word *semantics*. I don't want it back. Yours with much appreciation.

Washington, D.C.
September 28, 1942

Dear Bedi:

Please let me hear before I leave the results of your conference with the regents. Just have a wire from Burdine[1] stating that my leave was granted. Freddy[2] told me that Stumberg[3] wrote Dr. R.[4] a pretty hot letter, evidently intended for regential eyes. At any rate, I would like to have a report before I push off.

You may thank your good star that you live in Texas and in Austin rather than in Washington. This place is a madhouse with any sort of accommodations or help at a premium or unobtainable. Fortunately Bob Mason[5] took me in with him near center of things. Have been to British Embassy and find that I shall probably go on bomber instead of passenger plane. That suits me as I can ride passenger planes any time. Also find I may be able to take additional baggage.

This place dwarfs everything, even the New Deal. Down in Texas one gets to be known, and his doings are a matter of favorable and unfavorable comment, but here people are ciphers and most of them know it. The place must be lousy with experts who, to reverse the wisecrack, are important people away from home on unimportant business. But everybody is doing this much, pushing the war machine along. On railroads and in stations people are good-natured, patient, and forbearing, and the overworked staffs from redcaps up are as helpful as circumstances permit. Somehow one gets the conviction that we are making headway and are going to win. The cool assurance of the British Embassy staff, to say nothing of the musical voice of an unusually good-looking English gal secretary, makes you feel that these people cannot fail. Major Steward Richardson inquired *when* I would like to cross. I told him preferably between the fifth and tenth of October. "Oh," he said, "we may not get you on the regular passage, but we have bombers going all the time and there will be no trouble." Also mail and freight are going through now on fast schedule, about ten days or two weeks. There is no doubt that the submarine menace has been somewhat demenaced. Of course, dear Bedi, I may feel differently tomorrow, especially if the Russians are hard hit. Today I feel OK. Bob Mason may have something to do with it. Bob argues, and very well, that the war may be over in a year or less. I don't quite see it, but he is rather convincing.

You will have to act with your usual promptness if I am to get your letter. I'm going to New York Wednesday, and should be back here Friday. It's good to have a little leisure to rest. I really was about all in when I left Austin. Hope you will go out occasionally and look at the ranch. I think of it many times a day.

Sincerely yours,
W. P. Webb

Austin, Texas
December 7, 1942

Dear Webb:

I believe you have given us in your letters as intimate a view of the inside of Oxford as it is possible to give by the written word. If you were an artist or good cartoonist, you might emphasize certain features for people who have less imagination than I have. But for me your descriptions have the fidelity of a photograph taken in just the right light and from just the right angle. Our blood bond (if you will forgive a Nazi expression) permits us really to appreciate the English. I loved them when I was visiting there briefly in 1907; thirty years later my daughter spent a year in London, and loved them; and I can see that you are in a fair way to succumb to their charm, even overcoming the bad taste you acquired on a former trip. Your restrictions concerning the form of our letters to you rather cramp my style. As I attempt to follow directions, I feel pressing down upon me the burdens of war. I must crowd my spacious thoughts into a single-spaced, no-margined page, and seek to imprint upon this flimsy onionskin emotions that "do often lie too deep for tears." Anyway, here goes, and in addition I am *marking* not *making* paragraphs with that thing-a-ma-doodle (※) on the typewriter which no one has ever taken the trouble to name. All to save tonnage. You can't say I'm not patriotic! ※ You have sacrificed something, after all, for your English adventure: notably witnessing the chagrin of FDR haters when we really scored a touchdown in the Solomons. They have been glooming about for a month to the effect that we had lost practically our whole fleet in the Pacific. When Maas[6] returned and reported, they fairly gloated under their skins at what they supposed was the humiliation of the administration. They were in exultant, I-told-you-so top form, when suddenly the news of a smashing victory broke, and they literally turned themselves wrong side out trying to appear gratified. And then came the invasion of Africa. This really stunned them, especially when Churchill's generous credit for the coup was headlined. And curiously enough, a sour note came now from the other side of the orchestra, from amongst the liberals. They've been hounding poor old Hull[7] on account of his "appeasement of Vichy," and howling bloody murder for a second front. At one telegraphic flesh, appeasement was justified and a second front was established. They are caught with their prophetic breeches down, and they grabbed Darlan[8] as the best screen available to cover the indecent exposure. *The Nation,* the *New Republic, PM,* Dorothy Thompson,[9] all the pinks and near-pinks were caught. An editorial "Letter to Liberals," from Kenneth Crawford[10] in *PM* is the first sign of returning sanity. Willkie's[11] was the crowning asininity: "We should keep our diplomacy open and aboveboard, in the good old American way, and resort to no such contemptible tricks." Can you beat it! Sooner or later they all crack under the strain—all except Churchill,[12] FDR,[13] and Uncle Joe.[14] ✕ And let me say in a really tough aside that I get blankety blankety tired of being lectured by Ed Murrow[15] on the Darlan theme and generally on my duty to the British Empire. If he would confine his husky, quarrelsome voice to giving us news when there is any and just plain shut up when there is none, he would really make a great hit with me. ✕ At the last meeting, our dear old discussion club was at its dunderheaded worst. I let myself get out from under control and intimated that there were a bunch of ignoramuses not a thousand miles away, as well as some hypocrites, and that there were certain individuals who satisfied both categories. Imagine a bunch of men in Austin, Texas, solemnly, each one after another, declaring that he had never seen any indication of social or other discrimination against Mexicans in Texas! ✕ Your description of the cold makes me shiver here in my office where the temperature is now 85 degrees. You are a hedonist with Christian veneer, and the

veneer so thin that when I remind you of that vast pile of
sound white-oak crossties in my back yard which will feed
a four-foot fireplace this winter, your emotion will not be one
of "Thank goodness, poor old Bedi is comfortable," but rather
an envy as creeping and insidious as the cold which you describe. You see how little you have ever put over on me. But
nevertheless, as Will Hogg used to say, "I think of you often
and always with affection." Since you advise full signature (I
guess for the censor's benefit), I drop the *Bedi* and subscribe my full name: Roy Bedichek.

Queen's College, Oxford
December 16, 1942

Dear Bedi:

Order from Macmillan E. H. Carr's *Conditions of Peace*.
I'll take it when I come home, but I want you to read it now.
Brilliant, illuminating, meaty, and sound. You can make the
T. & G. howl, but that is not the point. The book is right. He
is main editorial writer for London *Times*. Much to tell you
when I return. A fine year to be here, and am tempted to stay
till the show is over. Made broadcast to America BBC Sunday
night. Cabled folks, but doubt if Texas carried it. Would like
to camp at F. M. Ranch with steak and coffee! Go look it
over and report. Have not seen U.S. paper or magazine. Mail
3–5 weeks in transit. Life here one of quiet and comparative
luxury. Very restful, but remote. Otherwise outside. London
is h—— No rooms in hotels. Queue up! Line up! How small
the individual in this mad, and wearying, world. The problem
begins with peace.

Good luck. Write me the news.

W. P. Webb

Queen's College, Oxford
March 24, 1943

I write at the "witching hour" of one to urge you to read—
if you haven't—Christopher Morley's *John Mistletoe,* an autobiography. He saw H. Steger[16] just before the last. Was here,
but the best is as a news hock and Editor, N.Y. The letter
of Steve O'Grady is sublime, though Steve wrote it when drunk,
or just after. This has been a great year, perfect peace under
the hum of planes—none tonight. I am doing some of my
best writing, though mine is always simple stuff in comparison
to the scholar's.

W. P. Webb

Queen's College, Oxford
December 23, 1943

Dear Bedi:

According to promise I should have written you earlier,
but I have broken so many obligations of this sort that the
sin rests lightly on my broad-shouldered conscience. Spending
Christmas holiday away from your own kind has its points
of leisure for rest and meditation, but also one finds some
dregs in the bottom of the cup.

I thought of you tonight as I was returning from the King's
Arms where I go to play bar-billiards in the pub with the
Professor of Egyptology. On our way in we walk down the
most medieval lane, made by the backs of colleges, that I
have seen anywhere. One end is called Queen's Lane and
the other New College Lane. It turns and twists, but finally
makes its devious way from the Broad to High Street. The
moon is brilliant tonight and the bare trees stand out with
every limb showing clear in the moonlight. I refused to come
in and went for a walk up High Street, which becomes London

Road leading north. I passed Magdalen College on the left, crossed the bridge over the Cheerwell (called the Char here), which runs through Magdalen Park where thirty or forty deer graze. I then passed a shopping district, not too prosperous, the street curving gradually to the left. This brings me to a residential section with more open ground and a gradual ascent by the road to Headington Hill. Here I came upon six or eight girls singing "Noel" and other Christmas carols by the gleam of flashlights, while overhead I could hear the drone of planes winging high and fast for the Channel and beyond. That's where you came in, and I just thought of all the possibilities for conversation that such incongruities could make. Don't you see what all we could say about any idiot like Hitler who would put a whole world in darkness, deprive people of food, clothes, toys for children, and medicine for the sick because he thought he could sandbag civilization with one swift lick on the head. Well, he's failed, for we are on the way now and he'll never be able to stop the avalanche that is rolling towards him.

As yet nothing exciting has happened near me since my arrival October 8. I'm not yet permitting myself to think of returning to Texas because the time is too distant and the psychological effect would be bad. I have not been homesick yet, and shall not be until the time I intend to go on passes. Do you realize that it was only two years ago that we spent a part of the holidays in the Big Bend looking for rabbits and arguing with Jack Wise?[17] Do you think it would be possible for me to look up Harry Steger's[18] record here and see what recollections I might pick up about him? What college was he in? What year? Also don't you agree that we should collect and edit those papers for which Calhoun[19] furnished the best title in the world? I carried what I had collected in my billfold for months, but decided to leave them in Washington, believing that you would have duplicates. I've written at least a dozen books since I've been here, all in imagination, and spent all the money they made, all in imagination, on the Friday Mountain Ranch.

The chaplain, who is just across the hall from me, gave me on loan a rare little book that you would find pure joy. The title is *Microcosmographia Academica, Being a Guide for the Young Academic Politician.* I can't quote much of this little gem, and it is hard to make a selection where there is so much excellence. But I choose the paragraph on Wasting Time as a means of obstruction in academic life.

When other methods of obstruction fail [and he has given them all] you should have recourse to *Wasting Time;* for, although it is recognized in academic circles that time in general is of no value, considerable importance is attached to teatime, and by deferring to this, you may exasperate any body of men to the point of voting against anything. The simplest method is *Boring.* Talk slowly and indistinctly, at a little distance from the point. No academic person is ever voted into the chair until he has forgotten the meaning of the word "irrelevant"; and you will be allowed to go on, until everybody in the room will vote with you sooner than hear your voice another minute. Then you should move for adjournment. Motions for adjournment, made less than fifteen minutes from teatime or at any subsequent moment, are always carried. While you are engaged in Boring it does not much matter what you talk about; but, if possible, you should discourse upon the proper way of doing something which you are notorious for doing badly yourself. Thus, if you are an inefficient lecturer, you should lay down the law on how to lecture.

I'll give you five bucks if you cannot name the man in our gang who is described here above. Try this:

Another sport which wastes unlimited time is *Comma-hunting.* Once start a comma and the whole pack will be off, full cry, especially if they have had a literary training. . . . But comma-hunting is so exciting as to be a little dangerous. When attention is entirely concentrated on punctuation, there is some fear that the conduct of business may suffer, and a proposal get through without being properly obstructed on its demerits. It is therefore wise, when a kill has been made, to move at once for adjournment.

It's getting late. There will be much to talk about when I come home. It's a good year to be here, but it will be good to get home. Don't fail to order from Macmillan E. H. Carr's *The Conditions of Peace.*

So long, Bedi.
W. P. Webb

Austin, Texas
February 23, 1944

Dear Dobie:

I have the advantage in that I get to read a good long letter from you every Sunday morning without having to bother with a reply. The *Austin-American* is quite faithful in printing your articles. It even printed the stinger in the tail of your article on conversations with English barbers, which I note you placed in a paragraph at the end apropos of nothing convenient for the blue pencil. I don't find this article in the Dallas *News,* although I mean to make another search for it. I am amazed at your turnout of good stuff—more amazed at the quantity you manage to get off without becoming dull. Is it the climate or the whiskey, or both?

Our life here is becoming more and more anemic. We are doing all business that is done, and performing all our functions with the leftovers, and they are a sad lot. When the human herd is subjected to one screening after another and you get down to the runts and roustabouts, the halt, the lame, and the blind (physically and/or mentally), there's not much left to fight with or for, apparently. You come to the conclusion that man is a mistake and should be permitted no longer to disturb the beautiful balance which Nature works out when this forked carrot of an animal, this interloper, this ingenious, egotistical anthropoid, is out of the way. Man delights not me.

We tried early in the year to find Mrs. Dobie at home for a Sunday morning in the woods with Sarah[20] and me, but finally discovered that she has been ill and is staying somewhere in south Texas.

Looking forward to your return, laden as some successful pirate's vessel, with the golden lore of the old cultures, I am, yrs.

Bedi

Emmanuel College, Cambridge
March 20, 1944

Dear Bedi:

God bless you for your letters, that of Feb. 23 arriving this morning—fast time these days. I have fifteen or twenty letters to write, but will begin with yours—and get no farther. I have all kinds of strong impulses to write letters but no will. That means no energy. Public talks, people, and burglars take all the juice out of me, and my system has not accommodated itself to sucking juice out of a diet very exclusive of meat. I wonder that you or anybody else finds the articles interesting. Sometimes I take pleasure in writing them, but often it is a chore. I have many encounters and impressions that are vivid at the moment; encounters and impressions that are dulling erase what I would store up and I am left empty. A man who writes should have nothing else to do, so that he can put the cream of himself into words before it curdles. I find that the curdling process is one thing very much accelerated by years. Webb said I would have lots of time to work; I never had less. Too much public; too many Americans, mostly Texans, like the boll weevil just huntin' fer a home. Several times as many as four and six have found that home for a little space in my room at one time. I generally like to see them, but they wring me dry. I woke up this morning half-dreaming that I was back home in Austin, had just arrived, and was telling my wife to phone you. She thought I might do my own phoning. NO, I said, "I don't want to talk over the telephone to anybody, but you tell Bedi that I want him to come and get me and take me out into the brush. I don't have a car any more and Bedi is always ready to spend a gallon of gas to get away."

I guess Mrs. Dobie is back in Austin by now. She had a long spell. I don't know when I'll get there—along in July, I guess. My work here is not over until towards the last of June. Old man George Dealey[21] is sending me the Dallas *News* now as a gift. He was so moved by the "Kind Hearts" (Christmas) article that he is sending a check for five pounds to be given to the bedmakers. I wonder if he has a feeling of repentance for not seeing that some of the hard truths, not at all kindly, I have written were not published in his paper. Anyway, when I read the Dallas *News* and see what is principally occupying the people at home who want to "return the government to the people" I am damned glad to be where the people have more of a sense of reality and are more sincere. I have a kind of loathing for returning to where I must listen to the lying babble.

Yesterday I had a cablegram from John Henry Faulk,[22] for whom I have a great fondness, calling on me to announce myself for governor and saying that organization to draft me is being formed. I don't guess it is much of an organization. There wouldn't be any oil millionaires in it to pay my radio expenses. I have not the slightest wish to be governor. I doubt if I could be elected. If I were governor I could not save anything or anybody. I am cabling dear Johnnie that I won't stand. I would like to get away off somewhere and write two or three more books about the Age of Innocence when coyotes howled free and men made razor strops out of

Indian hides. I have no desire to write a book about this country or to put into a book, your phrase, "the golden lore of the old cultures." I like and respect the people here—I wish to God I could respect my own people as well—but the sunshine is too pale and the spaces too crowded for my imagination to burgeon.

Tell Sarah that I liked her friend. She wrote and asked me the other day to go out to Girton for tea with her, but I had another tea or talk or something on. It is vacation time now. I am going to north Wales this week to make some talks for the OWI. Then I am going to a country estate in the Highlands and kiss the good earth. With affection, admiration, and appreciation, I am

> Your friend,
> Frank Dobie

> Austin, Texas
> April 10, 1944

Dear Dobie:

I think you did the right thing to turn down political activity in favor of continuing your present role as ambassador of goodwill. I don't think you could be elected anyway for the simple and sufficient reason that you could not get enough money ($100,000) in chips and whetstones from the real people, and I know you would not want to be obligated to any of the big financial boys for really substantial contributions. Besides, you are at present doing important work. Stay with it, as you intimate you will. Interpret the English to Texas, and Texas to the English. You are making headway, and getting better all the time. I have sent your letter of Apr. 10, published in *Austin-American*, to Bill Owens, on account of its letterlike quality, and I have sent him and others, others.

It doesn't make much difference what happens here at the

university. I am coming to Hitler's conclusion that intellectuals don't count anyway, especially cold-codded intellectuals like any number I could name and you would recognize immediately as entitled to the designation. There's one thing you could do which would better my personal relations with the British Empire, and that would be to catch Ed Murrow by the scruff of the neck and choke him with a hot potato every time he begins broadcasting and keep him hot-choked until the broadcasting time is up. What he says is often good; the way he says it is unendurable. His scolding, sepulchral tones, his accusing finger, his pose of omniscience, his curtain-lecture bearing and air of "now, children, quit being like you are and be adult like the English"—I tell you the man is a menace. God damn him forty times, and kick him to the devil.

Green grows the grass on the campus, bluebonnets abound, paintbrush, phlox mingle therewith, the odor of the mountain laurel has gone but other perfumes intoxicate. The post oaks and blackjacks have still the tender green (lots of yellow in it) and every shrub that lines the bank of Walnut Creek and the banks of every other creek in this vicinity is bursting with life. We've had a wet winter and a warm spell, and so, "comes Spring, with rose in hand." . . .

Bedi

Austin, Texas
April 14, 1944

Dear Dobie:

Yours of Mar. 20 arrived the day after I mailed you a letter dated April 10. The two discuss the same things and you may think when you get it that it is an answer to yours of Mar. 20, but it is not. The two letters crossed in the mail around about Hearne or Georgetown.

You are a sort of gadfly, and should continue to function

as such politically, and not attempt the actual duties of public administration. There's no getting around T. V. Smith's thesis that the politician is essentially a compromiser, a bringer of people of opposing views as near together as may be so that society may function as an organization and not as a group of warring factions. Take Sam Rayburn, for instance. He is an ideal politician in the best sense. He perhaps never gets what he wants done, but he gets *something* done. A Congress of J. Frank Dobies would get nothing done except a lot of broken heads, in all probability. The non-compromiser is just as important, but his function is entirely different. A man can hardly be an efficient advocate if he has in him that compromising strain which is essential to the successful politician.

Smith writes a book about this, but the above paragraph contains all there is in it. It is one of those things that is obvious the moment it is pointed out.

I wish you might have the peace and seclusion necessary to write your really, truly best, and I have an idea which will give you just that peace and seclusion. When you get back to Texas, it's going to be damned easy to get into jail. The Negro question is hot and getting hotter. The big boys are getting frightened. The slick magazines are preaching through editorials, fiction, articles, and especially in advertisements the desirability of changing nothing. The boys want to come back to things just as they were. Let's return to normalcy. That idea is getting set in a large section of the public mind. Over against it is the idea of a "brave new world." The clash of interests is going to get near to the revolutionary stage and it will be dead easy to get in jail. So my solution for you is to do something that will intern you indefinitely, and you will come out, as Cervantes did, with immortal works. Think of Defoe, O. Henry, and many, many others who could not get going towards immortality until they got in jail. The peace, quiet, hard fare, and protection from annoying visitors some way does the trick.

I have had a dream myself about writing a book for at least twenty years. There's a drawer full of scribbled notes on the theme which I have never had the courage to clean out and burn up. If I had just been sent to jail, it would have been written long ago.

Well, the office force is beginning to arrive, and I must chew this off. Good luck, you are doing a fine work. Stay there another year, if you feel like it and think you are needed.

Yours,

Bedi

Austin, Texas
June 22, 1944

Dear Dobie:

Yours postmarked May 11 reached here June 20. A letter that long "being delivered" is often stillborn, but not this one. It's quite fresh and readable. I shall not, however, take the same risk with this one. I'll buy for it a 30-cent pair of wings.

The 'twixt and 'tweenness of this, our American life, which you deplore is another of Swinburne's "burdens," but let us put the best face on it. There are bits of unspoiled native growths around Austin which puts one in mind of the untamed wilderness and the wide and glorious freedom for which you yearn. And occasionally in this vicinity one runs onto a civilized plot which brings before the mind's eye the old, old, places of the earth, warmed by generations of cultured living. So, with the stimulus of bits of Nature and bits of Man, let us create both enjoyments in our imagination, and not bluntly declare, as you do in your letter, "give me all of one or all of the other."

You are doubtless seeing England at its heroic best. War has cured unemployment and doubtless much of the caste atmosphere which I encountered there in 1907. I suppose that

Piccadilly Circus is not now thronged after nightfall with painted whores a-glitter with paste jewels like cats' eyes in the dark, as in 1907. If you turned a deaf ear to their solicitations, they cursed you with the foulest oaths. And there were beggars, pimps, and homosexuals in high-heeled shoes and corsets.

I strung along for a while with a young sleuth who was gathering statistics for the Yearbook of the London *Daily Express,* and his special assignment was to trail pieceworkers to their lairs and get the low-down on living conditions. We often found families of 4, 5, or 6 littered in a 16-foot square room two stories underground. I shall never forget the terrible sights. Never, before or since, have I seen humanity so degraded, and I worked once in the West Virginia coal fields.

Fresh from burrowing underground, I talked to the young Oxford swells and intellectuals who visited Harry[23] in our lodgings, and

> Then I perceived, that people had a dread
> That untaught should be taught, and starving fed.
> They were afraid lest taught and fed should rise
> Not on the horrors of their miseries,
> Not on their rags, their drunkenness and itch,
> Their lice and ignorance, but on the rich.
> This common dread among the general dark
> was social conscience's expiring spark.

Not that we can't find all this in our own dear country. I am saying, only, that perhaps 1907 was more normal in England than 1944.

But you see I was driven to quote an Englishman to get words with which to describe England's degradation; and thus it will ever be. There is no nation, I verily believe, which knows its own weaknesses so well, or is so sensitive to its own shame. Would that our bluster and braggadocio could be taught a little modety by our poets.

As to caste, England accuses herself thus:

> Two races trod the English turf,
> The (so-called) Norman, and the (not called) serf.

Do we have a poet in the South who rebukes our boasted democracy with such a two-edged couplet? You have been away for a year in an entirely new environment and I daresay you have become conscious of how we treat the Negro. Do you remember drinking fountains in every dirty east Texas courthouse labeled "For Negroes" side by side with those labeled "For Whites"? Nothing comparable to this exists outside of India.

Thanks very much for the clipping. My wife said the other column of wills interested her more. My hope is that the national traveling spree occasioned by this war will cure some of our provincialism.

Affectionately, and hoping soon to see you,

Bedi

Emmanuel College, Cambridge
July 25, 1944

Dear Bedi:

I am sending you clippings from this morning's *Times*. It would mean a lot if a man could have as good a newspaper every morning. No matter what the policy of the paper, it does not constantly insult intelligence. Within the last few days I have received about 20 issues of the Dallas *News*—gift of old man Dealey.[24] I have not opened them, but will save them as fresh packages for some homesick GI. The Americans over here have made a religion of being homesick, though the sickness has much diminished during the last four months.

Not long ago I sent an article in for the Texas papers quoting a paragraph from your letter about Negroes and the drinking basins in east Texas courthouses. You'll probably think I took undue liberties. I couldn't resist. You will live over the public exposure of your liberal ideas.

Here I am fiddling around when I should be going home and showing myself a 100 per cent American by being edified with the realistic arguments for free enterprise advanced by Rotary Clubs. I have a little hope that I may see the lights go on in England before I leave towards the first of September. I can't say when I have been happiest—living in the past, as I have lived in all my books, or in the present, as I have been increasingly living during the past four years. The weather has been hellish most of the time since the invasion opened. The sun is out today, though veiled. I want to go out into the fields and listen to the larks, though I'll stay in, end this letter, and try to strike a note myself. I think of you lots of times.

Your friend,
Frank Dobie

Yes, Piccadilly Circus is still a gauntlet for virtue. A million Americans have seen at first hand the "Piccadilly commandos." I wouldn't know what per cent of them have explored farther than what meets the eye. I hung around that vicinity for about two hours the other evening. It does not get dark until after eleven o'clock these summer days, double summertime. One private, perhaps from Indiana, said to another respecting a blondine, "But she is one of those five-pounders." I believe if he had started his bid at five shillings she would not have been insulted. Another commando got into a fight and had her mouth bloodied. A big crowd gathered. In the end a seedy-looking GI let her cry on his bosom. A Samaritan of some sort in uniform came along with a first-aid kit and gave her a powder. I understood she had fought with another commando. In the milling crowds there were many more spectators than actors, and uniforms predominated among the spectators. Alerts for flying bombs had no effect on the drama.

Austin, Texas
August 15, 1944

Dear Dobie:

Mrs. Dobie says you may get an airmail letter mailed today before you leave Cambridge for America, so I am sending this merely on chance with nothing particular to say. Mrs. Dobie seemed to think that I might be disturbed by quotation you published from one of my letters. Quite the contrary, I feel flattered, especially flattered by your kind and too enthusiastic remarks introducing the quotation. I never care for any of my letters to be quoted about *general* matters, but I seriously object to anything being quoted about persons. Sometimes I am a little rough in condemning individuals for doing or saying things that seem to me contrary to the public interest, and I talk much freer concerning them than I would if I were writing for publication. But on anything as general and important as the race question, I would write a lot if I thought I could get an audience. You gave me an audience on the remark concerning separate drinking fountains for Negroes. I'm all in favor of sanitary drinking cups, but under cover of a sanitary measure to insult a whole race is, to my mind, about as low-down as my particular race has ever gotten. We take food from their hands and drink from their lips as long as they are *servants,* but disengage them from that relationship, and we make out like every one of them is too filthy to drink at the same drinking fountain. Since national solidarity is about the only hope of survival in this jungle-world, I think that any group which seeks to alienate any other group of our population and set them apart as pariahs, destroying the loyalty they have to the whole group, is doing the work of our enemies—whether they know it or not, they are enemies of the nation, traitors, boring from within. This goes for anti-Semites, anti-Catholics, Lily-whites, and all the rest. In my opinion much of it is done by shrewd engineers of reaction, sometimes with the motive of weakening the nation in its foreign relations, and sometimes by employers who want to "divide and conquer" labor. In either case, it's a blow below the belt and calls for the severest condemnation by people like you and me who have had our eyes opened. While I am not sure, still I have a deadly suspicion that the recent Philadelphia Transit Company strike has some such sinister background.

I was hoping you would stay away until the summer heat has been somewhat mitigated, but you will hit it in full blast. This will try your loyalty to dear old Texas severely. But wait until the chill days of fall! You will "come to" again.

I think you have done a fine job with your articles from England. You will be accused of being an Anglophile, of course, but do not take this too seriously. We are in a sink-or-swim, live-or-die alliance with England, and one can afford to gloss over the failings of such an ally and play up her virtues. And I don't mean the end justifies the means. In times of great emotional tension, such as we have at present, we *honestly feel that way*. I do, and I know you do. I tell you that I wake at night, twist and turn in my bed, and my wife says I groan, thinking about that terrible shelling London is getting.

Well, much love, and safe voyage.

Bedi

Emmanuel College, Cambridge
September 20, 1944

Dear Bedi:

I don't remember what or when I wrote you last. I fully expected to be home before this. Maybe I told you about my book. Ben Hibbs of *Saturday Evening Post* wrote and suggested I do an article on professoring in Cambridge. After I wrote

it, I considered that it and all the other stuff I had turned
out amounted to a full-sized book's worth. My publisher said
to go ahead and he'd stand all the loss. I thought I'd just
add a little, subtract a lot, and change what was left and
turn the thing out in a jiffy. Nothing I ever tried to write
turned out to take less than two or three times the amount
of work I first figured on. It looks as if I would learn someday.
Anyhow, I am still adding, subtracting, and changing. I may
have ruined a horn and spoiled a spoon both. Lots of days
I have had a hell of a good time. Now I have written nearly
all the words the book should take and I still have a lot to
say and am going on saying it. I'm not trying to be coherent,
and if anybody wants to read the book he can pick it up at
one chapter as well as at another. If I just had sense enough
to cut out, I think it might be quite readable. That is a big *if*.
I'm expecting to get off early in October. Tomorrow I am
going to London, for the first time in a month, and that will
throw me out of gear.

I settled down a long time ago in one of the snuggest little
pubs in fair England—the Anchor. Six or eight of us use
the back entrance ahead of regular opening time, though it's
perfectly legal, draw our own bitter, and sit by windows
looking out on the Cam River and drink and talk. Two of
them are doctors, one still in the army and the other retired
after Burma; an old salt; a man that got shot up twice in
airplanes in the last war and always has a laugh in his heart;
an authority on Estonia—some sort of university scientist; a
young man in charge of construction, and he's in London
all the time now mending houses damaged by the pilotless
bombs, which were a lot more hell than the world generally
conceives. It is always painful for me to leave this jolly
crew to come to my college for dinner, but I have got so
that I don't mind being ten minutes late, which is the limit.
Academicians are the same the world over, and I don't find
the average of Cambridge academicians to have any more or

any less juice in them than the American academicians. They can be and are quite pleasant, but I never hone for them—as I do for the Anchorites.

The war is going so good that lots of times I forget it, though I know lots of good men are getting killed. If I had time to go to France, I'd get war correspondent status, which I could easily do, and take a look. I'm just a slave and have to get home someday.

Yes, I'm an Anglophile. Two Texas congressmen on a junketing tour over here came to see me yesterday, guided by a Ministry of Information man who was showing them Cambridge. Each wore a Stetson hat and neither one showed a strain of the good earth or of civilization. They were, at this distance, consumed with the petty details of the mechanics of politics, and gave no evidence of being interested in policies. There is something metallic and barren about an awful lot of American citizens. Their minds are puerile, like the funnies, the pictures, and the horseplay humor they feed on. I always will take great delight in people of the soil. Otherwise, I find that more and more I want them to be civilized. And nobody is more interesting or richer in nature than a civilized man of affairs with perspective and a sense of values. There are plenty of the type at home, but you have to pick them out, whereas they turn up often in Europe.

I have not seen an editorial statement about the presidential election in any English newspaper. Everybody is certainly hands off. But if the English could vote, I bet Dewey wouldn't know he had run. Isn't he a hell of a compliment to citizenship's sense of responsibility! Well, it will not be a dull world for quite a while after the last German and the last Jap have been killed. I'll be coming round the bend some day. I guess old Lomax is sulking in his tent. Here's to life! It never seemed more fetching to me. With lots of affection,

Your friend,
Frank Dobie

Austin, Texas
September 4, 1945

Dear Dobie:

The validity of the above address is dependent upon Mrs. Dobie's memory. I got it from her across the bluebells two or three weeks ago.

I have had writer's paralysis for a solid month, not of the hand but of the brain. Webb told me of your initiation of proceedings which are intended to free me from the office grind long enough to write a book, and you've no idea how this glimpse of freedom has inspired me and even tempered down the August heat. Webb seems to be carrying on but I haven't got any definite word as yet, although on his assurance I have been "gathering the forces" in way of many years' note-taking accumulations, letters, articles published and unpublished, etc., to serve as something to set to work on. In any case, I cannot leave this work before Nov. 1, as I am in process of training a young lady to get out the *Leaguer* and do other little odd jobs which I have been doing for a number of years in my sleep. If I get this "reprieve," I am going to tackle the big question of a proper approach to Nature and Nature study, hanging it, perhaps, on a thin autobiographical thread and relating the whole thing to Texas first last and all the time, as Texas is all I really know.

By the way, I saw yesterday the first authentic picture of Texas ever to reach the screen. You must see it if it comes to England. When you do you will taste the dust, see the sun-grins, smell the overflow of a raging Texas creek, and hear a perfect Texas cotton-farmer dialect.

This picture is badly named *The Southerner.* Its basic theme is the same as Pearl Buck's *The Good Earth,* namely the love of the land (on my theory, you know, the basis of all patriotism worthy the name). The lead is played by an Austin boy, Zach Scott, who won an acting award in his high school days in our Interscholastic League contests. This boy knows his Texas, knows its talk, its psychology, its stride, its anger, its trusting ignorance: He knows it all and he and he alone makes the picture really authentic Texas, although that French fugitive, Jean Renoir, directs it with genius. How he, a stranger in a strange land, interprets what he is told (he could have no firsthand experience with his subject matter) is another of the marvels of the play. Imagine yourself trying to direct a folk play of Bavaria! This man's sensitivity must be that of an exposed nerve. As you see the play, look for the country funeral; and the return from the funeral. The pedestrians are crowded by, i.e., *backed up against* a huge forest of sunflowers or ragweeds lining and confining the country road, as the vehicular traffic goes by, giving each one a sun-and-dust squint until the broken-down autos and horses and wagons clear out ahead and leave the lonely, narrow road to those afoot.

In an early scene, watch Scott's face give a Texas sun-grin. I have seen this grin nowhere else in the world. Only a certain pattern of wrinkles distinguishes it from the usual Gary Cooper counterfeit, and Scott gets this pattern. The woman, Betty Field, plays well, but her inflections, compared with the incomparable Scott, are manifestly phony. Note her pronunciation of such words as "winter." You soon see that she has donned a Texas garment; on the other hand you see that Scott has pulled the trappings of other roles (in none of which I considered him particularly distinguished) and there he is: a young, hopeful, attractive, fighting Texas farmer, with a kind of suppressed gaiety and native courtesy. Of course, Jean Renoir, being a Frenchman, had to lug in a whore, and she turned out to be of the big-town type. I could have given him some points on country whores. But the little slips like this are only specks on a really great canvas.

And there's no outright propaganda in it. It doesn't touch the terrible land question here in Texas except by faint indirections. Scott never realizes he is exploited, and this makes him all the more genuine. Revolutionary concepts have never penetrated the renter class here very deeply. The great privilege, the real privilege, they verily believe, belongs to them— that is, living and working under the sky and from dawn to dusk, in wind or rain or under the "splendid, silent sun."

Well, well, I sound like a movie reviewer, and I had no intention of telling you all this. I meant to say something about how things are going at the university, of a farewell cedar brake party to Henry Smith, of Rainey's radio talks, of my recent trip to the Davis Mountains where really, once again, "the deer and the antelope range." But of this another time. I miss you very much, and I know many others must miss you even more, for after all I am a sort of lone wolf who never gets really lonesome.

Yours,

Bedi

Austin, Texas
October 28, 1945

Dear Dobie:

As the divine child, Wordsworth, said of the sylvan Wye, "how often has my spirit turned to thee," so I of thee. I read in your articles in the paper a longing "to meditate on everlasting things in utter solitude." I judge you are not enjoying the hurry-scurry of the Army University as you did the academic quiet of Cambridge.

You are making an excellent choice in some of the correspondence you print. The English lady in Chicago who wrote you about her memories of England writes like a professional, and a good one at that. I am often astounded at the freshness and electric style of some letters I read in the papers from people who never apparently write at all. You never hear of them before or since, but they deliver a perfect gem of writing which the editor crowds down into the correspondence column, often a real jewel in a muck heap. I would mark those occasional glimpses of some secluded genius for black-faced type anyway. I judge there is more real literature in the world out of print than in it. Think of the oceans of correspondence during the war years—letters right out of bleeding hearts. Just yesterday this came to me in an incidental way:

At the war's beginning, a boy loved a girl who lived in Waco. He was assigned for primary training to airfield at Mission in Lower Rio Grande. He would leave Mission in a high-powered car every Sat. night at close of his training-day and drive to Waco, reaching there in early morning, spend day with sweetheart, and start back Sunday night to be ready next morning at Mission to resume training. He was an old west Texas ranch boy and stood this kind of thing, tough as a longhorn steer. Then away to the islands of the Pacific. Letters stopped. He was reported missing. Girl gave up, came to university and was graduated just this summer. Then they received word that he had been found in Jap jungle prison camp, but no word came from him. She knew he had got back to this country from collateral sources. Then came a weak voice by telephone from away off, asking if he might come to see her. "You'll have to have a mighty good excuse," she told him brusquely over the phone, and she could just hear something of a mumbled excuse but couldn't make it out. Anyway, she told him to come on. He was lifted out of the car in front of her door a mere skeleton. He couldn't open his mouth over an eighth of an inch, could barely make himself heard. In the jungle prison camp he had got a fungus in his ear that was slowly closing his jaws tight and starving him to death. Well, that was his excuse. Does he die in her arms? Is this tragedy, really? Ah, no. They married and are living happily now on a west Texas ranch. The day he arrived he got a telegram from some medic who had been treating his case, telling him to see Dr. Somebody at the airfield near Waco, as he was a world authority on this particular fungus and had treated it successfully. The girl and her dad bundled him out to this doctor in about fifteen minutes. The doctor looked him over. "You have been in ———— (naming some island in Pacific), haven't you?" The boy nodded yes. The girl was amazed. "How did you know?" "This island," said the doctor, "is the only habitat in the world for this particular fungus." He made up a bottle of dope and gave him treatment by pouring it into his ear. He got immediate relief. The doctor gave the girl the bottle with instructions as to how to administer it. The gal took him home and cured him. He toddled back from the tomb and got fit as a fiddle. Marriage. Curtain. "And now, Robert Browning, you writer of plays, here's a subject made to your hand." Ain't it so?

In the stories of the millions who have been jumbled about in this war throughout the world are volumes which it will take a thousand years of writing to exhaust, and that in every language in the world. The world will likely be blown up by an atom bomb before it is ever written, more's the pity.

Terrible slowdown here since war's end. Morale bad. National leadership poor, as you have doubtless noticed. Is it the same in England? I am disappointed with what the Labour Government is doing, but perhaps my information is too scanty to form a judgment.

Mrs. Dobie's little army of bluebells has been decimated by the fall weather, but a few are still standing up bravely, as I notice when I drive by. Had a glorious day on the coast last week at Rockport. Mrs. Hagar[25] and I shook the bushes and my, the birds we did see! Sixty-four species from sun to sun—'cluding not less than ten thousand geese settling in the marshes near Austwell, Lesser Snow, Blue, Canada, and the wonderful White-fronted geese which did some fancy rolling for us. I had never seen them do this before. In fact

I had never seen so many White-fronted geese before in all my life. We needed only the Hutchins's goose to make the goose roll call for North America complete.

Grant which you conceived for me and which Webb is industriously trying to execute seems assured. If so, I am going to take off Feb. 1, and myself "meditate on everlasting things in utter solitude."

Thanks for the papers. I have gone over them with interest.

Much love,
Bedi

Shrivenham American University
Shrivenham, England
November 5, 1945

Dear Bedi:

I think of you lots and lots of times, but get worse and worse about writing letters I don't have to write. Such are merely communications, not letters. It took me longer to answer Barker[26] than you, and I think that his letter and copy of my reply to it may interest you. Also, some things inside old Money Bags Crockett's[27] letter might surprise you, though they don't surprise me. With a gathering in my heart, I wonder if you have received the "reprieve." Had I not made myself such a persona non grata with financial men of the state, I could without difficulty, I think, have gone out and raised a fund to assure you the freedom that would assure society a beautiful and interesting book. I don't know if Webb's Rockefeller money is operating for you, or if any individual has matched it.

The Army has indicated that this school is to close early in December and that some "junior colleges" under strict military control are to be established in Germany, in place of this. The Army may change its mind. The Army is terribly afraid of ideas, but, believe me, a lot of these soldiers have them. They do not represent the majority, whose minds are permanently opiated, but the number of young men who are aware and alert is a great tonic and hope to me. Lloyd Gregory[28] writes me that the politicians are terribly afraid of the soldier vote; they have reason to be.

I am not going to Germany to teach in a junior college. Life is far too restricted here to suit me. I should like to go over for a short tour of lecturing and may. I don't know and won't know until the Army becomes definite. Otherwise, I am apt to go home within two months. I have lots of things to put into books, out of the old innocent days. I suppose that if I withdraw myself from current life, my imagination will take me into them as of yore. However, I can't get into them and remain interested in the rapidly evolving world that right now is the only reality to me. On the other hand, I am too damned ignorant to be effective in writing about the realities of the present. That is what comes from having spent nearly a quarter of a century of my allotted years in doing nothing but soak in the lore of coyotes and cowboys.

I don't know what this Labour Government will work out. There are two big facts in their favor. The leaders are able, and the masses are self-controlled and patient, willing to keep their belts tight and to be deprived a long, long time. The British always calculate on a long pull, and they seem to regard the present economic pull as being as long as any war pull could be. My admiration for them grows all the time, and of the way the elements are mixed in them. Out on a farm near here Saturday I came upon a badger's den that interested me more than the Roman baths at Bath. It is bigger than fifty dens made by Texas badgers. And after all these centuries, the people are still weighing the good done by badgers against the evil they do. Adios and a world of good wishes.

Your friend,
Frank Dobie

Shrivenham American University
Shrivenham, England
December 6, 1945

Dear Bedi:

I have missed writing a dozen good books and more good letters to you than that by not putting the stuff down while it was hot inside me. I am sure that in the way of writing in 25 years I have not accomplished 8 per cent of what my capabilities would have warranted. I had figured on writing a couple of magazine articles this month, following the close of the term. It closed yesterday, and there is so much fuss and flurry about getting away and breaking camp that I don't think I'll get anything written. I'm not sorry to leave. I have sucked very little juice out of my experience with the school, directly I mean. I am in the atmosphere of barren men mostly, the faculty, though, as I have said, the soldiers are the hope of the earth. If the Army just had a higher per cent of alert, aware, reading, questioning fellows like the cream we have here, I would not be depressed by the spectacle of America at home now. It seems to me that the country is going the exact route it went after the last war. The United Nations *spirit* in America seems to be as hollow and dried in a lime kiln as the religious spirit of a church supporter like Pappy O'Daniel.[29] Why talk about the subject?

I have two letters from you, the last one on your rejuvenated Oliver. I learned to peck on one and wore one out more or less. I still can't do anything but peck after having written millions of words. I don't think I could even peck on an Oliver now. Yet your type has a lucidity that comports beautifully with that of your mind. Go ahead and write the book and damn the publisher. You'll get the book published easily enough after you write it. I think Little, Brown & Co., my publishers, grand people and would like to see you and them collude.

Have you read Lamb's "Superannuated Man" lately? Lamb expresses finely your emancipated feelings. I have written in a variety of places. The three best have been my own study before I became a public institution and took to making talks and seeing people and gradually becoming responsible for other things than writing; a ranch down in Mexico where I had a great room, a great fire, a great steer hide on the floor, nobody to bother me except Mexican servants, and had a good horse to ride over an immense country in the afternoons; then Cambridge. Cambridge would have been perfect had it not been for floods of American soldiers who had found me out. I loved them and blessed them, but they cost me a lot more than they ever guessed. Many times the unsmelled and unheard emanations of certain people beyond a wall tie my nerves into knots, damn up all the flow of spirits within me, and constipate my brain. I pray God that you get a place wholly congenial to work and no compromise in any way.

You are mistaken about my having written Barker in anger. I had no anger when I wrote him, though I may have been violent. And I'll go on thinking that he is a monomaniac, though I should not for a minute call him crazy or insane. I truly regret to hear of his physical condition. I thought that De Voto gave him what was coming to him in the *Harper's* rejoinder.

The San Antonio *Light* has, after six years of helping to support my wife's garden, dropped my weekly articles. "The people are interested in picking up life where they dropped it, getting back to normalcy"—oh, accursed word. Yes, I shall have to go back to the coyotes.

Before I leave the Old World, very likely for the last time, I am going to Germany. I expect to report in Paris next week and there get assigned to some army area. In this I'll mosey around lecturing to troops, probably three lectures a week, a trilogy, in one camp, and then move on to another place. Three lectures a week will not kill me, and this seems to me a fair way of seeing and hearing something. I am going to give them a dose, three doses, on Citizenship and the Necessity for Thinking. I really watched myself make some lazy heads do a little thinking this past term. I'll have another APO, but anything directed to this one will eventually catch up with me—perhaps in Austin. I don't think I want to stay on the continent more than a month or six weeks. I could stay in England for years with happy feelings.

Well, Bedi, may you thrive. I had rather talk to you than any other man I know. That was a dramatic story of the soldier who had a fungus in his ear and his mate.

With love,
Dobie

Austin, Texas
December 8, 1945

Dear Dobie:

December's nights are cool and clear, and according to the old rhyme, they should usher in a fruitful year. I hope they do for you, since your fruitfulness is other people's pleasure. A merry Christmas in merrie England!

Events have been disturbing the even tenor of my life. Sons-in-law and now a son returning from the war, a new grandson, another grandchild expected almost momentarily, the settlement of one of my daughters in far-off Milwaukee, approaching marriage of my son, the coming to live with us of my mother-in-law, one of the dearest old women I have ever known, my approaching leave of absence and consequent change in my ways of living, the omnipresent atomic bomb with the sense of insecurity it brings . . . is it not enough to disturb an old man settled in his ways?

Really, the impetus called life is just that, however: a cosmic determination to allow nothing that proceeds upward along the way of life to become settled in its ways. Since animal life parted company with vegetable life eons ago, advancing animal life has refused to become "settled in its ways." Whenever it relapses into a vegetable reverie, it tends towards parasitism and eventual fixity. So I thank whatever gods may be that I am not allowed to settle down into slippered ease, but am compelled to push off as Ulysses did after the wanderings of a lifetime.

I hear from Lomax[30] that he has really struck a jackpot with his ballad-hunting adventures. The movies have made a contract with him and he is really "going to town" to a big town in a big way. The vitality of any kind of folklore is tremendous. After the *Reader's Digest* republished Donald Day's story about him, the Library of Congress, folklore division (which was referred to in Day's article), got as many as four thousand letters in one day, so Lomax tells me.

Edgar Witt[31] was by a week or two ago, drinking and talking very loud. He is obsessed with the Rainey controversy and becomes apoplectic upon mention of *The Big Money.* His rage knoweth no bounds. It has been a curious thing that indignation over the "obscenity" of that book has been in direct proportion to the general looseness and nastiness of the lives of the persons who feel the indignation. I suppose this would not hold true in all cases, but it does in the cases that have happened to come under my observation.

The Austin Garden Club under the stimulation furnished by Mrs. Dobie is doing well by the bluebells. The president of the club was telling me yesterday a remarkable story of how many householders have gone in for domesticating this flower. I talked to the Austin Women's Club yesterday on nature study. I met one very charming woman, a Mrs. Kyle,[32] who is matron of one of the university dormitories.

Barker,[33] I understand, is not going to say anything back to De Voto.[34] There is a considerable blowup here in the press over Maco Stewart's[35] man Ulrey[36] passing on textbooks for the State Board of Education. You would really enjoy this fuss.

Judging from your last letter you will be back before a great while.

Yours,
Bedi

Munich, Germany
January 13, 1946

Dear Bedi:

Handwriting is hard work for me, but I left my typewriter in Frankfurt 6 days ago so as to travel light. I have been down here in Bavaria talking to troops and tonight go on to Vienna. I can't think that what the troops get is worth what it costs the Government in money, and me in time. At any place I go I find a commandeered hotel, the best left in the city, serving the best food possible—in the hands of bright-faced waitresses, usually DPs (displaced persons). There will be a bar, and for lunch and dinner, music, sometimes by Germans, perhaps by Hungarians or some other nationality. The U. S. Army runs the trains and I have learned to manage against having some officer rank me out of a berth. For some occult reason, the Army chooses to run all its trains by night.

When I went from Munich south to Bad Tölz, in the foothills of the Alps, I experienced the first feeling of release I have experienced in Germany. The sun was shining from a cloudless sky; the fields were plains of snow, and the forests were patterns of fairy-white tracery. These Bavarians do not have the heavy sauerkraut countenances of the Teutons to the north, but except in the villages they are all in a hell of a fix. Many of the whole houses have been taken over for displaced persons and used for Army occupation. Amid the desolation any whole business house looms as singular as

Waco's skyscraper over the farm lands. I think Germany, aside from the processes of education, will need occupying 25 years from now more than it needs occupying at present. And, believe me, Germany is occupied.

The enlisted men in the cities have their night clubs, with wine, beer and women. The officers often waste more liquor than it takes to make a certain portion of them drunk. At Augsburg I met 2 Texans interested in German pistols, hunting, women and cognac. Two other young fellows I talked with were interested in art and ideas; they turned out to be Jews from New Jersey and Philadelphia, respectively. The colonel I ate lunch with yesterday was in righteous wrath against the labor unions and he did not conceal his displeasure over the speech I had just made to his soldiers. The morale of the Army is low, though it may get better. Too many people spend too much time harboring their privileges instead of regarding their responsibilities. Yet the Army has done a lot since the Germans surrendered. One big trouble with the whole outfit is that they don't get any newspapers except *Stars & Stripes*—a house organ. In England plenty of Americans never learned to read the English papers, which I prefer to the American. In France they can get the Paris editions of the London *Mail* and of the N. Y. *Herald Tribune*. In Germany we get nothing of news in the English language, and most Americans, like me, can't read German.

I have not been to any place yet where museums exist. I have seen little destroyed architecture that I regard as a loss to civilization. But the autobahn and other expressions of German efficiency in physical matters are probably responsible for more American sympathy than the fräuleins are. What I miss is charm and freeness, both common in France and England.

I hope that you will be in a weaving way on your book by the time this reaches you. I hope that you have found (no more ink up here in my room) a writing place that calls to you to linger and remember and expand. I can't think in the

damned, heavy, Teutonic, steam-heated room in a barbed-wire
compound assigned to me in Frankfurt. Just before I left
England, December 18, I had your good letter of the 7th with
copy of letter on Whitman. Intellectually I correspond with
Whitman, but he seldom warms me. I simply don't comport
with him chemically; yet I admire your regard for him, also
your mastery of him. Well, good composing to you!

> With love,
> Dobie

> Austin, Texas
> January 28, 1946

Dear Dobie:

Your painfully written letter mailed from Munich (of in-
famous memory) came the other day. So sympathetic was I
with your typewriter-less condition, that I almost got writer's
paralysis from reading it. However much I yearn with Morris
for the old handicraft culture, I make *one* exception: I don't
want to go back to "Nature's noblest gift, my grey goose
quill." And I like geese, too.

To think of your working your stubby fingers over those
two sheets (much of which I managed to decipher) was unpleasant, but the thought of your undergoing such a hardship
in my behalf, although it should have been still more unpleasant, was not unendurable by any means. Such is egotism:
the extreme case being that of the lovely and tenderly sympathetic lady who derives such *pleasure*-in-sadness remembering
the lover who died for her. Egotism is at the very core of life.

I am not in a weaving way with my book, but I at least
have my fingers loosened up; I am breaking disturbing contacts, and am in process of getting settled. I have some raw
materials assembled for processing. My leave begins February 1.

At the T. & G. last night the membership committee announced Dolley[37] to succeed Payne[38]: not a bad swap, but the committee in my opinion could have made a much better one. I had made a plea for Paul Boner.[39] He is young, articulate, and perhaps the most distinguished scientist in Texas. He talked on scientific weapons (radar, atomic bomb, etc.) at a proceeding of the club which everyone considered a masterpiece, and I had concluded that his election was practically certain. In my opinion, the committee yielded to the paper-prestige of a person who is prospective president of the university. Or, worse, it yielded to the pressure of the Gown members who think they derive a little personal advantage from having the higher-ups in university administration in their own club. Am I too cynical? Do you remember how the old boys used to capture Benedict[40] and later Rainey,[41] and even before that Splawn,[42] at their table: Well, Rainey came to a meeting recently, and was relegated to *our* table. Maybe I'm too suspicious: Maybe he sought our table. Anyway, with the loss of office prestige he becomes quite ordinary.

I think, with other contacts I am breaking, I shall drop my two clubs too.

I have tried, off and on, to get in touch with Mrs. Dobie, but without success.

I got Edgar[43] yesterday to invite him to a showing of a bird film here tonight.

There's a plethora of liberal papers here now. Newest is the *Texas Herald,* Vol. 1, No. 1, now before me. It is a curious sheet. It proposes to expound and uphold the liberalism of Jesus, but publishes the Washington column of Paul Mallon. It may be that it is financed by anti-labor interests, seeking to slip up on the blind side of the liberals by being liberal in everything else. It's a seven-column newspaper, 4 pages, weekly, well written, well proofread, and well printed. The editor's name is J. L. Dennis. I'll try and look him up.

Looks now as if Rainey[44] intends to run for governor. He inquired particularly about you when I saw him the other night.

We'll have to have a session or two on Whitman when you get back. Did you ever try taking a volume out in the open and reading aloud such pieces as "The Prayer of Columbus"? That particular piece stirs my emotions very deeply. Tears rise in the heart and gather to the eyes.

Well, well, enough and too much, as I am stealing this time.

Yours,

Bedi

Nürnberg, Germany
March 9, 1946

Dear Bedi:

I've learned to take my typewriter with me. Since I scribbled you from Munich, a time ago that now seems very remote, I haven't traveled in realms of gold and I haven't seen any goodly states, but I have been moving about. If my letters to the Texas papers get there and if you continue to read them, you have more or less kept up with my physical wanderings. I think that the best thing I have written on this side of the English Channel was a Letter from Vienna; certainly I enjoyed being in Vienna more than I have enjoyed being in any other place I've been. I liked being in southern Austria, in the Alps, also, though I have hardly been to any spot that I will in years to come lie upon my couch and return to with great gladness and refreshment, as I can and shall return to many scenes and personalities in England.

My week in Heidelberg was commonplace. Berlin was interesting, but much of my time there was ruined by ignorant, idea-less people in charge of my program of speaking. I wrote a long "Berlin Diary" of my own for the papers, don't remember what I said in it, have half an idea that it will never get across to its destination, and a year from now I will probably have forgotten most of my impressions except of destruction and the Russians. It was my impression three months ago that hardly an American soldier could be induced to volunteer for a war against the Soviets. My impression at present is that a good many could be induced to volunteer. We are all speculating here on Churchill's anti-Soviet speeches. Yesterday I met two lieutenants just back from the States, and glad to be back. One said his money evaporated over there like smoke, the other said a million ex-soldiers could be enlisted to fight Russia, not however because of anti-Russian feeling but because of their dissatisfaction with civilian life. In other words, they would enlist as soldiers of fortune; they have found that the Utopia they dreamed of while abroad is not Utopia at all. Heaven is still where they ain't. I had more association with Military Government people in Berlin than with Army people; a lot of them are strongly sympathetic towards the Soviets and are learning to get along with them. The only absolute and categorical conclusion I have arrived at in Germany is that the Army is absolutely incapable of operating in the realm of civilized ideas and that, therefore, the sooner the occupation of Germany for denazification purposes is turned over to civilians, the better will denazification be accomplished.

Churchill's eyes are in the back of his head. I have a great respect for what he was, but he now seems to me a pitiable figure, both tragic and dangerous. It is said that he left London because he could not bear to feel himself non-extant in the UNO proceedings. This view may be malicious. Anyhow, he has now betrayed noble dreams as grossly as Cabot and Borah and that group betrayed them at the end of the last war. Of course there are many Americans and also many Britishers, Tories of both countries, who never had the great dream. I can't think we'll go to war with Russia at any time soon, but we'll go someday if the UNO does not become a reality.

Hours later. I decided to go out to the Press Camp and learn something. For one thing, as anticipated, I found current

London papers out there, brought over, by air, by the British. Not a single American newspaper of any date, though it would be easy for our Army to bring in the Paris edition of the New York *Herald Tribune,* if nothing else. This damned Army spends millions on what it calls an education program and the men in the Army can't get any information out of newspapers beyond the *Stars & Stripes.* In both the London *Times* and the *Telegraph* I found Churchill's complete speech, and it read much better than the belligerent extracts selected out of it for publication by the *Stars & Stripes*—all I had been able to read when I wrote the first page of this letter. Nobody could be stronger than I am for our going along with England and the British Commonwealth of Nations, but I am still sympathetic with Russia. Every time she brings a Catholic country into her sphere, she has broken an iron band around the minds of a nationality of people, even though they don't have freedom of speech and freedom of the press after they get in her sphere. She is in a state of becoming, and I am confident that millions liberated from priest domination will in time become free to think and say what they will. If it comes to lining up with Franco and the Vatican against Russia, I am out, no matter if Churchill chooses that line-up—and that is the line-up he is choosing.

I have been to the trials here at one session only. This afternoon I got a pass to sit in the press section and will have a good view Monday. The newspapermen in this country—I talked to a few in Berlin as well as some here—are feeling very blue about the American form of isolationism that no longer has interest in European affairs. After the last war, the country deliberately chose isolationism; now we say we choose to collaborate with the other nations of the world and we have turned towards a provincial nationalism that absolutely vetoes our profession of faith in the UNO. These newspapermen say that the papers in America won't print what they send over concerning politics and economic matters in Europe.

I'm getting more or less ready to start to make some sort of move towards going home, but I hate to contemplate being tied to the pervading air of unreality there. The last two or three years have brought me to an understanding of Henry James's attitude towards America. I'll always have roots in Texas, but I have arrived at a state of development in my brain and nature where European consciousness of its own complexities is more interesting to me than American obliviousness to realities. If I had a hundred or so more years to live, I'd spend most of the time between now and the next war in Europe.

By now you are, I guess, away out somewhere listening to the coyotes howl and the owls sport free, getting authentic tidings of invisible things and interpreting through words certain visibilities that the tidings illuminate. I expect to get back home in time to put in a few licks for Rainey in the governor's race. Then I'm going to listen to, or at least for, voices. Good weaving to you. I'll always want to be making medicine with you.

With affection,

Dobie

Cedar Valley
Travis County, Texas
March 23, 1946

Dear Dobie:

Well, this trip to the mailbox yielded rich fruit, for from it I plucked your letter of March 9. Two of my letters to you have been returned for better address, and last time I was in town I called Mrs. Dobie to get the correction. Mrs. Smith answered the phone and gave me the same address I find on your letter, so I am hoping this will get to you.

Yes, I am keeping up with your articles. I read the Munich one with great interest and thought it one of the best.

Liberal thought in this country was outraged by Churchill's speech. What these Tories can't understand is that Russia has discovered an atomic bomb all its own, an atomic bomb in social relations. They set up their acquisitions not on a colonial but brotherhood basis, share and share alike, regardless of race, color, or religion, if the religion is not a political one. They are doing what we started out and intended to do with our territories. We did give all territories full and equal political freedom but have reduced many of them to economic dependencies. Russia, on the other hand, seems to be sowing broadcast with a free hand and will reap, in my opinion, a richer harvest than the imperialist countries. We at this moment are torn asunder in our own back yards. Our Negroes are palpably rebellious. Labor is coming to really hate management, and management returns the hatred fourfold. GM & Labor are at war. A committee claiming to represent every Knights of Columbus chapter in the country, and 600,000 individuals threatens the present administration with defeat if it continues to *persecute* Franco. Wisconsin dairymen are so organized that my two grandchildren living there are starved for assimilable fats, oleo, or butter. They can't produce enough butter to supply the market and they have a prohibitive tax on oleo— meantime, the health of children is permanently impaired. At a veteran's meeting the other night (officers) a proposal was endorsed to pressure Congress into giving the same retirement pay to Reserve officers as to regular Army officers, a measure that, if adopted, will cost the Government within a few years $180,000,000 per month, according to statisticians. In short, we are split into plunder pressure groups, silly racial alignments, cliquy social exclusions, "two and seventy jarring religious sects," and the armies of labor and capital drawn up almost in battle array. To make all this all the more dangerous we have a sense of false security in the possession of what we call "the secret" of the atom bomb.

Russia, meantime, affiliates and consolidates. I'd rather have her "atom bomb" than ours. England's imperialism is out of date. It cannot stand the atomic fission which Russia is applying in Asia.

I remember when I was a boy we used to have a game to beguile the time while waiting for the football game to begin. Two would get together and agree on a certain grip. Then these two in possession of a secret grip approach a third and demand that he give the grip. Upon his failure, the two grab him and paddle him good. Then at the end of the paddling, they give him the grip and make him a full-fledged member entitled to all the rights and privileges of the gang. Then the three seek a fourth, initiate him. Presently, the group is formidable in size, and initiations are taking place all over the field. There is no organized rebellion, because each one is taken into full fellowship. This is what Russia is doing, and there's no stopping such a movement. Colonialism breaks up; sovietism consolidates.

But the chief criticism of Churchill in this country is of his apparent attempt to destroy the UNO. This he disclaims, but the whole force of any "alliance" proposal is offensive to and incompatible with the United Nations idea. As you well say, his eyes are in the back of his head.

Yes, many of the soldiers want another war. They have come back home to live in huts and trailers, to take jobs, many of them at half or a fourth their Army pay; and competition for jobs is getting more strenuous every day. They will fight any antagonist, Russia especially. But it is well to remember that the soldiers are only about a tenth of a nation's fighting force. Without the labor which makes the equipment, the best army is helpless. And it is among the laboring classes that it would be hard to stir up enthusiasm for another war. There is no FDR to lead them and no Hitler to scare them with. Indeed, so far as Russia is concerned, they have a rather vague and unintelligent sympathy with her. Did you notice a threat in England of a general strike if war came with Russia? Production, ample production, depends upon the spirit with which production is undertaken. "Slow down" has become an art. In my opinion, it would be national suicide to engage in another war unless the whole people were stirred with the deepest enthusiasm for it—something like the wave of popular support that gave us such unprecedented unanimity when the Japanese attacked us at Pearl Harbor.

Don't, I beg you, become expatriated. The mind and the emotions have to have a home, just like the body. For better or for worse, in health and in sickness, etc., etc., a man is born into (i.e., married to) a country, and with all her faults, he must love her still. Think of your brush country and of the paisano, and of the friendly people who talk with just your own accent, and of the good and noble things your countrymen have done and said. As Whitman said, "report everything from an American point of view." Because that is the only possible point of view you can have, for after maturity a man doesn't get another point of view. He may think he has but he hasn't, any more than he has a genuine liking for light bread having been reared on soda biscuit. The whole bread-world is judged necessarily from the biscuit point of view. So with ideas.

I am set up quite pleasantly in Webb's old rock house 17 miles out of Austin on the Camp McCulloch road. I am far from an auto highway, can't hear a car even on the country road, and 3 miles from a telephone. I go into town once a week. I write of mornings, and browse around in the hills for a couple of hours or so afternoons, and read somewhat at night. I cook for myself, as the owl says he does. The large open fireplace provides ample facilities for preparing the simple dishes upon which I subsist. You know I am largely vegetarian so the difficulties of keeping meat without artificial cooling are avoided.

My writing so far is of the love-and-admire Nature order,

and some of the pieces, I think, are pretty good. I am hoping to turn out a book of about 300 or 400 pages by next February 1. It will not be systematic, but will have unity of point of view and subject matter. As you know I am almost a mystic and the study of Nature (such as I have made) has seemed to feed rather than cure my mysticism. Nature to me is a living presence, not a mere mechanism. Facts of science, as my favorite American poet says, are fine, hurrah for exact science, but they are but the "area of my dwelling," that is, merely the yard and approaches, not the dwelling itself. I don't know if any publisher will think it fit to publish, but it will be in type nevertheless.

Rainey has got the dog-water scared out of the old Texas Regular bunch.

Yours affectionately,

Bedi

Cedar Valley
Travis County, Texas
March 30, 1946

Dear Dobie:

The *Austin-American* headlined, or rather, subheaded, your Munich article "Ingrained Slant of German Mind," which is not bad, although a more accurate use of the language would not suggest that the slant is ingrained, inasmuch as you furnish the slant on the ingraining of the German mind. But this is more English-teacher carping. The big head is good: "Even Munich's Heroic Monument to Peace Conveys Veneration of Force and of Victors in Conquest." This is set in two lines balanced across three columns.

I envy you your ability to deliver sharp body punches in a casual manner. The remarks about the crucifix really jar the beastly Catholic superstition pretty hard and are in the authentic iconoclastic tradition.

I transmitted to Rainey your expectation of being here for the finish and a little before, since he inquires every time he sees me concerning the time of your return. He is developing political sense or has surrendered himself to good advisers, perhaps both.

Some days I am greatly encouraged with my work. Other days are gloomy, and it seems to me the thing I am attempting is not worth doing. Today it happens I am about fifty-fifty. I am hoping to be able to find a tough enough string to bind what I say into some sort of unity. The random character of my writing so far is what discourages me more than anything else. When I think of it as a *book,* it doesn't hold together. What I miss is "the continuity, the long slow slope and vast curves of the Gradual violin."

If you have access to files of the *Sat-evg-post,* be sure to look up two articles by Alva Johnson, issues of March 16 and 23, entitled, "Television: Boom or Bubble?" It gives the inside on radio and movie advertising, invaluable for a person writing for the general public, as you are. I thought I knew something of the extent to which all our present-day art, amusements, philosophy, and religion is directed and dominated by advertising, but as the saying goes, "I ain't know nuthin' yit" till I read Alva Johnson.

I am renewing my acquaintance with the sun and stars and especially with the sky itself: clear, cloudy, partly cloudy, lowering, smiling, in all its aspects, dawn-tinted and evening-glowed, darkling and purpling, blackouts and star-bespangled. A man might write a book about the sky, just sitting down on a rock out in the open and noting its everlasting and never-lasting moods and changes, with, of course, a larding in of appropriate reflections from a human standpoint, growing discursive occasionally by recording what he imagines a dog, or a horse, or an armadillo sees in the sky and what they think about what they see.

Did you ever notice how Wordsworth plays with the sky? More memorable, I think, than the lines universally quoted from "Peter Bell" are those/ occurring early in the poem:

> At noon, when, by the forest's edge
> He lay beneath the branches high,
> The soft blue sky did never melt
> Into his heart; he never felt
> The witchery of the soft blue sky.[45]

Well, this is nearly April, and after showers there is that sky and that witchery for hearts warm enough to permit its melting therein.

This letter was indefinitely prolonged until I found out that I was writing you an article not a letter and I chopped it off. I may enclose a copy of what I was inadvertently inflicting on you as a letter. If so, you will not find yourself under any obligation to read the enclosure.

Yours,

Bedi

Lancaster, Pennsylvania
February 15, 1948

Dear Bedi:

Late yesterday afternoon after I concluded the last of the four so-called Appel Lectures at Franklin and Marshall College here, I repaired with four bright young men to a small old tavern with more geniality in its atmosphere than I have found in any other tavern this side of the beloved Anchor in Cambridge, and talked until the stars were out and the starlings were chittering on the electric-lighted roosts up in the cornices over the street. One of the young men asked me something about

Lomax,[46] and while not telling them, I was thinking what a pity it will be if we do not sometime for our own delectation set down the warty realities, along with hearty and not-warty other realities about Lomax. You know twenty times as much as I know and have about seven times a better memory. I hope that you kept carbons of all the letters you wrote to Lomax; if not, try to get the originals. What a bully little book you could make, calling it *Me and Lomax!* He never struck me as being anything like the letter writer that he was talker.

It took me two days to come to Philadelphia on the train, and I enjoyed all the ride, reading a life of Grey of Fallodon. Wednesday I spent several hours with the *Holiday* people and came away with all their manuscripts on Texas, which I have been reading. I have not read yours yet, nor is there any reason for my reading it, editorially, though I shall. I have inserted your correction and emendation. The latter had already been made. I am going back to Philadelphia this afternoon and tomorrow shall consult the editors. The Texas issues are to be October, November, and December. Hart Stilwell wrote them three good articles. I'm going to New York for two days, then lecture in Summit, New Jersey, to an old literary club that has been after me; thence to the Universities of Omaha and Nebraska, which desire samples of my wisdom.

It does me good to get out of Texas. I think it must be the damned provincial-minded, fearing-of-intelligence newspapers there that depress me. Anyhow, I had just as soon live in New England for a while. This is a lovely part of Pennsylvania. I wonder why and how I used to think that I could not live happily anywhere but in Texas and wanted no other intellectual pabulum but Texas and surrounding territory. Intensity can certainly make a fool of a man.

> With affection,
> Dobie

IX. A Book Corralled

By 1945, both Dobie and Webb had made international reputations as writers and teachers. Bedichek, who had probably written as much volume as either, certainly so if his correspondence is included, was known only in Texas, and mostly to the Texans who read *The Interscholastic Leaguer.*

From my early acquaintance with Bedichek, from the time I was able to gauge somewhat the breadth and depth of his personal experience and observation, I had urged him to write at least two books: one, his autobiography, the other, a kind of miscellany that would give to the world some of his anecdotes and thoughts on bird life and animal life, and the foibles of mankind.

Dobie and Webb, I soon discovered, were urging him in the same direction. They succeeded. In their case it was an example of young bears teaching an old bear how to catch fish. At the time he started writing, Bedichek was sixty-eight, Dobie and Webb fifty-eight. Mortality was beginning to hang heavy over all three. There was so little time, and Bedichek feared he had waited too late. So did they.

Bedichek could easily have waited longer. He had only

two years till compulsory retirement. He could have stepped down at the end of a professional career that would have ensured him a place of honor in the history of education in Texas. Instead, with a grant of $4400, equal to his annual salary, he went to Friday Mountain to write a book. Dobie, by his own admission, was able to help only a little in raising money for this grant; he had become persona non grata with too many of the wealthy men in the state. Webb went to work and raised it from various sources, knowing that the University of Texas could easily have afforded to subsidize all three men the rest of their lives. They needed time more than anything else, and time was penuriously denied them.

Years later, Webb was to summarize Bedichek's experience at Friday Mountain:

You used the old stone building as a hideout to write your first book, *Adventures with a Texas Naturalist.* You spent a year and a day there, but you came out with the finished manuscript. Your picture hangs in the room upstairs where you did your writing, sleeping and eating. You cooked your own food in the open fireplace or on a hot plate; occasionally you insisted on eating things you had cooked in the ashes. The potatoes and eggs were all right, but I drew the line on brussel sprouts and spinach, which I don't care for when cooked proper. There was not even running water in the house, but you made out. We still have the big round table you used, one that Captain Ernest Best of the Texas Rangers took out of a gambling house.[1]

In warm weather Bedichek bathed in Bear Creek. Good weather or bad, he roamed the hills and valleys, thinking his own thoughts, then painstakingly setting them down with the aid of his old Oliver typewriter, from time to time getting advice and criticism from Dobie and Webb. Their letters tell most of the story of how this book was written; their advice to each other on the problems of writing and publishing could serve as an informal textbook for young writers.

Bedichek extended the story in taped interviews:

The man I've corresponded with I think most here in Austin is Webb—Walter Prescott Webb. Of course, you know him almost as well as I do. I'll tell you this about Webb. He is the most ideal teacher that I ever came in contact with. I can certainly understand that, and I don't wonder at his success as a teacher, for the reason that he does what Socrates declared should be done and that is bring out what is in the person already. It's not his theory. I don't suppose he has any theory about it, but he's so sympathetic and he's so gentle in his criticism, and when he praises anything he praises it so judiciously that you feel he is sincere.

He is a master at giving encouragement to people. As I told you the other day, I never would have written a book if it hadn't been for Webb because I would never have had the nerve to write a book, to put it out on the public when there are so many millions of books they'd rather read. Anyhow, he encouraged me to the point where I really got to work and wrote a book.

Bedichek told how their friendship developed:

When I came back to the university we gradually became better acquainted with each other. We found that we had similar tastes and so on, and we would write each other notes, little notes, about this or that, whatever happened to occur to us, and just gradually grew into a very fine friendship. I feel a very deep friendship for Webb and I'm sure he does for me. We have written more to each other than two people would usually write who live in the same town.

All the time that I was out at Friday Mountain, writing
that book—that's about fifteen or twenty miles out here in the
country—every time I thought I had a brilliant idea I'd sit
down maybe and write it to Webb. Webb'd write me back and
so on and we had considerable correspondence during that
year. That was 1947, I believe. But for many years I know
that we have exchanged letters and you'll find quite a volume
of stuff and I've got some more accumulation since I took that
over there. Between Webb and myself. I saw the files pretty
big there just now. We always just ranged over many topics
and so on and there's no gossip in it I don't think a-tall.

In reviewing his correspondence with Dobie, Bedichek
understated the case:

Now you'd be disappointed, I think, in any letters that you
find between Dobie and me, because Dobie and I talked and
were both writers and—I had become a writer before I got
acquainted much and began correspondence with Dobie—and so
I just have never written Dobie very much that I was in any
way satisfied with. And he had never written me. We have exchanged letters. You'll find some natural history and stuff and
one thing and another between Dobie and me. Dobie and I
have talked endlessly, you know, whenever we get together to
talk.

No self-consciousness. I feel that he is not very greatly
interested. I don't feel that interest that I would have if he
reciprocated. I'll tell you, a correspondence is like a conversation, and people who just think they can write letters and be
done with it—that's all poppycock. They don't write real letters.
They just exchange gossip or something like that. It has to be
reciprocal, back and forth. You will write some people and
they will acknowledge maybe the date of the letter and yours
received, etc., but they say nothing else in connection with it.

Correspondence is a development, you see. It has to develop along just like a conversation. I feel so thoroughly the obligation to the correspondent that when I write a fellow and ask him something definite and he doesn't reply, it is an insult. It's just as if I had gone along the street and spoken to him cordially and he hadn't returned my greeting. I'll never write to him again. It makes me sore and I just don't pay any more attention to him.

I'm not that way with Dobie, of course, but Dobie's and my correspondence doesn't amount to anything. Now of course Dobie, he pours himself into his books and when we got acquainted on a letter-writing basis, why, I was doing some writing, too, and just didn't feel able to do it.

Month after month Dobie and Webb read manuscript with Bedichek and advised him. Both experienced in the ways of the publishing world, they made contacts for him and saw that chapters got to editors who might be interested. He needed their help, isolated as he was, one old man, working against time, writing what might interest no more than one out of a hundred editors whose only background was the city.

The one turned out to be LeBaron Barker of Doubleday & Company, Inc., a man whose own experience made him especially susceptible to Bedichek's style. Webb took him to Friday Mountain Ranch and, after some talk, the manuscript was brought out. Barker began reading and Bedichek, too embarrassed to stay with him, took a walk. When he came back three hours later Barker was still reading. He looked at Bedichek and said, "I think we've got something here. We'll give you a nice advance."

Doubleday published the book as *Adventures with a Texas Naturalist,* and Lee Barker became Bedichek's editor on two more books.

May 4, 1945

Dear Dobie:

The inscription on the flyleaf of your book (received today) touches me very deeply. It would be curious, indeed, if, under your friendly stimulation, a sun about to set should find a fissure in the cloud and send a few beams across the prairie, wouldn't it? I must go around to Doc Ellis and get him to tell me again of people who have done worthwhile things in old age. He has all the statistics (or, rather, the instances) at his fingertips.

I am reading the book in leisurely fashion, as I like to read good books, and I am enjoying it. You have put a lot of yourself into it.

This State Meet is now in its dying throes, and I hope now for a few months to have more time to cultivate the "humanities," of which you are one.

Yours,

Bedi

New York City
July 24, 1945

Dear Bedi:

The army in control of millions of men has to adapt its machinery, I suppose, to non-intelligence. That may be because the adapters have such an excess of non-intelligence. I can't remember when I was not setting out on this expedition to England. Instructions to get my old passport from the State Dept. went to Washington when I signed the first papers —back in June. I got here July 15, spent the next day signing more papers and being patronized by a peanut captain. I was to sail July 17, but no passport came. It arrived today; I shall sail tomorrow. I have had some congenial talks with a few

New Yorkers I know and like, but mostly I have been tired and bored and often in a bad humor with the damned noises and the everlasting crowding. Yet I realize that the fellow standing up in the middle of a subway jam that encompasses a million people is as human as old Rol Rutledge camped alone at the mouth of Reagan Canyon on the Rio Grande, a hundred miles from a street sound, a radio, and anybody that wants to sell anything.

One of the editors of *Harper's* magazine that I met gave me the enclosed to be published in the August issue. I have quoted a paragraph from it for my Aug. 5 article, just sent off. Circulate it as you please. Also I send what N. Y. *Times* published this morning. I am more sanguine every day of Rainey's chances to be elected governor. All this is on his side. I actually think that if we liberals get behind a good man like Rainey—there is no other, of course, like him—the Coke Stevenson Texas Regulars will be driven into a hole as deep as Hitler's.

I read *PM* up here, but I can't get a tenth of the information from it that I get from the N. Y. *Times.* My thirst for knowledge and something of civilization would make me perish with nothing ampler than *PM,* though it certainly has its function. Well, I sure hated to tell you goodbye.

They say that my address is APO 24418, care Postmaster, N.Y. I'll get another APO number in England. This army persists in trying to make us believe that we don't know where we are going, that we don't know what boat we shall sail on, and that everything is to be kept as dark as though the Atlantic were swarming with German submarines. Damn petrified minds, and bless you.

Dobie

Austin, Texas
July 31, 1945

Dear Old Scout [*Webb*]

I miss you. Not that I have had any daily association with you this summer, but I have had a feeling that your benign presence was available if I took the trouble to trail you down. It served as a sort of prop. I find company now amongst Austin's quality roasting their fat buttocks on the cement curbings of Barton's Pool and deploring the repudiation of Churchill, and sounding warnings and prophesying doom. This association fails to cure my loneliness in any great measure.

Your proposal in the lobby of the Stephen F. Austin Hotel has been subjected to the digestive juices of my enfeebled mind, and I imagine now and then, even in this withering August heat, I feel the stir of glands I had forgotten I had, and I catch myself dreaming that maybe after all conception and birth is possible in exceptional cases long after the mental menopause. At any rate I have been mulling over notes that I thought were cold to find them still exhibiting signs of life. I find myself eyeing a cozy corner in Johnson Institute as I imagine a cuckoo does the warm and comfy nest of his prospective host. A strange egg I would lay there.

Just at this moment, however, I am answering telephone calls, expecting Ox Higgins by to sell me an old rattletrap car for my son-in-law, who must have one in his new assignment, hearing complaints about the janitor from Miss Thompson, listening through the window to one of Kidd's fish stories, etc., etc. More anon.

Bedi

Minneapolis, Minnesota
August 23, 1945

Dear Bedi:

Your Drummond[2] news story is returned. Very interesting, and an example of what will go on around there for a long time. Two weeks ago A. C. Krey[3] and I made a trip into the lake country of northern Minnesota. On the train we met a Dr. Bradley, either a Congregational or Unitarian minister from Chicago, and a very able man as one could tell in even a short conversation. When he learned I was from Texas he commented on the Texas situation, saying that an Illinois college of which he is a trustee had just elected a president from Texas, Lay. "I had to go to bat for him," he said, "because some of the board objected to him because he was from the University of Texas." Those who think that recent events have not hurt the university and those connected with it may ponder this item. A less able man than this Dr. Bradley would not have been able to stand against the "good businessmen" of the board and Lay would not have got the job, and neither would Drummond. Of course by such a process of elimination the opposition at Texas is worn down.

Pictor[4] sent an invitation to an able scientist here to come to Austin for an interview. This man is back and I had a long talk with him. He was entertained by the right people and no unpleasant topics were discussed. Brogan and Parlin are the only non-scientists he met. He got the offer and is now considering it. I asked him if he got an idea about who would be president. He said he did, and thought the mantle would fall on a scientist. So there we are. Science, engineering, and business are to be built up, and the social sciences are going to get the scraps from the rich man's table. This is going to be done by a group who maintain stoutly that they would do nothing of that kind. No indeedy.

Yes, Dobie initiated the business in hand, but left before it got far. He wrote me from New York, and, as the English say, I carried on. Better not write Dobie until I get back and talk with you. I must still get the approval. While I think this is a matter of form, one cannot be absolutely sure these days. A delay of a few days will make no difference to Dobie. Take no further steps until I see you. I have made up my mind and you are going to do this book. Go ahead with your preparation of your notes and papers, but do not discuss your plans and do not take any official action just yet.

Your synopsis thrills me. I think this is going to be a real book, one that flows directly from life onto the pages without having the thought obscured by the foggy particles emanating from other books.

You certainly are skittish about a little physical work. Of course if a blizzard came up making it impossible for me to bring you some canned beans and lollipops, and the cattle were starving and hay was within twenty feet of them, would I or would I not hope that you would roll 'em out a bale? How could you ever raise such a question in my mind? As for making you a literary exhibit, perish the thought. The fact is that you are going to get so damned lonely that you'll be glad (though you will conceal your gladness under rough and abusive words) to see any human being turn up there.

Letters from Austin tell me that you have had a pretty mean summer. I'm glad I missed it. The temperature here this morning is about 65, and the haze of the northern autumn hangs over the landscape. I wish I could remain here until October, but I'll be seeing you about September 3.

Sincerely,
Webb

G. H. 102, University
September 19, 1945

Dear Bedi:

I would suggest, and in fact I insist, that you prepare an application to be submitted to the Research Council for a grant of $2200 or less for the preparation of your work as a *field naturalist*. There is no necessity for you to discuss other work you propose to do, except to state that you plan to take a full year's leave. The half year will no doubt be consumed with your field investigation and writing.

Since the application goes before a group of some dozen people, it is desirable that you be as specific as possible in reference to the material you have collected, the notes you have on hand, the place the study is supposed to fill in the educational vacuum, and the absolute impossibility of doing the job while looking after the routine of your present office. You might also hint that time is a factor, and say that you are now ready to go.

I am on the subcommittee to pass on applications in the social sciences, and therefore it is desirable that your application come through this committee rather than through the science committee. I am also on the larger committee of which Brogan is chairman. It is my opinion that your proposal will meet the approval of the scientists because J. T. Patterson is on it and he knows you and your work well. I know the nature of the mill-run projects submitted and there is no doubt that a grant will be made, and made gladly.

Please get up this application and let me see it before it is turned in. Please don't nerve me up by arguing. I'll try to see you within a week.

Yours,
Webb

Austin, Texas
November 17, 1945

Mr. Roy Bedichek
University Station

Dear Mr. Bedichek:

The committee on grants for the Texas State Historical Association has authorized a grant of not to exceed $1875 out of Rockefeller funds to enable you to do a book on Texas nature and subjects.

From other sources we have received funds bringing this amount to more than $2200, enough to assure you of a half-year leave with pay. This money is now in hand and will be available as you need it and when you need it.

In addition, I have received assurance from a thoroughly reliable source that another fund amounting to more than $2500 will be made available to provide for a second half year. This money is not actually in the hands of the Association now, but we have every reason to believe that the check will come in within the next few days. All funds will be deposited in a special account under the custody of the Texas State Historical Association. Two of the following officials of the Association can make out checks on this fund: Mrs. Coral M. Tullis, Mr. H. Bailey Carroll, and W. P. Webb. (At least two of these should survive automobile hazards.)

It has been provided by the Association and others that you are to receive the sum of $4400, or the amount of your salary, with the understanding that you are to have twelve months' leave for work on the book you have outlined. There may be an additional amount for expenses incident to typing, but that has not yet been authorized.

To sum up: We have in hand enough to guarantee a half-year leave with pay; we have been informed that the balance is in hand, and will be forwarded to us in a few days. You will be notified when it is received. You can therefore count on the full amount and make your plans accordingly.

> Sincerely yours,
> W. P. Webb
> Director

> Austin, Texas
> November 20, 1945

Dear Bedi:

You will find herein the formal statement, as formal as I can make it to one with whom I have rarely been formal. If I can believe the word of an individual who would not dare break his word, the $2500 is in his hands and will be sent in as soon as he returns from a business trip. I have this word by telephone and also by letter.

> Yours,
> W.P.W.

I note with pleasure that even in a very formal, consciously formal, statement to me you cannot refrain from introducing parenthetically an informality—namely, your grim references to the likelihood of Mrs. Tullis' and Mr. Carroll's surviving auto hazards at least to the point of one or the other being able to sign checks, even though you should again decide to charge into a concrete abutment.

The formal statement is all that I could ask. I am busily tuning myself up for a year's adventure. I am, indeed, having trouble tuning myself *down* to the necessary office routine.

> Yrs.,
> Bedi

It takes two to sign checks—two out of three—a wise provision which guarantees corporations eternal life.

Austin, Texas
November 24, 1945

Dear Dobie:

I was digging around in the piles of junk in an old garage the other day and found an Oliver typewriter which had not been in use in ten years. I dragged it out, took it to a typewriter repair man and told him to put it in operation again. He did and I am now writing you with it. It has a triple shift and you will find in this letter many strike-overs, but it's the only typewriter I can get ahold of to take into seclusion with me on my leave, so I am determined to learn to write on it again. By the way, I like the type, don't you?

Webb says he regrets that he cannot take credit for getting me the grant (full year on full pay) but that he must turn whatever credit there is in it over to you. Webb is so secretive in nature that I cannot really be sure whether this is the truth or no. Anyway I am making vast preparations and intend to write a book to suit my damn sweet self. I am dickering with a publisher, but on an independent basis since I've already gotten my pay and a publisher can take it or leave it. Ah, what a grand and glorious feeling.

I haven't pressed Webb to find out just where the final money came from and come to think of it, I don't care to know more than that this is *through* the Texas Historical Association. The first part came from Rockefeller funds.

I have been scouting around in the hill country to find a place to "seclude" in. Webb is kindly offering me a room in the old rock building which used to house Johnson Institute. It's just about the right distance from Austin, just about the right distance from a telephone (3 miles), and is off a highway and thus away from the noise of heavy traffic. Walls are two or three feet thick, and I notice they exclude the sound of everything except that of an airplane which traffics between Austin and San Antonio at fairly regular intervals. It has many attractions and I may set myself up there. On the other hand the room is upstairs with no sewage connections. There's a family living downstairs and living like hogs. I contemplate establishing wherever I go a fair-weather camp, and spending a good deal of the time in it. I like the Edwards Plateau better than any other part of Texas.

I am hoping as you do of yourself; "I suppose that if I withdraw myself from current life, my imagination will take me into them (the old innocent days) as of yore." Blessed contemplation! Have you noticed in "the lives of great men" how retirement has so often produced wonders? Compulsory retirement to jail produced *Don Quixote, Robinson Crusoe,* and I know not how many other masterpieces. Of course, one must be modest and disclaim any such intentions on his own part, but let's not be too damn modest or we might lie.

You have been forced by your own warm heart into public discussion in fields for which you have not been prepared. Your natural good sense and your realization of your lack of equipment, as well as a virile and fearless pen, have served you well. His strength is as the strength of ten because his heart is pure. But I think your longing for seclusion should be heeded. It is not retreat to rest up for the battle of tomorrow. You have been losing some of your audience, I mean of your old audience, and maybe it's time to lure them back within striking distance with innocent tales of cowboys and coyotes.

Your exchange of letters with Barker[5] has a violence in it that shocks me. His intimation of cowardliness in your attitude of course touched off your temper and he got an earful of the kind of thing he has always stood for, i.e., utterly brutal frankness. Reduced to its lowest and simplest terms he says you're cowardly and you say he's crazy. You are neither of you right, and you both know it. Did you ever read Browning's sonnet to Fitzgerald, beginning "So you thank God my wife is dead"? I believe Browning finally excluded this sonnet from the final edition of his works, and when you and Barker come to edit your own letters, you will each decide to exclude this correspondence. The last time I saw Barker to talk with him, he was unutterably miserable. He is afflicted with a universal itch. The whole body was itching, and he was constantly shifting his position, and trying to scratch here only to shift his hand to another place more drastically affected. It was terrible. And he couldn't keep his attention on the conversation. His eyes wandered and when you caught them with yours, there was a vacancy there which was relieved only temporarily. He had had what Kreisle[6] had called a heart attack sometime previously and had been confined to his room for three weeks. He later went to Houston, I understand, and got a discouraging diagnosis from some expert there.

The letter from "Old Money Bags" is not surprising. Hitler, you know, was the tenderest of individuals in his animal contacts.

Well, I've decided to go fishing this afternoon, and must get rid of this morning's letters before I go. So so long, and I'll be expecting you home soon.

Affectionately,
Bedi

Austin, Texas
December 1, 1945

Dear Bedi:

Thanksgiving I skulked around your office, drove by your dismantled and unfragrant garden, and at various times I telephoned to see if conversation was still running out of the tap. But no tap.

Yes, I should think you would want some fixin' before your sabbatical begins. But me, I'm paralyzed, and I wanted to tell you you would have to make the first move—and the last—

in getting your necessary plunder to the ranch. My auto is in the shop and probably will remain there far into 1946. I'm willing to go along, glad of the chance to get a free ride, and I might even volunteer a few directives. As for real work, I, like you on many occasions, have retired.

The beds in the log cabin are usable, but not the last word in Sealy or Beautyrest. We have some good rugs, tables, cowhide chairs, good kerosene lamp, and a fancy set of bedroom utensils which have long gone out of style, namely, a pitcher, catcher, etc. Wood ought to be got up, but for such cooking as you do you should have a hot plate for use when it is too warm for a fire or you are too lazy to build one. At present there is no electricity in the room, though it can be obtained. I have a notion that the ingenious neighbor, Mr. Garrett, who lives on the adjoining place, can devise a way to get electricity into your room. He would also be willing to use his truck in getting the plunder over from the cabin, but he would have to have help, especially if we bring the cookstove, for which, I take it, you will have no use. I can furnish Abe, who is a good heavy man, and the whole job can be done in a half day.

The hot plate you should provide at once, before the Christmas buyers gut the market. Of course a better way is to hint around to the family that you would like to be remembered on Christmas with a hot plate, being careful, of course, to locate and identify the model you want.

I have an old cedar chest which I brought from England which will be a real ornament to your quarters, and a great convenience in storing bedcovers and such personables as might embarrass you if left in the open. This chest is plain, rugged, beautiful in its functional simplicity, and very substantial as is everything the dear English build out of wood. If you object to its stains and scars, I'll furnish a soft rag and some oil with which it could be shined up by any industrious individual. I like it just as it is, and would not voluntarily exert myself on it. Come to think of it, it is probably not cedar, but walnut or some other hardwood. On cold, rainy nights you can turn your imagination loose on that old chest, bought in a Jew trunk shop on the corner of Oxford Street and Southampton Row, and have a good time.

Here's hoping you do.

Yours,
Webb

Austin, Texas

Dear Bedi:

I brought a good cow horse out here that belongs to a friend of mine. I'll probably buy him. In the long room downstairs you'll find a sack of horse feed by the east door. I will appreciate it if you will give the horse a gallon of feed each day, preferably at about the same time, either night or morning. He is gentle if you want to ride him.

Yours,
W.P.W.

He likes sugar and apples.

January 12, 1946

Dear Dobie:

You will probably not receive this note before your return; but, anyway, off it goes in pursuit of you. I read last night your fable in the *Saturday Review of Literature.* Something of that nature may really happen.

I heard Paul Boner[7] last night tell of the atomic bomb which, in its terror and destructiveness, is the visible anger of God Almighty against civilized man.

Had this pleasing idea ever occurred to you? that maybe civilization has become so cursed, and the little manikins that run it so foul of character, that maybe it's right from a cosmic standpoint that it be wiped off the face of the earth.

Evolution has taken a wrong tack, depending on intellect instead of upon more kindly instinctive direction. Positive Science with its partial view of life has succeeded in blighting the little prong of life which we call civilization. This experimental prong is therefore pruned away to keep it from sapping the strength of the tree.

As Einstein has pointed out, this bomb can't wipe out human life. He estimates two thirds, which, of course, would mean the civilized two thirds including the great cities, which are really strangling life slowly anyway. I am sure they should be considered cancerous, i.e., cells running wild. This is an idea to play with until something comes of it. It has been sound philosophical basis at least for speculating purposes.

We are developing a *priesthood* of positive scientists. They are assuming airs. They put you off with mysterious nods, like the priests of ancient Egypt, or like a physician, his country-bumpkin patient, or like a preacher insisting on the reality of the Trinity. They are proud to bust at having devised and exploded that vast firecracker, and brag that it's not a patchin' to what they will do, given a little more time—and money. Really, Paul Boner, hardheaded scientist that he's supposed to be, last night gave human life no hope—we are to be destroyed (i.e., mankind is)—in short, after all the higher education which has been poured onto science, this high functionary of science declares the same thing that the Seventh-day Adventist preacher does, bawling out there under a brush-tabernacle in the cedars of the Jollyville plateau, before an audience of gaping and frightened hillbillies. So there. What has it all come to?

I note your wish, publicly expressed, that I be confined to the penitentiary so that I will be forced to write books to dispel the ennui of such incarceration. Thanks. I am going into voluntary confinement February 1. A tornado tore the roof of my intended habitation last night, but I take this as no unfavorable omen—rather, a thunderous welcome.

Well, I must get busy. One thing more: I understand Johnny Faulk,[8] God bless him, has excellent chance of being taken by CBS. He has just returned from New York where Alan Lomax[9] exhibited him to the bigwigs of the radio world, and they like him.

There are a hundred more things in my mind to write, but I must remember that you will not get this letter until you get back, so really I'm wasting time writing to myself.

Yours,

Bedi

January 24, 1946

Dear Webb:

Thanks for carbon of letter to Tom Gooch.[10] You seem under impression my leave begins March 1. In fact, it begins next week, Feb. 1. Quarterly payments are OK. I'm fortifying myself to do my damndest. I'm a little troubled about whether I will get to start on the scratch, or not. I believe I'll go out and establish myself as soon as I have a "roof over my head," and drive back and forth for a few days, because I know once I get settled there'll be something every day that I have forgotten.

By the way, can I get cut of Friday Mt. Ranch? I should like to make up a private mailing card for use while I am out there.

See you Sunday.

R.B.

Austin, Texas

February 1, 1946

Dear Bedi:

I am inclosing check for $1100, first quarterly payment on the fellowship. I also inclose a letter which you might desire to file, pending rendition of income tax for this year. It seems obvious that income tax is not payable on grants made to promote knowledge. Your grant would without doubt be interpreted in that category. If you do not wish to keep the letter please return to us.

With all good wishes for a real New Year, beginning today, I am

Yours,
W. P. Webb

Austin, Texas
March 13, 1946

Dear Bedi:

Thanks for your delightful snapshots of spring at floodtime on Friday Mountain Ranch. I have never seen the creek at flood, such are the penalties of ownership. Joaquin Miller once said something like damn all owners, for all they owned was his to enjoy, or something like that. I was out Sunday with four men, including Little Garrett,[11] but we worked all day rebuilding the string of fence on north side of Driftwood Road. I gave out about 3:30, doing nothing. I put Garrett in charge of the crew and it would have done you good to see how efficiently he got the job done, and he never gave an order to anybody. The more I see of that little guy the better I like him, the more respect I have for men who know how to do things.

Before the week is over, take a walk into the north side. Go to the new gate up the road towards Driftwood, and pass the place where we sawed wood. Continue north by a dim road which winds a great deal. There are two treats for you on this trip *at this time*. First is a cove or break where you can from one place count a half-hundred redbuds in bloom. I have never seen more in one place, and you must not miss it. Then continue by the road until you come to my north fence. The pasture beyond the fence has not been grazed by goats or sheep, and there are hundreds of wild flowers blooming right at the fence. The contrast is remarkable, the division as definite as a barbed-wire fence. You may see the flowers later, and in other places, but you must see the redbuds now and there.

I left a five-gallon can of kerosene near the well, under an old trailer. If you want to burn a few stumps, hop to it as soon as they dry off. If you don't want to, then do as you damned please. The kerosene was your suggestion. When I come out we will haul up a little tender to use in burning the stumps. I had intended to come next Sunday, but the abundance of rain may make work impractical. In that case we'll build some more fence.

Wallace Garrett told me that you had developed a slight indisposition. I feared you might be laid up at home, but resisted the impulse to make inquiry. I had intended to call the office, but your letter answers all my questions. You better take good care of yourself.

Keep an eye on the kids and take keer yourself.

> Yours,
> W. P. Webb

> Cedar Valley, Texas
> March 13, 1946

> *In re miracle*

Dear Webb:

A gentle rain started on the corrugated iron roof a moment ago and I pulled the curtain of the southwest window to take a peep at Friday Mountain in the rain. Suddenly as a flash on a motion-picture screen an *upright* rainbow in full and vivid colors appeared on the third tier of hills to the right and stood there bolt upright like a soldier. I was so flabbergasted I forgot for a moment the cause of a rainbow in the sky and

stood there transfixed, a witness to a miracle. Then from the
tail of my eye I caught a yellow gleam on the window casing
and glanced eastward to see a rift between cloud and horizon
that let in the rising sun—a clear sunrise in the rain! But, like
Burns's snowfall on the river, "a moment white then lost
forever"—so the rainbow. Even as I turned my eye again in
its direction, a low-lying cloud swept over the sun and the
gorgeous apparition vanished as suddenly as it came.

And all this time you were asleep!

Is it not clear why all of us people who spend our lives
hedged in, cabin'd, cribbed, confined, with purblind eyesight
poring over miserable books are so goddamned deadly dull?

R.B.

Austin, Texas
March 14, 1946

Dear Bedi:

Thanks for the breath of glory from Friday Mountain in
rain. I read it entire to a class of fifty advanced students, even
to the goddamn. Bailey[12] says, "If he is writing like that, it's
going to be all right." Hill,[13] one of the young men in our
department, says if you're doing what you are doing you
should not miss Caddo Lake, a neglected wonder in the annals
of Texas nature. He says he can fix you up with a cabin,
and that there are Negro "pullers" who man the boats to
thread the cypress mazes and know how to get the greenhorns
home from the swamps. The bird life, Hill says, is gorgeous
and abundant. Why not crank up and spend a week there,
unless you have already covered the lake, which I doubt because I never heard you speak of it. Hill will jump at the
chance to go over with you, about 300 miles from here, but he
would have to come back for classes by Monday or Tuesday.

He knows the country and is of it, and is worth having along for his lore and introductions.

Joe Prouse of the city recreation department phoned this morning for permission to take a municipal walking club to the ranch next Sunday. They carry no dogs, guns, or axes, and are well supervised. Please mention it to the Garretts. They are not supposed to molest the house, except to report their presence. I hope you do not mind having your privacy invaded this much. D. E. McArthur is, I understand, the lead ox, and therefore you ought to be able to keep up with them if you want to horn in to their party and show them the wonders of the place. They have seen it before, so this is a return engagement.

If weather permits I plan to be back Sunday but will be working on the north side, finishing up putting posts in the fence line. The rain should make the post hole digging a little easier, down to the rocks. Be sure to visit the north side this week to see the redbuds in bloom. They won't last much longer than your rainbow.

Well, I'll have to close and go back to writing recommendations for people who want something. I've heard of the grace laid up by unselfish service, but I've just about got a bellyful of grace.

W.P.W.

Austin, Texas
March 25, 1946

Dear Bedi:

I warn you that your notes on Friday Mountain, goats, devil's elbow, et cetera will form grist for something I may write about the place eventually. It is in view of this use that I bear up under your insinuations and abuse. I have had some experience in offering hospitality for work, and like all other

get-rich-quick schemes, it is no good. The only work I ever
got out of anybody out there is, of all persons, out of Fred
Duncalf,[14] who helped me build the first little dam in the
ditch—a dam long since buried under the soil. Fred and I
gave out after casting a few stones and spent the rest of the
evening sitting on the grass and looking at the landscape,
soaking up something which can be found only in the country.

Recently I read a book by Duff Cooper entitled *David*.
Yes, the biblical David, and what a man! It seems that David
had stashed his men in the trees to ambush a bunch of
Philistines, and he had to find help from Jehovah in getting
his men to fight the Phillies; so he told 'em that they would
know the time to strike because of a sign, the sound of men
marching in the trees, or leaves of the trees. Now he knew that
at a certain hour at that season a breeze sprang up and that the
rustle of the leaves sounded like marching men. (He evidently
learned that herding goats.) Well, the point or excuse of the
story is a quotation Duff Cooper used which is about like this:
"A man never knows how many voices a tree has until he
comes up on it in the desert." I recommend the big poplar just
above the cave on the south bank, the fastest-growing tree I
have ever seen. Four years ago it was a switch. It is bare now
but will soon be in full murmur at the breezes.

No, I never intend to ask any damned professor to do any
work out there, and what's more I wouldn't even tolerate it.
I prefer Abe, who is getting old, Paul, who is young enough to
look forward to the night and humorist enough to find fun in
work and sex, and to slight little Garrett, who can relate his
experiences all day long and never repeat himself and who
lives on his nerves.

But you see, Bedi, it is good, as David knew, to stand with
the Lord. Yesterday we scattered the fertilizer, and much
depended on the type of rain that followed. A hard rain and it
all washes away; a gentle rain and it soaks in. This morning a
gentle rain! If me and the Lord will just keep combining

fertilizer and rain we'll make that place look like something. The way things are there I think it's going to take both of us to get the job done.

I called on you in your office this morning, but your secretary said you didn't live there any more, and that she thought you and Kidd were off drinking beer. She seemed to be glad of it.

I would like to restore the wild flowers. Is there any place where they can be had? I doubt that the goats will bother them. What do you think?

W.P.W.

Cedar Valley
Travis County, Texas
March 27, 1946

Thanks, thanks, dear, dear landlord, for the equine companionship thou has furnished me with. Sugar, however, is rationed, and apples this season are runty and expensive, so with your permission, I'll try salt and the simple blandishments I learned as a boy. At sundown yesterday when I returned and found your note, I began looking about for the animal and found him on bluff above the cave. He is apparently a pet, for he welcomed my approach. I tied a string around his neck and led him back to the house where he got the gallon of feed which you directed he be given. This morning when I was taking a sufficiently motivated stroll over to the wooded section, he spotted me and came up for a pet or two. I tried one of my runty apples on him, which he disdained; then I tried sugar, which he sniffed and refused; then he rejected salt, also. He wants merely human companionship. I'll see that he gets his gallon of provender once a day.

Yours,
R.B.

P.S. (Mar. 28) Little Garrett and the two women tried to get goats off Friday Mountain and bluff above cave yesterday but couldn't. Say pen will have to be built across creek for shearing, as kids won't cross creek and nannies won't come without kids.

By the way, a cowboy was once afflicted with fleas, and when asked did they bite, replied, "I don't so much mind what they eat, but it's what they tromp down." That's what you will mind about the pony. He's restless as a caged tiger. You find his tracks everywhere you go on the place. He's tromping down twice what he eats.

Frankfurt, Germany
April 11, 1946

Dear Friend Bedi:

Your letter of March 23, concentrated on Russia's own "atomic bomb," is such a masterpiece that I sent it to Tom Lea in El Paso, with the understanding that he will return it. I hope that you and Tom Lea meet someday. He has the elements of nobility in him, has the seeing eye, and may be a great artist.

Now comes your letter of March 30. I read it as soon as I received it about 5 P.M. and as I read it constructed a wonderful letter to you, but I had to go make a talk—perhaps the last I shall make in the ETO—and now what I would have written could I have sat down at once to a typewriter seems to have largely evaporated. . . .

I got back last week from the last trip I shall make before going home. I was in the Bremen Enclave for a week and then took off for Denmark, where there are too many Lutheran hymns to suit me. It came to me when I got to Bremen that I was ready to go home. Every day the conviction is stronger. I have seen all of Germany I want to see. I have learned a lot, though not what to do with Germany, unless we sterilize the Germans, which might be charitable and would certainly be rational. I have a letter from Fred Simpich[15] suggesting two articles on Germany for the *National Geographic*. If I do them, I'll do them after I get home. I'm burned out on the subject and burned out on the Army and about burned out on myself; I dislike the way this Army is run more than I dislike anything else *right now*. I am standing to heel like a moronic rookie waiting for the Army red tape to get me away. You have no idea how helpless a man is in this country without complying with Army whims. An order came out the other day, for instance, that all civilians take brass buttons off their coats; they had to be on the coats when I came over. It's easy to say that the Army can go to hell. I have said it. The Army says, "You can't enter this mess hall with the brass buttons on your coat." The Army has a military policeman at the door to look for brass buttons.

We have had ten days of mostly sunshine. The miracle of spring works here in Germany also. I want to see mesquite green though and a roadrunner, though several birds talk to me in English. I don't think the blackbirds and larks know how to sing in German at all. The German poets above all other poets of the world have translated them. I'm going by England, which I love, but I wish I were in a rocket to be shot straight to Austin, Texas. I fervently hope to get away next week. So don't write me any more here. I long to see a sample of your composition. In this last letter you spoke of "inflicting" an enclosure and then, to my disappointment, did not enclose.

With a great deal of faith and with affection.

Frank Dobie

Cedar Valley, Texas
April 23, 1946

Dear Webb:

We have had here a glorious rain, really a ground-soaker. Creek is up some, and the swag down the road between house and creek fooled a spotted sandpiper into believing that it is a marsh. This is going to bring on a flower crop that will tempt me too often away from the typewriter, I'm afraid.

Bedi

Friday Mountain
April 25, 1946

Dear Webb:

Item: Blaze-faced filly returned by Little Garrett yesterday clean-nosed, hungry, and—what de ye know—hossin'.

Item: Caught half-grown La. bullfrog on creek under red mulberry during my bath yesterday. On release, jumped six yards, or thereabouts—didn't measure it.

Item: Baby blue-eyes are blooming.

Otherwise, life among the hills moves on steadily, phlegmatically, with majestic deliberation under the splendid silent sun.

Yours,
Bedi

Cedar Valley
Travis County, Texas
May 16, 1946

Dear Webb:

We had last night the hardest rain since my coming here. In an hour or maybe a little over there was not less than two inches fell. We do not have a gauge, but my guess is pretty good. There are "washes" showing all over the place, particularly in the auto tracks down across the field to the tank. The mud-trap is three fourths full, and the bottom of the tank itself almost covered. Ridges of clay left in the bottom still show. It will take a lot of rain to fill the tank. The ground was already soaked when last night's rain fell, and still there was not enough runoff to make a start at filling the tank, or more than a start. It's still cloudy and threatening.

Creek is up and very muddy. Indeed, creek has been running muddy water for two or three days; in other words, the countryside is bleeding.

Yours truly,

R.B.

May 17, 1946

Dear Webb:

I steal this moment out of Sacred Time, time set aside in which to give genius an opportunity to burn; but the clouds have rolled away with last night's rolling thunder; the skies are clear; the wind is balmy; the water in the mud-trap is almost clear; and the little clump of *Dianthera americana* just above crossing over the creek is again erect after three successive and torrential mud baths in the last two weeks, showing delicate white flowers clear and clean above the water.

How would *Around Friday Mountain* do for a title?

The creek itself is clear, the dew is clear, the song of the Carolina wren is clear. My mind is so clear that it imparts a clarity to everything I think about, invests the object with gathered light as it concentrates on this or that. I should be able to turn off some good paragraphs after I get this note clear of the typewriter.

And it's out right now.

Bedi

Austin, Texas
May 17, 1946

Dear Bedi:

I am returning the Lynn Landrum[16] screed. Like so many writers, and some singers, Lynn has become fascinated with the ping of his own paragraphs and songs. There is nothing we can do about it because Lynn is at heart a bigot, a delightful one in many respects. In the Reformation it would have been his gaunt form that would have been illuminated by the flare of the fagots around the shoe leather of some dissenter, and as a dissenter, he would have fried for his own faith. Such persons are safe in this democracy, and for that we can be thankful. He may have been tipped off by your little "d" democracy. Who knows where a fanatic gets inspiration for the airing of his own views.

Sorry the rain damaged the old fields, poor old fields! I'm waiting the day when grass, called by some genius "the forgiveness of nature," mantles the wounds and rebuilds sound soil below.

Later, May 19. Really, Bedi, I did not see any serious washing, not what I imagined from your letter. This morning I found your purple paragraphs of May 17. As I read them I thought again of the matter we discussed, the injection of learned quotations into writing. You have so steeped yourself in the 18th century, and earlier stuff, that you may have taken on some of the manners of that day in writing. It always annoys me to have a writer, who is doing all right on his own account, reach into somebody else's till to get a fine exhibit, not of how good he is at his craft, but of how much he knows, how learned he is.

I doubt that I know much about art, but I think I have a philosophy of art which has validity for me. To me art consists in shearing off the superficials until the simple, elemental truth is left in clean, clear relief. I like "clean" as an adjective there, for it means uncluttered, sharply defined, like that skyline beyond Friday Mountain and its guard of flanking ridges on a morning after rain. My own best writing has always been done with my heart bursting somewhere between my gizzard and my gullet. Only then come the overtones from depths which we know little of, and in those high moments I have never thought of a quotation or of other men's ideas and phrases. My own have for me then far more meaning, and the force with which they emerge seems to clothe them in appropriate language garb. And this brings me to my theory of style, which is expressed in the next sentence above. I think ideas and not words create style—and that may be why so many learned people have none at all. I do not object to their turgidness, but I do object to their stubborn insistence that turgidness is in itself a merit. Muddy thinking comes from muddy minds and can have no other source.

All this is full of the appearance of ego, and the appearance is not deceiving. Any writer must have ego in order to write. It provides that delusion which is essential to hold one to his chair.

After leaving you yesterday, I went out to Struhall's[17] and I guess I bought a registered bull calf, a square-built son of a bitch whose reach may be a little short, but whose ambition ought to enable him to mount almost any obstacle which he desires to tackle. He is a pet and you and he ought to become great friends, with something but not much in common. Little Garrett will bring some cows out this week to keep him company and furnish him an outlet for his surplus energy. He has a name, recorded in a book in K.C., but I may call him Friday because he will be so useful in helping out with the chores on a ranch, and perhaps give some comfort to Crusoe, who is stranded there. Little Garrett has two good stories you ought to get out of him at an appropriate time. I ribbed him up to go to a livestock auction over towards Dripping Springs, and his account of it is most amusing. The other story has to do with his run-in with some game wardens and self-appointed g.w.s one night on his way from town. What a man that little guy is! How much life and drama and near tragedy go on in a small community. And city folk think all the excitement is in town. Don't miss these two stories, but use your best gumption in bringing them out.

Adios,
Webb

Cedar Valley, Texas
May 22, 1946

Dear Webb:

Your Doric theory of art set forth in a letter which is itself an exemplification of the principles tempts me to give over this morning to answering it. But no, I have set my hand to the plow, and there's going to be a 400-page book (God willing) by Feb. 1; or at least, a typed and arranged ms. which I myself consider a book. I shall carefully insert your letter in my "WP" file, and don't jump to the conclusion that "WP" stands for "Walter Prescott." In the shorthand of my famous filing system it means "Worth Preserving."

The best thing ever said on the issue you raise is "style is the man." You see how readily I break into quotes. That's modesty. You didn't know it, but I'm so extremely modest that, when anything particularly wise or witty occurs to me, I try to give someone else the credit for saying it first. Others, the Mencken school, for instance, get off ancient aphorisms, twisted, disguised, and sometimes fearfully mutilated, as their own. I one time marked an article by Nathan[18] and Mencken,[19] and found 90 per cent of its witticism either devised to shock (as to say among the very religious that Jesus Christ is a bastard), or the lugging in of obscure references (as much as to say, if you don't know what this means or where it is found or who said it under just what circumstances, you are an ignoramus and have no business with our work in your hands); or simply the "topsy-turvical" device, i.e., converted or reconditioned epigrams, usually paradoxical, at which, by the way, Gilbert Chesterton was a complete master.

Of course N&M disdain to quote anyone directly, but in fact the whole spirit of the article is quoted, or I should say copied, mostly from Shaw, who happened to be the rage just then; and how much Shaw got in the same manner from Oscar Wilde has never been set down in print. I suppose another generation or two will have to pass giving Time a sufficient term in which to deodorize the name of Wilde before we shall see in some solemn English journal a scholarly and conclusive article titled "Shaw's Debt to Wilde."

I don't go the whole way with you on cutting everything to the bone, and neither do you in practice. I know the Doric column is beautiful and holds up its share of the building at the same time, as your letter is and does, but an Ionic column may be beautifully made. Some writers quite worth reading seem to have taken the Corinthian for a model.

Nevertheless your theory that the art of writing is the art of blotting out, pruning, rigid exclusions, severe discipline of the fancy, etc., produces more really great writing and great art generally than any other. It's safe, classic, and *French*. Flaubert wouldn't permit his pupil, de Maupassant, to publish a line during the ten solid years of his apprenticeship: too much exuberance, too much excess. I know nothing of the history of French literature, but I guess Flaubert was influenced by Gautier, ten years his senior, who set this criterion down for any art:

All things are doubly fair
If patience fashion them, and care:
Verse, enamel, marble, gem—
  Chisel and carve and file
  Till thy vague dream imprint
  Its smile
On the unyielding flint.[20]

(That's word for word but the lining is evidently wrong.)

If I might find two or three other such inspiring correspondents each able to write even once a week such an intelligent, soundly styled letter as yours of the 17th, I'd have
enough to fill up the 400 pages by Feb. 1 and I'd devote
myself entirely to stimulating my correspondents.

Yours,

Bedi

P.S. No contact yet with young bull whose exuberance (you
slyly suggest) I may enjoy vicariously when "his reach ex-
ceeds his grasp," or view with the despair of age, according
to the mood of the moment. I find the white-faced bull, the
Jerseys, also, cropping hymenopappus avidly; and I note the
billy too aristocratic to associate with the herd, scratching his
back with the point of a long, twisted horn, and stalking
about like an Arctic Russian clothed in an astrakhan.

R.B.

Austin, Texas
June 3, 1946

Dear Bedi:

For some time I have had the chore of inquiring of you
about the cut of Friday Mountain Ranch house. We always
have matters of so much more importance to talk about that

I am never able to think of it when we are both present. Therefore this letter.

It may be that you returned it to me, but I have no definite recollection of it and I find it easier to inquire than to make a search.

I spent last evening with Harold Young, secretary to Henry Wallace, and with the editors of *The Spectator*.[21] The boys are getting to the end of their financial rope, and need such aid as may be forthcoming. From a purely abstract point of view, there should be room in Texas for one free, liberal paper. In addition to this, they are giving a high type of journalistic reporting. It seems that a liberal must always have the help of a conservative in carrying out his liberal ideas. It's that necessity that makes me a retiring—almost retired—liberal.

I have expected to have a letter saying that the goats are still in the sudan. Well, I am sure they are. I may get out Sunday to stretch another line of fence and perhaps close them out. Little Garrett said he saw a kid with worms in his ears, or one ear. Please make such casual inspection of all the stock as you can without overexertion, and if you see any signs of wounds, blood, or worms, let me know and also let Little Garrett know. Stock that are infected should be penned if possible. Garrett will doctor if they are penned. One more thing: I left a gate down which I wish you would put up. The gate is to your left as you walk towards the fern bluff. It is in the corner 100 yds. east of your rock and root. When I left the gate down I did not know that there is a single wire stretched across the field. This is very dangerous for the colts. As soon as we can build one more string of fence cutting off the little field, we'll take down all that ramshackle fence.

I am anxious to see some more chapters and may drive out most any time.

Yours,
W. P. Webb

Austin, Texas
July 31, 1946

Mr. Roy Bedichek, E.L., R.N., B.F., and B.S. mainly:
Commander in Charge of Friday Mountain Expedition
Cedar Valley, Texas

Dear Bedi and Staff:

I am very well pleased with your latest report on the observations of you and your numerous staff, but I still note an absence of any evidence of anything more substantial than mere looking, hearing, feeling, and smelling. If you would animate these sensory responses with some action, after six o'clock in the morning, I could not wish for more.

The pump last night completed its first task and may now have some rest. Had I had your report earlier, and realized that we had only a three-inch margin, I would have saved last night's gasoline. A heavy rain now would actually damage the place by overflow, but it looks like dry weather. Please set some gauges to mark the rate of fall of the pond so we will know whether we have a holding dam.

There are some long green bullfrogs, partridge size, in the new water. I saw one who hopped in, and then sprawled himself out in froggy lassitude on the surface, somewhat in the attitude of a marriage-minded gal among the sofa pillows. Yesterday at dusk the doves were watering there, the first I have seen, and last night the bullfrog, who inhabits the north side, was muttering his love song at a croaker on the south. Both were using instruments that I have not heard in the running water. Please mark this and see if the frogs change their notes with a change in environment. I can't imagine how those bullfrogs got up there, though Little Garrett says they smell water and go to it.

Please don't spoil that bull Friday—so named because he helps out around the ranch—by being afraid of him. He grew up with human companionship, and he craves affection. He likes to have his side scratched, and will allow you to walk up to him. Of course, having just been introduced to new company, he finds much to interest him. It may be that his popularity has gone to his head and that he is uppity, but he will soon settle down to normal life. There is really a lot of class about that fourteen-month-old calf and he can easily elevate the quality level of Friday Mountain Ranch. He can't do it by chasing women and broken-down authors, and I don't want them fooling with him unless they are willing to meet him on an equal basis. It's all right with me for him to knock the billy goat into the creek, or over Friday Mountain, but I sure don't want him to waste his energies on authors. There is no percentage in such activities.

By the way, I have a name for Kidd's[22] camp.

CRUSOE CAMP

on

FRIDAY MOUNTAIN RANCH

(An Island of Beauty)

Yours,

Webb

Cedar Valley

Travis County, Texas

August 16, 1946

Dear Dobie:

You lucky dog. This is the hottest, driest summer we have had in twenty years, and you sitting up there among the cool, cool lakes and almost arctic breezes. I am still hammering my old Oliver in an attempt to produce the great American classic in the field of natural history. Some progress, but not of the jet-propelled variety by any means. I'll send you some stuff for criticism soon.

I have been diverted for a day to write a radio speech in behalf of Rainey,[23] copy of which is enclosed. I am under no illusions as to outcome of the race, but I thought this was a good opportunity to do general educational work concerning tricks and wiles of the conventional politician.

Yours,

Bedi

Cedar Valley, Texas
August 17, 1946

Mr. J. Frank Dobie
English Department
The University of Minnesota
Minneapolis, Minn.

Dear Dobie:

Your kindness in submitting "Denatured Chickens" (along with, I doubt not, a persuasive sales talk) has borne fruit in enclosed note which comes just at a time when I am in sore need of encouragement. The editor seems to think, however, that it is the book you want him to consider, not serial publication of a chapter of it.

Well, I'm comin' along, and hope to increase pace as soon as it gets a little cooler. The first norther of fall is always a vast inspiration—nothing quite like it. Fall is my favorite season.

Yours,

Bedi

Cedar Valley
Travis County, Texas
October 5, 1946

Dear Webb:

As I was getting my mail from the box yesterday afternoon about 4, a man drove up in a covered truck and disembarked a beautiful sorrel mare. He said she was for "Dr. Webb." It was starting to rain and threatened a real downpour. He said the mare should be put in a tight lot for the night as she had just been taken from her colt and would likely pace that north fence all night if left free in the pasture. I told him we had a tight lot, and he looked at the clouds saying, "but I'll get wet taking her up there." Thereupon, I agreed to lead her up to the tight lot and place her therein for the night. He was much gratified and beat it back to his truck, but not before I asked him to explain some daubs of dark-colored matter on breast and right shoulder. He said it was medicine for "a little irritation." I told him the other mare had a deep cough (a matter that has been reported to your veterinarian) and he declared that was something new, that she had no cough when he delivered her. He said something about doping them with "sulfa" something or other for such a cough.

I led this beautiful animal, far superior to the other sorrel mare, and put her in the lot. I watered and fed her and tried to soothe her feelings about the loss of the colt, but to no avail. She whinnied all night.

This morning I led her down across the creek and into the meadow where the thickest buffalo grass grows and took off the hackamore. She was so avid for grass that she skinned an area within the swing of her head down to the bone before taking trouble to lift a foot. My reason for putting her across the creek was to be sure that she had the water well located, and besides, the other mare was over there.

This is one of those beautiful horses with which human

beings are wont to fall in love. She has that comprehending glance which makes you talk to her without reservation. I found myself saying complicated sentences to her, full of dashes and dependent clauses. The goddam geneticists to the contrary notwithstanding, the horse is one animal to which man has communicated a part of himself, the best part. Well, well, I begrudge this time. I haven't caught up on my schedule yet.

Yours,

Bedi

Austin, Texas
November 12, 1946

Dear Bedi:

I happened to think yesterday that you have started your fourth quarter and I have asked Mrs. Tullis[24] to make out the check. I hope you have not suffered too much from this oversight.

The flickers may be rewarded for their impertinences. Sunday I let the contract for a deep well and the drillers are supposed to move in today. I am sorry you missed Lawrence Oliphant Sunday. He is Jane's brother, visiting from Chicago. Having retired, he spends his time gardening and has become interested in birds. He has found some bird feeders (and has promised to send me one for the place) and has an interesting story to tell about the sparking habits of the cardinals. It seems that for several months of the year, the mates have nothing to do with one another. The male (as I recall) will not permit the female to come near, and will not permit her on the same bush with him. He always eats first, and nary a bite for her until his gut is full. Then he goes away and she comes in humbly for what is left. As the mating season approaches, this attitude changes, very gradually. Soon the two are sitting on the same bush, but rather far apart. Next they are sitting close together. Now she is permitted to eat along with him, maybe at the first table. The climax comes when he actually carries the food to her and puts it in her mouth, being rewarded, no doubt, by the paralyzing odor of her sexual breath. I think you can depend on these observations as being accurate as the birds have become very tame, feeding just outside the Oliphant window at 1819 Noyes Street, Evanston, Illinois. I give the address in case you want to obtain authentic records. It may be that Lawrence will get out to the place again, though it now seems doubtful because he leaves Friday and has a pretty full schedule until then.

By the way, Lawrence got a good picture of the palomino Sunday. He was cutting didos on the tank dam. He certainly is getting to be a hoss.

Why don't you write to LeBaron Barker[25] about illustrations? We have enough money left in the fund to take care of a respectable artist's fee. I plan to see Ward Lockwood. We may not be able to find a Texas artist, and the book should not be delayed on account of illustrations.

Kidd is getting deep into this camp business. And, for that matter, I am too. By the bye, how well did you wire that chain to the little boat? Please look. I half expected to find it in the Colorado after Saturday's rain. If you let that boat get away, Texas is going to be minus a field naturalist.

Sincerely yours,
W. P. Webb

Johnson Institute
Cedar Valley, Texas
November 20, 1946

Dear Webb:

I heard this morning amid the cawing of crows in the still air the sound of three waterfalls, one far and rather faint on the Archer place, one from the old dam, and one from the new: thus a little family of tones.

Since in modern music, however, things seem to go by eights, I find the musical possibilities of the waterfalls sadly restricted. Among other very *practical* suggestions you are receiving from sympathetic (or envious) observers, I hope you will consider mine, namely, that you build five more dams, making altogether an octave of dams and increasing the happy little family of tones from three to eight. Of course all these structures should be within hearing distance and audible with only a moderate flow of the stream, so that when I walk out on a still morning with my senses keened up by a night's refreshing sleep, to enjoy the sunrise, to see the mist arising from the Pond of the Open Eye and from the sinuosities of Bear Creek, to receive the begging nicker of the sorrel mare, and for other purposes, I may hear while so engaged a somewhat elaborated music of the waterfalls: this would just be lovely! And hoping you will pardon the suggestion, I am

Yours,
Bedi

Austin, Texas
December 2, 1946

Dear Bedi:

Off to Oklahoma tomorrow. Take care of everything while I'm away—such a long time, three days.

Last night I got to thinking of things no business of mine, including a possible title for your book. This on the assumption that you may want to use Friday Mountain in the title. Far be it from me to suggest that you use the name, but I should be pleased if the best title you can think of had Friday Mountain in it. It seems to me that a title should suggest, and if possible, pique, but never give information or satisfy curiosity.

The titles below came out of a bad night when the mind does strange and unaccountable things:

A Bird on Friday Mountain

Of course this is Hudsonian—*A Hind in Richmond Park.* Variations: *Bluebird on Friday Mountain; Redbird on Friday Mountain; Friday Mountain Mockingbird.*

Of course you would have to provide a bird on Friday Mountain, or near it, to be literally correct—which is not at all necessary, since the title means nothing, and asserts nothing. The bird may be purely imaginary, a peg on which to hang your observations.

Another idea occurred to me, doubtless the result of your gift at giving birds human qualities. It is a chapter on "Birds and Men," in which you treat the antics of the birds with which you are familiar, and do it in terms of human antics. For example, did you ever watch the pantomime of a conversation which you could not hear—and note how silly it is. Did you ever see a good-looking gal preen herself, deftly touch a stray strand of hair, exhibit her hands in conscious or unconscious graceful movements, or lift her foot in a way to reveal the lovely lines of an inverted baseball bat? Lawrence Oliphant commented on how like people birds are, and based his remark on the sparking habits of his redbirds, or cardinals. Birds must strut, show off, primp, bathe, and at times raise hell just for the hell of it. I don't know, but I would be interested in a chapter that told tales on them. They may have prima donnas, braggarts, bullys, and liars. What is your crazy quail but a liar? And natural liars have always interested me, I having some affinity for them.

I dread the trip to Oklahoma.

Yours,
W. P. Webb

Del Rio, Texas
January 12, 1947

Dear Bedi:

Here I have been five days and feel as in place as one of the millions of rocks around me. I have a good cottage belonging to the Central Power and Light Company situated by a dam at the head of one lake and at the foot of another, which they made and use for power purposes. I don't think the company people know I am here. I came through Bob Snow of the Texas Game and Fish Commission, and a game warden lives in another cottage and has charge of the grounds. The cottages are used in summertime by the CPL people. This one has a good wood stove, electric lights, electric cooking stove, hot and cold water. The room I work in has two long tables and one short one. My coyote papers are arranged by chapter heads on the long tables, and I brought in a fourth one with sawed-off legs to use for the typewriter.

I did not know I had so damned much on coyotes. I have been accumulating stuff for 15 or 20 years, and this fall have been gathering material in a scientific way. I have three or four or maybe a half-dozen items that your coyote-elk observation will fit in with, helping to strengthen the case for the coyote's taking advantage of the situation, whatever it is. Please send it, with notation as to source. All the writing I have done so far as been in patches. I keep having ideas. But I am ready to write my first chapter, which will be on the *voice* of the creature. There are going to be some strange things in this book. It is going to be a strange book. One of my best chapters will be the spiritual attitude of the Indian towards the coyote and the wolf.

When I think about the way you have made writing a habit and have lived richly and creatively this past year, I am full of admiration for you. I left with your papers at my house a letter from David Stevens of the Rockefeller Foundation. Henry

Smith out at the Huntington on a fellowship might help you get a fellowship from the same source. You have more to write. You are rich and ripe inside yourself, and I profoundly hope that you get another year very soon. The helter-skelter life I have lived for the past several years, pulled by causes, has made continued composition a stranger to me, although I always miss it. Things are beginning to come to me in the old way, and I think that very soon I shall be living for nothing else but writing. That is the most satisfying happiness I have ever known.

This place seems to be a haven for birds of many kinds. The cottage is on a kind of peninsula jutting between a lake on one side and a spring-fed creek on the other. There are good trees, oaks and pecans especially on the creek. I have seen two kinds of wrens that I don't know. The evening before last I walked up along the upper lake, past an old river rat's cabin; he sells minnows, rents boats, pets his dog, lets his hair grow prophetically long, talks when he gets a chance, knows the badger's secrets, and is a character. At dusk near his cabin I saw a small bird about the size of an English robin and with a reddish breast scratching in leaves in the manner of a thrasher. It kept scratching leaves downward on a rough bluff of rocks. I had been watching myriads of blackbirds, many redwings among them, going to roost in cattails along the edge of the water. It was time that all birds were in bed, but this quite little fellow kept scratching. He seemed not to want anybody to see him go to bed. He kept getting lower down, and at dark he went into a small hole under the bluff. I put a small stick close to the opening so as to mark it for another evening view. When I did, he came out, gave a few more scratches, and then went back in, at slap dark. It was too dusky for me to get a good view of his form, though I am sure he had a ruddy breast. It could not be a canyon wren, could it? The little fellow's quiet and prolonged scratching and his automatic cunning in getting into his hole fascinated

me, and I have thought of him dozens of times since. I intend
to go back to watch him.

Your first duty after going back to slavery should be to
come out to the Devils River Lake to inspect the school department of this area. I may still be here when February
comes. If I am, you must come, but you mustn't come while
you are writing. Nothing, nothing is so precious as time when a
man is using it to write in. God, the writing time that has
been stolen from me! or that I have let go, feeling falsely that
there would be time forever.

With lots of good wishes and with affection,

Frank Dobie

Cedar Valley, Texas
January 16, 1947

Dear Dobie:

A confession: Your letter felt so thick that I thought the
envelope contained merely a clipping. Dobie doesn't write more
than a 1-page letter, I said, and tossed it unopened on my
table. After my frugal meal—tomato soup and toast—wiping
my fingers and licking my chops, I slit the envelope and un-
cased a delightful surprise: two pages, single-spaced, telling
all about yourself denned up like a lone wolf in a canyon to
write about the sliest of the whole wolf confraternity. Really
this is more than I deserve, and I have never been modest, as
you know, in appraising my deserts.

I had a little pinch of conscience that I had not written
you immediately I ran across the self-explanatory letter signed
David in the file you returned to me. I saw that you had been
"active in my behalf" and should have written you at once to
express appreciation. But you know how stingy a fellow is
with his typewriter when he is writin' a book. He cheats and
skimps and becomes a regular miser.

Are you acquainted with the Arctic towhee? From this ground-scratching you describe I would judge that's the bird you find on the cliff scattering the leaves. Did you notice if he jumped forward and scratched back, and then jumped forward again and scratched back, repeating? The "ground robin," i.e., the towhee, does this. He's smaller than our robin and has a reddish breast, and black head, esp. the male.

You make a trip to Devils River sound mighty attractive, and when I get a collar on again I'll have to go where I'm driven.

I sent you a copy of the paragraph about the coyote and suppose it crossed your letter in the mails. I picked up what seems to me a bit of folklore about the coyote yesterday from County Judge Archer. He told me to tell you that the coyote is one wolf that doesn't nurse its young, but feeds them altogether by regurgitation. It has always been my understanding that the babies have a really short nursing period, say about six weeks, and then mother begins bringing to the den solid food for them. Please tell me about this. I told the Judge that you knew your coyotes, but he said there was something somewhere in what you had written that seemed to him to indicate, etc.

I hardly know Henry Smith well enough to ask him to do anything for me in the way of getting another leave. I am sure the Rockefeller people are quite right in wanting to see what one year produces before providing for another.

I know that your book is going to be a knockout. Let causes rest and do that book. By the way, I never told you how splendid I thought your speech at race-meeting was. It was utterly fearless but showed damn good judgment in its approach to the subject. Well, it's mail-time.

Affectionately,

Bedi

Cedar Valley, Texas
February 3, 1947

Dear Mr. Dobie:

I'll return the copy of *Biological Survey of Texas* to Mrs. Dobie before your return. It has been helpful and I wish I owned a copy of it. The page with the Hollister signature is inserted in about the middle. It was detached when I got the book.

I read the coyote article with delight; the bass article with not so much. I think your mind and soul (if any) is at present with the animals.

I have been going like a house afire, at present between eighty and ninety thousand words, and am sending the publisher three chapters revised (following many of your own suggestions) per week. He is politician enough to say he is delighted with the manuscript, "charmingly written," "very interesting," etc. He has excerpted for *Reader's Digest,* which he seems to think will take some. The eagle chapters he sent to the *Natural History* magazine.

I miss your valuable criticisms and your sensitiveness to sentimentality, tangling and dangling participles, verbosity, and your forthrightness in saying so.

Yours,
Bedi

Box H, Univ. Station
Austin, Texas
May 8, 1947

Dear Dobie:

I have lost my voice and should therefore be pretty good company. So, unless this ailment becomes much worse, I shall wend your way Sat. about noon, reaching there in the afternoon, if the old Dodge functions as it generally does.

This loss of voice is saving a women's club a bad speech today at noon, and is saving this office force or certain members of it from bad temper which I feel rising already, although it's only seven A.M.

We are all so damned lonesome in this world that we get pleasure out of finding out that someone has done or felt as we have. Thus your acct. of destruction of old diaries pleases me for I thought I was the only one who had ever felt the terrible disgust of looking over an old diary, and dumped it in the fire. And every time I start one I remember and lose heart, knowing that in a few years it also will arouse unpleasant emotions. So I rarely nowadays do more than make a false start or two. How the hell have some people written such interesting diaries?

You are making a fine start this time by being completely objective. I have kept objective nature notes for many years and reread them with pleasure. It's when one becomes subjective that the danger of posing and mawkishness arises.

Enclosed is Lomax'[26] answer to my letter about his book. Please return it.

I would prefer not to publish my letter to Rayburn. It would sound as if I were trying to make use of a great name to get a little space in the paper for myself; and besides, it wasn't written for publication. I have received no reply: not even from his third or fourth secretary.

Have you seen Stassen's interview with Stalin? Quite the most significant talk I have found published about this whole Russian business.

I guess Mrs. D. has told you of seeing the scarlet tanager. Maybe that was before you left for Kerrville stay. Rare bird. I have never seen one here, although they are common on the coast. Strange how birds keep to restricted ranges with no natural obstructions to bar their roaming. For instance, a crow has never been recorded at Rockport.

I'll tell you one favorite food of the armadillo, at least of those I watched around Webb's place last year—1000-legged worms.

Letter from publisher says publication date on my book has been set for September 25. I'm hoping it won't be messed up as Macmillan messed up poor Lomax' book. I have never seen a more flimsy, shoddy job come out of any respectable publishing house. I didn't have the heart to say anything to Lomax about it in my letter to him, but I know he feels it.

Your diary about armadillos is the kind of thing Hudson must have done much of. Wouldn't you like to see some of his "in the raw," so to speak?

Well, barring adverse decree of destiny, you may look for me along Saturday (May 10) afternoon, towards the shank o' the evenin'.

Yours,

Bedi

Austin, Texas

June 9, 1947

Dear Bedi:

Yesterday was Sunday and I spent ten hours of it in bed, at least seven asleep or dozing, and then topped it off with eight hours last night. I think it is the relaxation following the six months' strain of getting Captain Kidd launched on his adventure. My conscience never keeps me awake, as yours does. No, I do not recall Swinburne's piece—only that about death which ends up with "death lies dead."

Unless your memories you've written are better than your posturing about letting me read your manuscript, then I am sure Barker will send them back. Do you recall that about

1930 I asked you to read some manuscript on a book entitled *The Great Plains?* I needed some good counsel, perhaps a little encouragement. What I got was a smart kick in the pants, a "No, I just don't have time; I have to read so much." Knowing how you feel about reading manuscripts (and I do not blame you a bit), I can understand your coyness and timidity about your own. Someday I'll come by the office and demand to see it. Ah, these shrinking artists who have to be coaxed! But they don't fool me.

W.P.W.

Austin, Texas
June 10, 1947

Dear Webb:

Your perspicacity in penetrating my "posturing" is sleuth-like. I intended my note from the *"dear mentor"* to the last paragraph (intended to arouse sympathy) as an invitation to a kind, fatherly critic to read and criticize the ms. of a distracted genius. Indeed, I have been little short of amazed at your capacity for being bored. You're one professor of my acquaintance now alive who really reads Ph.D. theses—I suspect every other one (with the possible exception of the painfully conscientious Barker) of skipping through here and there with just enough attention to pick up a thread to talk about and make the naïve writer believe his work has been read. The other man of my acquaintance who reads such theses is dead. The doctor called it something else but he was bored to death. I have periods when even Thoreau bores me, and a sonnet of Wordsworth's tastes like beer that has stood in a glass too long. Ah, me, the days approach when the grasshopper will become a burden, and the writer of Ecclesiastes didn't fumble his figure, either, as many moderns suppose: the orientals of his day got as much pleasure from the songs of insects as we do from the songs of birds. So I should translate it, "and the mockingbird shall become a burden." By the way, I believe the campus of the University of Texas is the best place in the world to hear the mockingbird. I have kept count this spring and I have not visited the campus a single time that I have not heard from one to three mockers singing. And yet the dumb publicity department of the institution has never mentioned it. There is rarely another bird to be heard there. I wonder if all the others have surrendered. It seems so. I used to hear a canyon wren singing about the eaves of the biology building, but no more, and when the old shacks were there, the Bewick wren, it appeared to me, sang about each particular shack. I had to stop a handball game in the old gym shack once to let a Bewick wren get out of the court. The shacks are coming back and maybe the Bewick wrens will come with them. It's an ill wind . . . And so on. Let me babble. I have imposed on you. You've read one of my ms. without knowing it. And now, dear mentor, never try to penetrate me again: I'm far too subtle. I find a way of circumventing you.

Kidd said you were out at the camp Sat. afternoon "beaming." And well you may.

R.B.

Austin, Texas
October 1, 1947

Dear Bedi:

I am savoring the book a little at a time, as one should drink good wine in order to catch the full effect of taste, aroma, and the fine combination of being soothed and stimulated all over at the same time.

As yet I do not know how the public will receive it immediately. The ultimate reception is in my opinion assured, and I have tried to be objective about it. A book, you know, like character in an individual, finds its own level. Each has its own buoyancy and range. Some rise like a kite and fall like a bullet; others rise gently and 'at just the right altitude level off for long and well-sustained flight, sometimes to immortality.

I have just read your second chapter, on "Co-operatives," an atrocious title which almost repelled me—in fact I did not note the title until I had finished the piece. Though it is difficult, I shall try to give the effect. It was that of repeated jabs of disappointment because the pleasurable sensations were ending too soon. You may recall from the dim past a comparable sensation which accompanied kissing a very beautiful girl. Please bear in mind I said "comparable" and not "similar." The difference is partly that of voltage.

Sincerely yours,

W.P.W.

Why didn't you put your Austin address on Preface? Do it in second printing.

Austin, Texas

December 17, 1947

Dear Guide, Philosopher, and Friend [Webb]:

The flop hasn't come yet, but it is in the offing and I am prepared to go down in good spirits into the trough of the wave and remain. At present, with all the Christmas autographing and gratifying reviews still dribbling in, I feel damned important. If I were a redbird I would be carrying my crest erect.

Enclosed is a four- or five-sentence review which came yesterday from the Hartford, Conn., *Times* which does me more good than the many longer reviews because it gets exactly at the thing I was trying to do. Please *return* it.

Is it good manners in the bookish world to write a reviewer (a stranger) an acknowledgment? If it's no violation of etiquette, I think I shall drop this man (or woman) a line of appreciation.

I hope the coin-card which I returned yesterday remains yet in the place I told you to put it.

Yours,

Bedi

March 27, 1948

Dear Bedi:

Alan Hutchinson, a brilliant Scot who is doing graduate work in history, sent your book to a friend of his, Dr. Frederic P. Lord, Hanover, N.J. It seems that this Lord is a naturalist of parts. At any rate, he wrote what strikes me as the best appreciation of your book that I have seen. Good, because spontaneous.

You will observe how this man skirts around Texas, giving you credit in spite of your Texas background. Actually, I am beginning to feel twinges of shame over being a Texan—not because of Texas, which I suppose I am very fond of, but because of the blatant yapping about it that goes on in all quarters. There is a vulgarity about this so-called Texas spirit that reminds me of the flashy tie, the "Hot Springs diamonds," and the "refined" manner of a spieler in front of a sideshow exhibiting the headless or tail-less woman. Those of us who take it remind me of the gawking yokels who spend their dimes to find out that they have been fleeced—and never learn that they have. Why do we do it? Why is it that when some individual does write a distinguished book—and one does appear occasionally—true reception of its quality comes not from within but from without the state? I have never had the courage to inquire into the decision of the Institute of Letters (Texas, of course) to pass your book up for the one they chose. My feeling in this matter is not based on my regard for the two authors involved. It will take about ten years for Texans to begin to see that quality is what makes a book. I'm afraid they will see only after the thing to see has been pointed out to them by those who can understand something more subtle than a galloping horse, a howling coyote, or a whoring Negro prisoner.

Well, maybe I am going out on a long limb, but a long limb gives you a good ride, and so here we go with my Texas culture theory. I have not seen the letters you have received about your naturalist book. But let's separate them into two piles, those from Texas and those from without Texas. Many of those from Texas are from personal friends—people who feel that they must say something nice to Old Bedi because he has written a book. The whole pile will not show any considerable comprehension of what you were about. There will be little criticism, much faint praise, and practically no constructive suggestions.

The pile from outside the state may be smaller, but what a difference. Those readers do not know you and owe you nothing in the way of courtesy. They do not all agree with you, and many of them will supplement your information and perhaps correct your mistakes. But they do recognize that here is something genuine and in places very fine. How good is my theory?

Selah,
W. P. Webb

Austin, Texas
March 31, 1948

Dear Webb:

It would be a good gamble that your theory is borne out by the facts. I have kinda felt this without putting it into words. Someday when I have time, I shall make the test.

I am simply busting to get turned loose on a new book.

I think I have had enough criticism of the constructive sort to do me a lot of good and believe that I can write a much better book. Did I tell you that Barker said he would give me another contract on same basis as last one. Perhaps you were present when he made the offer. I have taken him up and submitted the prospectus he required. You know my prospectuses are misleading and may bear no relation whatever to the finished product.

Anyway a prospectus and a contract starts me off and when I get started I can't be stopped—I don't know where I'm going but I'm on my way. My only fear is that this damned job I am in will squeeze the last drop of energy out of me before it turns me loose in June. I am carefully conserving myself, however, like a miser with a limited amount to spend. I have at last got a den where I am free from any fear of interruption, and am managing to get in two or three hours' good work before I go to the office. I'm in it now at 7 A.M. I flirted with the idea of trying a syndicated nature-column for newspapers, but have given it up. One thing which gives me heart with a book is the vastness of the canvas—I don't feel cramped. I could always take a deeper and more enjoyable breath out on the open prairie than in woodlands because I seemed to feel that the air there was inexhaustible. If I had been an artist I don't believe I could ever paint a miniature or model a figurine.

I miss very much the calming and reassuring effect of association with you. Much of my company these days is depressing.

This letter from Dr. Lord gives me a great deal of pleasure. I am particularly pleased that he says the book is good outloud reading. When I used to teach literature back in the morning glow of youth I told my classes that literature that could not be read aloud with pleasure was not literature; that there was a vocal literature eons before a written symbol was ever made and that all the deep responses of one human being to another lie in those ancient and ineradicable tracks of the mind traced there indelibly and forever by the human voice. Writing is an upstart, simply a device for a quick-freeze of thought to be released and made palatable as the human voice warms it up again. Much writing stays frozen. Attention to sound accounts for the fact that the most divine language is always in every literature to be found among the dramatists.

But this is getting a little too highbrow.

Yours,
Bedi

X. Books, Books, Books

In the years from 1945 on, in the years left to them, all three of the friends worked diligently to get down on paper the thoughts and experiences that had occupied them a lifetime. All had major projects to complete. Their letters are more than usual concerned with their writing projects and the techniques of writing. Dobie said in an interview, "I find that God Almighty didn't start me off with enough power to paint the portrait in writing that I want to paint." Either of the others would have as readily expressed self-doubt.

As their friendships deepened, their help to each other increased. Each book became in part a communal effort. Each idea advanced by one stirred the others to deeper thought; each new chapter took final shape only after close scrutiny and careful discussion.

Literary friendships had been part of the lives of all three. But theirs was more than literary friendship; it was a working partnership.

Bedichek, perhaps more than the others, made literary friendships, even under circumstances as unusual as the following:

There's another man that you'll find I wrote to many years ago and it's a literary correspondence largely. His name was Leonard Doughty. I had a curious acquaintanceship with him. One summer I was helping my brother-in-law sell milk coolers. My brother-in-law was quite a trader and he had gotten ahold of some mules and he was trading around there and he suddenly decided that he would go to Greer County, Oklahoma. It was Greer County at that time. He left it up to me to bring those mules up there, so I started out with my mules. First stop I made was at Goldthwaite. It was Star, Texas, from which I went. Star is a little village out of Goldthwaite a piece, fifteen or twenty miles.

I stopped there at the wagon yard and I had heard of Doughty from someone, and I had seen some of his verses somewhere. He was a poet, so I went up to see Doughty in his office. He was a lawyer. Had offices over the First National Bank on the corner there in Goldthwaite.

I went up to see him and I found him to be a magnificent-looking man. He just looked like he was out of a picture book almost. He was so wonderfully constructed. His face was a great long face with a powerful moustache and a wonderful jaw and a decisive look in everything about him. He kind of scared me when I first saw him, but he was quite courteous and we started to talking and immediately I saw that he was pulling the conversation around to some literary subject.

So we got to talking about literature and just at that time, why, Omar Khayyam had gotten into circulation down here in Texas and all the intelligentsia knew something about Omar Khayyam. I thought I'd show off my knowledge of Omar Khayyam when the occasion came up talking with him, so I quoted five or six quatrains right off the bat. And he was astounded. See, I was in cowboy clothes driving my mules up the country and he had no idea that I could quote poetry.

I remember just how he looked. He looked right square at

me. He didn't say a word. He got up and he said, "You stay here, just a little while," and he walked out of the office. He came back in about five minutes with a quart of whiskey. He reached up into a cupboard he had there and took out two glasses and he said, "I'll tell you," he said, "I think we ought to talk more about Omar Khayyam." He poured each of us out a drink and we began drinking. We drank and quoted poetry throughout the whole night. At dawn the next morning, why, we were still going and he had more literature at his fingertips than any man I've ever met before or since. I was just swept away with him. And he was a wonderful story-teller, too. At dawn the next morning I remembered that I had some obligations to my mules so I went down to the wagon yard and fed my mules and went on my way.

This was a friendship that lasted a number of years. Bedichek and Webb talked about Webb's writing. Listening in tells us something about both men:

BEDICHEK: Webb, you know it's a commonplace to ask an author how he ever started to write a book, and I've always been interested to know how you ever began to write *The Great Plains,* which has been going now for about seventeen or eighteen years, and I understand the sale of it is as good now as it was when it was first written.

WEBB: That story is—it interests me because there wasn't any planning in it. I believe you said I was something of a mystic. I think you said instead of directing your way through life, you stumble; and you stumble in the way that you're thinking—maybe subconsciously thinking. Wanting to write, when I came to do a thesis, an advanced work, I desired to have the subject that people would be interested in and I went in to Dr. Eugene C. Barker to get an assignment of the subject and he gave me the history of the Texas land system and it had no attraction for me. Fortunately I had to get out and teach and spent two years dreading the subject before I got started. And in that two years trouble developed on the border. I was living in San Antonio and Jim Ferguson was governor of Texas. He sent the Rangers down there to clean up—to stop the raids. The Rangers committed almost as many crimes as the bandits did. That is, they were very brutal towards the Mexicans and they got to where they didn't discriminate between good ones and bad ones. J. T. Canales of Brownsville was elected to the legislature. He came from a very old Mexican Brownsville family. He started an investigation of the Rangers, and every day the papers would come out with screaming headlines about the atrocities that were being committed by the Rangers on the border as this trial unfolded.

I read this paper and the question that came to my mind was has anybody written a history of the Texas Rangers. I went to the Carnegie Library and checked up and found out it hadn't been done. So I came up to the university and asked Dr. Barker if I could change to that subject because I felt that it was something that I could work on with interest. I started working on it and I found myself. I found the first topic of the frontier which has concerned me ever since. In the process of tracing the history of the Rangers over a century, I became familiar with their weapons, their habits. I became more or less familiar with the nature of the state. I had received permission from an oil company operating out of Fort Worth to write a series of articles about the Rangers and their activities in cleaning up the oil towns. Borger, Ranger, Breckenridge, and others. In preparing to write this article I read Emerson Hough's *The Way to the West,* and in that book Hough said that four instruments had been of primary use in the conquest of the American frontier. They were the boat, the rifle, the horse, and the canoe. In the meantime, I had become familiar with the dependence of the Rangers on the six-shooter, and it seemed to me that Hough had left out something—that the six-shooter had also played a role. Then I saw in a kind of a flash that when the Rangers came out onto the open country, the prairie and plains country, they met the Comanche Indians and the Apaches, and they were mounted Indians. The revolver was the ideal weapon for a mounted man; the rifle was no good. I knew in an instant that I had something original that was mine. It took me about a year and a half to work out the details and get the facts to prove what I knew immediately when I thought about it. I wrote an article about it which was published in *Scribner's* magazine, and that was the genesis of *The Texas Rangers.*

The next step came when I began to look for other things. I felt that there was more than just the revolver as a new weapon when men came out onto the plains. . . . In order to get the material on the subjects which had not been noticed by the historians I had to open up correspondence with the barbed-wire manufacturers, the revolver manufacturers, and the windmill manufacturers. When I had worked out the story of the windmills and the fences, I found a parallel between what had happened to the procuring of water and the making of fences. I found a parallel to what had happened in the case of the weapon. These three pegs, as it were, sat in a row. I saw that I had a case for the thesis of *The Great Plains,* which is that when civilization came out of the woodland—out of the eastern woodland onto the open country, onto the great plains—that a complete revolution had to be made in the ways of living, in the ways of farming, in the ways of fighting. Water law, land law, and the rest of the book was merely—consisted of taking up one institution after another and following it from the woodland as it emerged onto the plains.

Of course, the whole thing was the story of the influence of an environment on a culture, going back to the teachings of Keasbey. Now Keasbey never put any emphasis on the great plains. He hadn't seen that, but he would have understood it immediately. I wrote the book in about four and a half months with the exception of maybe the last chapter. I got a leave of absence, and I was just ready for it. I don't think I've ever worked with the exultation that I did in writing that book. I had all the material and I sat down the summer before and made the outline, from which I didn't vary very much. I was so excited about *The Great Plains* that I threw the Rangers aside and finished *The Great Plains* first.

It's a question in my mind. I don't know today how it will rank in comparison with *The Great Frontier.* If I were required to destroy—if the dictator said, "Webb, you're going to destroy all of your books but one, and you can take your choice," I wouldn't have any trouble with the two of them, but I haven't been able to decide whether I would save *The Great Plains* or *The Great Frontier.* There is this difference: that *The Great Plains* has already been accepted, widely accepted. *The Great Frontier* is today a matter of controversy, and there've been some pretty bitter criticisms of it. Of course, there were some pretty bitter criticisms of *The Great Plains,* but even so, with *The Great Plains* accepted now, I still don't know which one of those two I would choose to survive. I think it would take about ten years to find out whether *The Great Frontier* has the same influence on thought that *The Great Plains* does have. *The Great Frontier* is much bigger in scope. It's not as well buttoned up but it's tremendous, I think, in its implications. Whether people will accept the thesis sufficiently to go on and make the further investigation which I have suggested, but wasn't able to do, is a matter that only the future can determine.

Webb's own evaluation of his relationship with Frederick Jackson Turner follows:

I found out two years ago what my intellectual ancestry is. When I came out with *The Great Plains* and later with *The Great Frontier* people always said, "Turner. Webb's a Turner man, and this is a continuation of Turner thought." Well, I never saw Professor Turner. I only had one letter and that was about—when he was ill—when he was near the end. When I got the notion of *The Great Plains,* at the time I got the idea, I didn't know much about Professor Turner before and I didn't read him at all while I was working on it. I never have been able to see—looking within my own process of thinking—I've never been able to see that I got anything from Professor Turner. But I never could say that because it would seem ungracious. It's true that we worked in the same field, but he didn't know anything about the great plains country. The West that he knew was Wisconsin, and the country east. I think that I would have done the same thing that I did had Turner never written.

I found out two or three years ago what this intellectual ancestry is; something that did satisfy me. I attended the American Historical Association, and in the process of reading a paper on Turner, a man mentioned an Italian economist, Achille Loria. I made a note on it: Achille Loria influenced Turner. I came back to the university and went to the library in order to get a volume that Loria had written. I believe the title of it is *The Economic Foundations of Civilization.* Lo and behold, it was translated into French by Lindley Miller Keasbey. I read it and it is completely in harmony with particularly *The Great Frontier.* There is my intellectual ancestry. It didn't come through Turner at all. The extent to which Turner was indebted to Loria—I doubt he was indebted to Loria very much. I suspect that Turner got his idea and then he found Loria after he got the idea. But I'll always, probably always, be ticketed as a Turner man. It isn't true. We dealt with the same subject; we came to some of the same conclusions; but it's the differences that need to be explained and I think I would have done the same thing had Professor Turner never written.

There was one book, however, that never got written. The best record of what it might have been appears in the taped words of Bedichek:

I will tell you one thing that is the most annoying thing I have ever had happen to me, I think, in my life. It just made me so sore that every time I think of it now I get angry—really angry. It happened in connection with Webb. We were both members of the Town and Gown Club and one night down there Dr. Payne,[1] who was a folklorist—he's dead now but he was a folklorist—Leonidas W. Payne was talking about folklore and while he was talking a brilliant idea came to him that there was a folklore that had never been collected in Texas or anywhere else that he knew anything about. He humorously proposed that there should be a collection of privy poetry. That is, the poetry that you find scrawled on the walls of defecating places—where you go to defecate—the toilets in hotels or country inns or anywhere else. Now, of course, it's a rich assortment of stuff and John Calhoun[2] got off a famous witticism at that time. When it came around to him to discuss Payne's paper he confined himself to this suggestion that Payne made about the collection of poetry from privies. He said that when it was collected that he would like to suggest to Dr. Payne a title for it. We asked what the title was, so he said, "Well, I hope Dr. Payne calls it *The Privy Papers of Sitting Bull*." That brought the house down.

Then Webb and I, stimulated by the idea, we commenced to see what we could do collecting this privy poetry, and we got the darnedest assortment of it that you ever heard in your life. But we were ashamed to sign our names to it. We always referred to it in veiled language in our correspondence so that nobody could tell what the dickens we were talking about. I kept insisting that he transmit to me and I transmit to him this poetry on toilet paper—not on any kind of ordinary conventional sheets. It seemed more appropriate to have it on toilet paper, and I did. I wrote him a whole lot of this stuff that I had picked up on toilet paper and we had quite an amusing—when you run into that you will see we had quite an amusing lot of stuff, except that some of it was stolen.

That brings me to the point. I had a very attractive woman in my employ in the office there and she was a sort of publicity creature. She handled the publicity in the office. She was a writer and quite an attractive woman. I didn't know how mean she was. Oh, I don't say mean, but I mean injudicious. I was out of town maybe for several months at a time at that time. She was assigned the job of writing up a sketch of me for the papers. Some editor out somewhere wanted it. She thought she was going to do a thorough, honest job, so what did she do? She went to my private files, my letter file. I hadn't thought of locking them, having there in my office Miss Thompson, my secretary, who knew it was a private letter file—personal. It was marked personal on the outside. She, without any privilege from me or from Miss Thompson, or anybody else, went into my private letter file.

She found this stuff between Webb and me and it just fired her with curiosity. She just wanted to know what the dickens it all was. That woman actually took that file to my wife in my absence, and you know that it aroused suspicions in my wife. She couldn't understand what all these veiled allusions and all that sort of thing. When my wife mentioned it to me I just flew all to pieces. I said, "That damnable thief." I said, "Did she go into my private file and bring letters out here?" She said, "She had a file of letters between you and Webb."

Well, sir, I was just so outraged. In the meantime, she had gotten another job somewhere and gone, and I have missed some of those letters. I have looked for them very carefully and I think that woman right now has those damned letters in her trunk or something. It's almost inconceivable to think that a woman would do a thing like that, but I know she did. She shall be nameless and I hope she is never identified because she's a well-intentioned creature but she's just lacking judgment and she lacked taste and she lacked everything else that goes to make a person livable—to live with a person like that.

The extent of their literary partnership is indicated but not measured in the letters that follow. In between the letters, there were often hours of talk in which they discussed general principles of writing as well as the works each had in progress. This talk is lost. Fortunately, each had the habit of crystallizing in letters the thoughts that grew out of discussion. Thus at least a part of the best from each is preserved.

> Austin, Texas
> November 5, 1940

Dear Webb:

I quote from page 2 of Audubon's *America:* "These are America, as it was, as we remember it, as, in some measure, it still is. Who can say why our sky is not the same as Europe's? Why our soil is not like China's good earth, why are the prairies not the steppes? The canyons are carven deep in us, and the broad rivers run in our blood."

Pish. Tush. Forsooth. I call this *precious* writing, and worse than that, New England precious writing.

> R.B.

> Austin, Texas
> August 14, 1942

Dear Dobie:

Am rushing enclosed letter back to you to avoid temptation of showing it to someone, and to prevent myself from copying down some of those corking expressions that sprout only in West Texas. One or two of them will naturally stick in my memory anyway—if Boyce House is a storyteller then my a— is a sugar bowl. Say, I heard a good one the other day from an old cowboy cook out near Kerrville—I am literally stealing time to write this. It seems two cowboys had been out on the range a long time by themselves and were getting (as men will under such circumstances) very quarrelsome. Nothing one did pleased the other and neither minded telling the other just how he felt about everything. They fell to quarreling about how to make sour-dough biscuit, and finally one made up a batch his way. The other refused to eat them and declared that the damn hound which was with them—lean and hungry— wouldn't eat them either. The maker of the biscuit believed he would and they made a bet on it. The leftover biscuits were thrown to the hound, who proceeded to gobble them up, then turned after finishing his meal, as hounds sometimes will, and licked himself. The maker of the biscuit said—"You see, he et 'em all right." "Yes," said the other, "but he had to lick his ass to take the taste out of his mouth."

Yours,
Bedi

Austin, Texas
August 16, 1942

Dear Webb:

Here is a note for your article on "Prison & Literature." It is taken from "Tonio Kröger" published in German in 1903 [1897], and translated into English in 1940 [1930], published by Knopf, 1941 [1936], occurs page 105 of volume entitled *Stories of Three Decades,* by Thomas Mann.

. . . I know a banker, a grey-haired business man, who has a gift for writing stories. He employs this gift in his idle hours, and some of his stories are of the first rank. But despite—I say, despite—this excellent gift, his withers are by no means unwrung. On the contrary he has had to serve a prison sentence, on anything but trifling grounds. Yes, it was actually *in prison* that he became conscious of his gift, and his experiences as a convict are the main theme in all his works. One might be rash enough to conclude that a man has to be at home in some kind of jail in order to become a poet. But can you escape the suspicion that the sources and essence of his being an artist has less to do with his life in prison than they had to do with the reasons that *brought him there.* A banker who writes—that is a rarity, isn't it? But a banker who isn't a criminal, who is irreproachably respectable, and yet writes—he doesn't exist.

The italics are Mr. Mann's.

Do you see why we readers never produce anything? We know too much. A good idea comes into the head, and the immediate reaction is, oh, that's too good for someone not to have thought of it before. Of course, it's been written up. Perhaps I saw it somewhere and have merely forgotten now where I saw it. Usually we are right. Here is your idea with an added twist to it, and a good twist at that.

Bedi

Austin, Texas
August 30, 1942

Dear Webb:

On page 426 of September *Harper's* you will find your "frontier democracy" thesis worked out in the case of Costa Rica, as if it were a designed and controlled laboratory experiment.

Bedi

Austin, Texas
April 11, 1943

Dear Dobie:

You certainly scored a knockout in your article published this morning. It's sweetly reasonable, it's salty, sensible, and there are spots of sweet, rich earth in it like some of the disquisitions of Sancho Panza manured two seasons ago with proverbial wisdom. Really, I'm more enthusiastic than I seem. I almost pulled my wife out of bed this morning to make her read it. I am glad you have absorbed semantics without using any of the unspeakable jargon semantics has created, "frame of reference" for example, of which our good friend, Dorothy Thompson,[3] is guilty. You must have read "Germany's Master Plan"—if you haven't, I'll loan you my copy. *Talk about planning!*

This and much more I feel, dear Dobie, with your sound sense and tough Texas guts.

Bedi

Austin, Texas
September 1, 1943

Dear Webb:

I have no idea I can get away on November 19, but I am putting date down on calendar, and will strain a point or maybe two or three points to make it. How long do you intend to be gone? One thing: unless you are to be entertained in a private home, you had better write now for accommodations, and then they are liable to cancellation without notice.

I happened to hit a page of Parrington devoted to my pet abomination in American literature, James Russell Lowell— a literary snob, a poseur, a shallow, rhyming nincompoop, a very striking example of Ingersoll's crack that a university is a place where pebbles are polished and diamonds are dimmed. He was a pebble to start with and not a very large one at that. Well, Parrington takes his number in about ten scorching lines— really about all he is worth, if that. Lowell in 1884 "took God's side against evolution," called Whitman narrow and unoriginal, couldn't understand why anyone would waste time reading a book like *Progress and Poverty*. Like the Republican Party he was wrong about everything, and posed (and was so accepted by literary New England) as *the* critic of his time. Parrington doesn't spare him, and I have almost decided to buy the complete set of *Main Currents*—if I do I'll return your copy—if not, I may keep it.

Yours,

R.B.

Dear Bedi:

This paper is not sufficiently heat-resistant to stand up under the things I would like to say to you (or did want to say) for phenagling me into promising to write this review. I'm damned tired of being impressed into service, compulsed into doing things I hate to do. I hate to review books, and I ain't going to do much more of it. Still and all here's your &&'*" ?, ... review, and I hope you don't like it. It ain't exactly Mellin's food for babes, and it may get us both carpeted, and me canned. I'm just tellin' what he told.

I wrote Oberholser,[4] told him the truth, that we are poor but ambitious. Had a lovely letter, a peach, a beauty. He would rather have Texas bring out his book than any. And what a work! And how Texas! All I want now is $40,000. The odd cents we can supply. But if somebody else does not publish his book, the Texas State Historical Association will. What a mark we'll make. Bedi, do you know where is forty thousand dollars to put into something that has actually cost in real money between $75 and $100 thousand? Let's me and you tap a capitalist. I want you to see his letter, his outline, map. Only three of his drawings have ever been published, and in an obscure govt. publication. Make a mark on the calendar of this day, kick a hole in the door, knock out a window-light—do something to commemorate the date of my high resolution. Damn you, Bedi. Damn all reviews. Above all, damn poverty.

Yours,
Webb

Austin, Texas

Dear Bedi:

What injustice we do our children! I remember your telling me in one of your sober moments that you had had little influence on B.,[5] and that he had gone his own way. Well, here he turns up with bird lore that is not only intrinsically interesting, but that really conveys a message to the initiated. I am returning the letter at once so as not to be tempted to disobey your injunction. I like to show good things around.

A student of mine turned up recently with a letter from an unknown writer to an unknown recipient. I have had copies made and am sending you one. You may have more if you like.

Thanks for your attention to the Curtis Walker[6] matter. He will be tickled and ought to come across with all the information you want.

Did you by chance see my little screed, "The Meaning of Academic Freedom" in the *Alcalde?* I enjoyed doing it, partly because it cleared up my own thinking. Even with the limited circulation of the *Alcalde* it is attracting about as much attention as anything I have done. It is to be reprinted in the *Outlook,* and there should reach the teachers—who read the *Outlook.* Of course I shall not know whether it reaches a high mark until you have turned your devastating eye on it. You know, of course, that I like to write for the common man, which lets you out. I would rather bring a tear to the eye of a sheep-herder with words than upset the stomach of a sophisticated critic with a book. Just one of those personal whims, some-thing inside one's guts.

Tomorrow I go to Friday Mountain to meet two agricultural agents from San Marcos. We are going to do a little light work, but if you can go we will leave you to your own devices. We will have lunch on the ground, and it won't cost you a red cent.

Yours,

W. P. Webb

January 4, ~~1944~~ damn it, can't I ever get rid of 1944?

Dear Webb:

You have touched the heart of this sheepherder several times, so you should be satisfied. If you weren't angling for a compliment I would tell you that I read your *Alcalde* article *twice,* took it home, made my wife read it. We discussed it and agreed that it was one of the best things we had read on the subject. I then marked it, and sent it to my sister in Portland, Ore., and if you are so damned avid for praise I shall send her reaction to you when it comes—if it is favorable. You surprise me. I thought you were blasé so far as praise for literary work was concerned.

In your undated letter, you say, "Tomorrow I go to Friday Mountain," etc. and invite me to come along. Now if you had said, "Friday I go to Tomorrow Mountain," I should have been able to locate the fourth dimension of your trip, but without dates, I don't know but what today is your tomorrow.

Yes, Bach[7] surprises me with his photographic memory.

He certainly rescued this bird note, for I can't find it in any of my notes, and I had forgotten it completely until he brought it back to my mind. It is an excellent case of symbiosis, cases of which I am collecting, interesting to all naturalists.

Thanks for mimeographed article. I haven't read it or the letter with it, but shall.

Yours,

Bedi

Austin, Texas
January 10

Dear T. R. Bedi:

You see, I have given you a new initial to indicate that I can still see through clear glass. Everybody who knows you, your views on literature, your familiarity with Whitman, Tolstoy, Shakespeare, and—I almost said the scripture but here I am not sure—will know that only one man in the university could have writ so to John William Rogers.[8] But that boy did a swell job, and what he did doubtless deserves wider circulation than it will go. He ought to send it to De Voto of *Harper's*.

What do words mean? The subject has always fascinated me, since I was a kid. They lie, all of them in the dictionary, and yet in most hands they are dead, inanimate. Yet others have a photoelectric cell, a brain which when stimulated causes these words to leap to life and come in trains, in a million formations, creating all the glory and misery that man has known.

Well, I'll quit before I go haywire. I'm about to add 100 acres to Friday Mountain Ranch, so you see I am carrying out our Big Bend determination to do something foolish each year.

Sincerely yours,
W. P. Webb

Del Rio, Texas
February 1, 1947

Dear Bedi:

Your letter of January 16 is just now reaching me. It seems to have been addressed to the wrong box number. Anyhow, as always, I am delighted to read anything you author. I have been accomplishing a good deal but not finishing much, though I have written three chapters. One of them, "The Voice of the Coyote," seems mighty good to me. One of the others has too much quotation in it. I have made writing a habit again; the habit of writing will carry any person to the composition of a book, though it will not guarantee that the book was worth forming the habit for. During long periods of my life I have missed writing in the morning as much as I miss a morning bowel action.

I'll be here until Feb. 9 or 10—just a week or so more. Then I am going west to consort with two or three Coyoteros. I may have to go to Alpine; if so, I could run on to Fort Davis to see your friend Ross Graves. Then I'd like to swing back through the brush and consort with coyotes for a night or two. The sheep have eaten all of them—absolutely all— out of this country. There is nothing natural that sheep do not eat up.

Yes, that little hole-under-the-rock dweller would jump forward and scratch backward, losing ground gradually downhill, like the frog that kept falling back two feet every time he jumped up one foot, getting out of the well. I guess it was an Arctic towhee, but he seemed smaller than the book dimensions of that bird.

Thanks for coyote-elk account. I'm obliged to Judge Archer also, but a coyote does not have tits on her like an old sow to suckle her young. I am well acquainted with the folk belief that coyotes do not suckle their young.

If you have my Bailey's *Biological Survey of Texas* at hand,

I wish you would mail it to me. If you are now in town and it is out under Friday Mountain, never mind; just bring it in the next time you come and leave at my house so that I can consult it when I get home about middle of month.

You have up enough steam now that no chains binding you to routine can hold you back from finishing the book. More steam to you. Meanwhile be formulating in mind what your next book is to be, and we'll make medicine. It is Saturday afternoon and I think I'll go to town and buy a newspaper and notice again how God-damned—and I use the word reverently —it is of either spirit or intellect.

Your friend,
Dobie

Kerrville, Texas
April 24, 1947

Dear Bedi:

I have thought up two good titles for essays—one in natural history and one in human affairs. I don't intend to pursue either unless incidentally. The first is, "Who Is the Early Bird?" Up here the redbird is rivaled in heralding the morn by a wren, probably Carolina. The other title is occasioned by the enclosed clipping—"Ways the Worm Can Turn." I give it to you; you can have the other also. Your own matutinal habits make it proper to you.

That is a bully letter you wrote John Lomax.[9] If you don't have another carbon, I shall return this. I had your reaction on his "poor white trash" twaddle. I meant to jump him about his yodeling cowboys, away back there 65 years ago or so. I feel sure that at that time there was no yodeling among people of the soil anywhere in America.

I'm in the middle of a cedar hill but hay fever time is about over. I should not have had it here two weeks ago had there been any rain. I have little, very little now. This country may be in for another cycle of drouths. It's about time. We are more able to stand it than the Russians, and according to all accounts, they have had almost the most disastrous drouth in history. One thing the American people can't stand is too much prosperity. Although I am all on the side of labor, it bothers me that the millions of union men seem in the long run not to desire anything different in quality from what their masters have; they just want more of the same thing. They are not essentially interested in freedom of intellectual enterprise; the majority of them have no more spiritual content than the average supplement to our Sunday newspapers—or than the average money-making businessman.

I'm gradually getting strung out on coyotes again. I'd never heard before of their knowledge of the weather being a determinant of altitudes at which they den, though they are famous weather prophets. Prairie dogs are supposed to have foreknowledge of floods and to move up in anticipation of high water. I am gradually getting strung out on my coyotes again. I don't know if anybody will want to read *all* about them.

This country is astoundingly prolific of armadillos. I can walk out a few hundred yards any time and see them. I send your copy of a file I am starting on them.

Dobie

Kerrville, Texas
June 12, 1947

Dear Bedi:

Your critical notes were exceedingly pertinent, perspicuous, and incisive. I think I have acted on all of them. The line from Keats was in my mind also, concerning the badger and coyote on the bowl, but would not coalesce with badger-coyote pursuit; however, I finally worked in a phrase from it.

Until today I made good headway. This has been a worthless day so far as writing is concerned. I finished a chapter yesterday, and was simply stifled this morning. The trouble was that I went to reading Schlesinger's *The Age of Jackson* last night, and all the goddamned fascists of the present in this country were revived for me. My God, what a time for mediocrities ignorant of history, incapable of thought, and empty of nobility to be running the country and trying to run the world.

I guess I'll stay here till July, and then right after that I have to head west, having very foolishly, months ago, when I thought I should have oceans of time, contracted to make talks at universities of New Mexico, Denver, Montana, and Wyoming. I think I shall get a bellyful of driving. The sad part is that I shall drive away from an uncompleted book. I'll have the natural history part about finished, however. Most of the tales are already written. The chapter I finished yesterday is on "Scent and Curiosity." That essay on "Love at First Smell" remains yet to be written; it could go in the book but does not belong in it. I may send you this chapter for your lancing instruments.

It's hot here too.

Your friend,
Frank Dobie

Two self-pious letters from old Lomax.[10] Bedi, you'll never grow old in outlook, nor I either. That's the payoff age gives for keeping the mind open. How empty life must be for those old men like Hackett[11] primarily concerned with keeping their own bowels open and other people's minds closed.

Austin, Texas
April 3, 1948

Dear Bedi:

The Committee of the Research Council will be so delighted with the novelty and unconventionality of your application that they will vote the $500 as spontaneously and enthusiastically as a group of scholars who have had the wine of human interest pressed out of them by drudgery ever did anything. (Ain't that a sentence?)

I am filing your application and "outline" for the purpose of comparison.

One thing I missed in your application is a statement of time. Perhaps you can insert that you consider the job a two-year chore. This will leave your foot in the crack of the door for another application.

You have always thrown darts at venomous innuendo at me for being commercial. Well, now, here you are canvassing your fan mail to catch a popular scent. I hope you do not carry this tendency any further than your Negro friend did his wife's virtue in the East Sixth Street conversation you relate. Don't do this except on Satdy night, jes to help out. It's dangerous to soul and spirit. But I won't preach because I think in the end you will write *what* interests you, and that in spite of hell and popularity.

I have not invited you to F.M.R. because I have been going through such torture that I am not fit company for cantankerous persons like yourself. Trying to get the damned place ready for Uncle Rodney.[12] Don't put any obstacles in his way, for if he fails I am ruined. Even now out there the little frogs quote the big ones in saying "Too Deep! Too Deep."

W. P. Webb

Austin, Texas
June 10, 1948

Dear Bedi:

For thirty days I have been tied up in knots, living three unparalleled and tangled existences simultaneously. You wrote a brief and cryptic note suggesting a renewal of acquaintanceship, a suggestion I ignored because I did not want to appear to bad advantage. I wasn't fitten.

Then yesterday came your letter suggesting that scholars should take out after all the little current balloons that seem important at the moment. I noted the foreign legion by another name, and thought of Rome and Carthage, of almost any imperial power that does this somewhere on the road to decay. But why aren't you practical and sensible? What would I look like if I became a wolf crier among academic sheep? Is it not better for the scholar to stick to his scholarship, work out some well-integrated fragment of truth, and let it go at that?

There is a chap named Bedichek who knows something about birds and nature. What of him? Is it better for him to write a good book on birds and nature than to cry out alarms in the hope of keeping the world in its orbit or preserving an empire? How puny his efforts! How feeble his cry! The result would be some amusement, some raised eyebrows, and damned little respect anywhere.

What if writers of books do not directly exert influence? As long as they point the truth, the influence takes care of itself. They educate the professors; the professors educate the people, even radio commentators and newsmen. Surely you would not argue that a professor of medicine is no good because he does not cure the sick. His function is to teach others to do it. And so with the professors, real educators, thinkers, and writers—and all this you know just as well as I do. I suppose you wanted to preach at somebody and you picked me as a target. Go along wid ye, and leave me be in the obscurity of my own cocoon.

Back off to a safe distance and come agin.

Yours,
W. P. Webb

Stratford-upon-Avon, England
June 30, 1949

Dear Bedi:

Yesterday evening, exactly one minute before the post office here closed, I posted off to Cambridge, for copying, my long-struggled-with long article on Cambridge. I stayed there a month and had no more energy than a despairing earthworm, most of the time. But I never get too low to read or to listen and I laid up seepings, and massed all sorts of disconnected notes. I did manage to finish while there my article on "Hyde Park Orators." It was to be about 2500 words long and I wrote over 5000. The editors say they are well satisfied with it. I came to this place on June 12 and began to recover my energy. I had a cough as wracking if not as deep as profoundest hell, but I suspect that sixty years is what I really have. For over a week now I have been writing without any interruption beyond going to a Shakespeare play now and then. It is better to have too much to say than too little, but in the end I had a bitter time leaving out some of my knowledge and wisdom on Cambridge. Now all I have to write is a short essay on Stratford, not so much as I write in three weekly columns. I expect to do it in London early next week before setting out for home about Friday.

Your saying that you read one of my columns with pleasure buoyed me up. I know that some of them have been leaden. I wrote one this morning, however, on my old friend Jack Barrett, proprietor of The Anchor in Cambridge, that suits me all right. It's troublesome to have to stop once a week to write that column, but the necessity for it keeps me observing. Sometimes I enjoy the exercise. The pay is a considerable help. So, all in all, I am glad to have this stint hanging over me, perpetually though it hangs.

Your letter was and is a benediction. You should be doing a lot of weaving all alone—the only way a writer can get the best association with himself, whence the best of his writing comes.

I have not seen much new in England this trip. I have come to the conclusion that the Labour Government is acting the fool trying to nationalize steel and iron. It has already taken on more than it handles efficiently. A lot of English people are not facing realistically the disproportion between exports and the inevitable imports. I don't know if the country can ever balance the books. Meanwhile she is going the path towards bankruptcy, it seems to me, despite the great rise in exports during the last few years. She may not be going as fast as she was towards bankruptcy, but going. The only thing to develop is labor, and labor seems to think that nationalization is the sovereign cure. Nobody thinks that nationalization will increase production in anything, except in coal, as it has done. Thinking on the matter makes me feel low.

Some spotted flycatchers out in the garden and lawn of my hotel, the Avonside, right by the water, make me feel brighter. A little brown wren here has just brought off her brood. A family of little owls, not screech owls, I judge, make queer, subdued noises among trees. The other night after the theater, *Midsummer Night's Dream* it was, I followed them into the churchyard, adjacent to the hotel grounds. Their talk and soft flight outside the church harmonized with the curse-protected bones of Shakespeare within.

I am sending this by steamship mail because the clippings weigh too much for air. I sent you a note just as I was leaving Cambridge. I may beat this home. I hope that when

I get to London tomorrow I shall find that my steamship ticket has been exchanged for one by air. I want to go by Dublin and stay thus in a new country for two or three days. I don't have any respect for the typical Irish mind, and the Irish in American politics have given me a disgust that comes near tainting all Irishmen in my mind. But I like Irish ghosts and folklore and fiddlers and expect to like Dublin if I get there.

With affection always,
Dobie

Boulder, Colorado
August 23, 1949

Dear Bedi:

Thank you for the liberal paper, news on the heat, a short note, and thoughts that you did not put on paper. We'll be home by Monday if not before, and as always I'll want to see you first thing. I have led a highly unsatisfactory life out here, despite some cool weather and warmhearted people. There were too many students to be casual with and the examinations nearly killed me. I have done no writing and financially I was a fool for coming. I thought we'd have a real vacation with expenses paid. I've never worked harder for less money. The next time I seek a vacation I'll take my typewriter to where nobody can prevent me from writing an article that with two weeks of work will bring in more than six weeks of absolute slavery to what is called an institution of learning. I've had grad people here, but the Ed. Dept. is filling the universities up with untrained numbskulls. I have flunked several "graduate" students. Tom Lea,[13] with his wife, was here last weekend and we mixed grand—too many grands— medicine.

Dobie

801 East 23rd
Austin, Texas
January 22, 1950

Dear Dobie:

The picture of you in the Houston *Post* Jan. 1 is the best I have ever seen in print. Your face in reflective mood far outshines your good-humored phiz as good as that at times is. And the article by Fuermann[14] is one of the best summations of what you amount to that I have seen.

Sorry I let you get away without any "Hail and Farewell." Matter of fact I was tied up with kith and kin of the blood, as weak as the spiritual ties may be. There are points of spiritual contact with my son, however, that I treasure greatly.

Don't forget to look up a personal friend of mine there in the Del Rio neighborhood—the Texas kingfisher.

Yours for the greater glory of the mustang!

Bedi

P.S. Our mutual friend Webb has quit his conservation and cattle ventures, leased the place to a goat-rancher who proposes to "goat" the brush to death. Meantime, Webb is resuming authorship—actually threatens to take a year off next year and extend his frontier speculations. Hope he does. He will do a great book if he sets his bald head to it. His "Future of the Republican Party" is going like wildfire in the East.

R.B.

Devils River Lake
Del Rio, Texas
January 23, 1950

Dear Bedi:

I drove to town this afternoon, 23 miles, received your letter, and after getting back to my house took a toddy. The letter was better than the toddy—and will stay with me longer. I thought that Fuermann's article got down into essentials, myself.

When I was out here three years ago, refuging from hay fever and writing the first chapters of *The Voice of the Coyote,* I often saw your little friend the Texas kingfisher. My house is on a peninsula that juts out between the Devils River on the west side and a creek on the east side, in which water from the lake backs up a short distance. Along this water the kingfisher was constant. I have not located him this time, though once I thought I got a glimpse of him. A big belted kingfisher is constant now.

I think of you every day and wonder how your work proceeds. One thing I meant to speak to you about before I left Austin is the use of one or more of your chapters in magazines before book publication. I am sure that such use does not injure the sale of the book. I rather think that it is favorable to book sales. I told Allen Maxwell[15] about some chapters; he replied that he wrote you and that you seemed not interested. If your contract forbids you to make magazine use of chapters, you could, I should think, get a release from Barker. *Natural History* magazine might take a chapter. Maybe I like publishing in magazines too much for a book writer; I do like it.

It is good to hear that Webb has released himself from the burden that Friday Mountain had become to his mind, so far as using it creatively was concerned, and is going to write his book. I don't see how he can write it unless he does take off. There was a time when I could do a good deal of writing and also teach. I can't do it any more. You have to teach in the mornings and something is always hanging over you. I came out here with all the membranes in my head in a wretched state and did not get into a chapter until recently, though I was working all the time. Ordering historical facts always has been hard for me, and it doesn't get any easier.

However, I have finished one of the two most stubborn chapters, and after I get the mustangs to galloping free, I think I shall be able to do a good deal of galloping with them.

Interruptions don't interrupt here. Nobody comes to see me. There is a locked gate up the road if anybody tried to get through it. There is no telephone. But I don't like the incessant roar of the water over the dam, the machinery of the power plant being out of order and no water going through the hydro plant's spillway. I want absolute silence, except when the owls make it more beautiful. The harsh scenery gets on my nerves. If I walk out, I have to walk up and down. There is no such thing as a trail to saunter along. Sheep took the country a long time ago; there are no coyotes to sing and few surprises in the form of nature to be expected no matter how far one scrambles about. Altogether, I can think of many much more congenial environments in which to retire and work. Still, I'm getting somewhere. I wish we had a bracing norther now and then. It's positively hot out here every day.

With affection,
Dobie

Austin, Texas
April 25, 1950

Dear Bedi:

When I get a commendation on a book review (the least estimable of all forms of writing) from two such honest and hard-boiled individuals as R.B. and E.C.B., and when they come spontaneously, I feel quite set up for the day.

At Oklahoma City, Friday April 21, I uncorked for the first time before an American audience of scholars the frontier thesis. The reception was not unfavorable. I think I can go ahead with that assurance which a writer *must* have, and I believe I can finish the job in a year. If I can do it right (and that is everything) it will equal *The Great Plains* in originality and surpass it in scope. I am living again with a sense of power not felt in 15 years—a fine state—

W. P. Webb

Kerrville, Texas
May 2, 1950

Dear Bedi:

I am sending you the attached letter for its coon picture. It is also a human document. I have never met the writer, Earl Butler.[16] A few months ago I had a letter from him beginning, "I write this for the good of my soul." It was very appreciative of some of my books, and the writer asked for two others autographed. I sent them; later he sent a post office money order in payment. This led me to judge that he does not have a bank account. I sent him a package of old *Harper's* magazines and some other reading matter. I guess I'll write him again someday, though there are many letters that I want to write and never begin; anyhow, you might return the letter.

I told my wife to give you a copy of the *The Ben Lilly Legend*—not my title and not to my taste, but I let the publishers have their way on titles to my books, though they can't make one as good as I can. Don't feel under compulsion to write me that you think it is good. It is not, I know, anything like as rich a book as the ones I have written on longhorns, coyotes, lost mines, and Mexican folklore. It may be fairly well written for what it is, but I would never write it now. I had it fairly towards completion when I left for England seven years ago this fall. I did not look at it until after *The Voice of the Coyote* was off my hands. Then I found I could read the manuscript and decided not to waste what was done. I may wish I had wasted it. Actually my only interest in it now lies in hoping that it will sell enough to clear the publishers and reimburse them for the advance royalty. It will not advance my stature; I hope it won't lower it.

I left Austin with a knee that had been bothering me a lot. It got worse up here, and I went to a good physician. He drained enough fluid off it to drown a rabbit in and told me I had strained it. I knew when I did. For nearly two weeks I have been saving it and it seems about all right. Today I have done better work than on any other day I have been up here. But damn a book that is made up of ten thousand separated particles that feel absolutely no magnetism for each other and have to be hammered piece by piece, particle by particle, into a mosaic of unity and of what I'd like to be called spirit. A pound of good horse manure on the grass would be of more value than a book about mustangs without spirit.

Your own book is being woven, I hope. I think of you lots of times and crave conversation with you. That was a delightful paper you read at Town and Gown. Wasn't Old Paterson[17] an ass? I don't comprehend Barker sometimes, but he's right on "the former and the latter." I doubt if I'll ever use that expression again.

> With abiding affection,
> Dobie

> Kerrville, Texas
> May 19, 1950

Dear Bedi:

My sensitive membranes and the look of the air told me yesterday that I was breathing Panhandle dust. I've been breathing it all spring. That looks like a drouth to me. My sister and her husband, farmers in Willacy County, have had only two or three inches of rain during the last several months, are feeding their cattle, and fear they will make no crops this year. I wanted to go to my old home in Live Oak County this spring, but was told that there were no flowers—only a brown ground. There has been too much rain in some parts of central Texas for farmers to plant, but there has been no general rain all year over the state. I don't predict the weather for Travis County but for Texas.

A letter from Angus Cameron[18] has this message: "Tell Mr. Roy Bedichek that I saw the good results of the Texas air on the whooping crane. I shall never forget his wonderfully pertinent remarks about the relative unimportance of the widely publicized Bergman-Rossellini and Hayworth-Aly Khan romances when one involving the survival of the species was actually going on in northeast [sic] Texas."

Your letter about Ben Lilly has cheered me enormously. It and letters from Tom Lea,[19] Dudley Dobie,[20] Ed Crane,[21] and two or three other individuals whose opinions I respect have made me feel mighty good about the book. My former indifference towards it is becoming a pride. I have thought sometimes that if I were not so set on writing more books, I should take a stock of what I have written and peddle them over the land to the common people of Texas—people who do not usually buy books but buy mine when they get a chance. Many of them have never been in a bookstore. Today my dear sister Martha and her partner, who set up a small bookstore in Kerrville something over a year ago, had an autograph party and sold about 40 copies of the *Ben Lilly* here, besides several copies of the other books. I don't think I really could peddle.

I am working on *Mustangs and Mustangers,* but have not yet got to where the mustangs are running wild and free. The first part of it is terribly learned, too learned, I imagine, for popular reading; but I am writing it as I want to write it. I have been impressed by the enormous amount of sloppy, snide, journalistic writing there has been on horses in America. This nation has not produced one noble work on the subject, whereas England has produced several, in which the elements of learning, horsemanship, humanity, and humanism are beautifully mixed. I am not writing in order to raise the American standard, however. Not a great many Americans want it raised.

I'll be home June 1, only to leave shortly, however, for some bread-and-butter speaking arrangements. However, I hope to see you then and inscribe *Mister Ben Lilly.*

Dobie

Kerrville, Texas
September 3, 1950

Dear Bedi:

I think I owe most of what I know of Henry George to you, and I think that you are right in saying that a just tax system is the only alternative to revolution, by the communist route, in the long run. You don't exactly say this, but the implication is there. Tom O'Connor, who died a few years ago, said that the public had done nothing for him and he owed the public nothing. His eldest son says the same thing. The first O'Connor bought that huge ranch for ten cents an acre or something like that. Now some of it is worth thousands of dollars an acre—oil. The only reason it is worth more in 1950 than it was worth in 1840 is the public. There are lots of Tom O'Connors. When population reaches a real density in this country, the people, if they still have a vote, will tax the big estates out of existence; if they don't have a vote, they will seize them.

I see report on Webb's frontier thesis. He is leaving the Industrial Revolution out of the picture, and he seems to make capitalism and democracy synonyms. He has a big idea, but to me it is not so clear as it is to him.

I guess I'll go home Friday for two or three days but won't have that chapter copied for you for some time. It is trying to rain here and did rain a week ago.

That is a very fine picture on Lon's[22] page today. I had seen it elsewhere. I think that Lon is getting too patriotic on Texas writers. Some of the books he nominates as important will not be worth the paper they are printed on.

Yours,
Dobie

I ran into Bill Johnson of Dallas (Time-Life) three or four days ago here. He is reading galleys on *Karankaway Country* and finds it delightful and rich.

January 20, 1951

Dear Webb:

I enjoyed your exposition of the frontier thesis last night.

The primitive man has tabus which bind him in many merciless and idiotic toils and entanglements, as one of the commentators said. Quite true, those are *his* institutions after ten thousand or more years of pioneer life. But they are not the institutions which the Western European develops on the frontier with his background and experiences with civilized institutions and with a culture of high order dating back to Homeric and pre-Homeric centuries. It is the result of pioneer conditions not upon primitive man but upon *European* man that you are talking about.

As you answered, the "frontier" has come to be merely a metaphor in much of the writing and talk of economists and sociologists. "Oil a new frontier!" The oil worker moves to Houston to work in a new field. Does he change his way of life from that of Tulsa where he last worked? The automobile according to these "thinkers" is a new "frontier." A man moves from Pittsburgh, Pa., where he screwed on nuts in a machine factory, to Detroit where he screws on nuts in an automobile factory. He has a letter from his church in Pittsburgh to his church in Detroit. He attends the same movies, chews the same tobacco, eats out of the same tin can, has protection of a similar police system, etc., etc.

Your frontiersmen organized their own police system, established their own rules of conduct, what was right and what was wrong in their new environment, conducted their own business in their own way, employing themselves, shedding their masters, and out of this came the institutions you are trying to trace and evaluate, democracy, capitalism, etc. What these critics mean by a new "frontier" is a new field for making money, a new way of advertising a gadget to make it popular, discovering an old material which may be made to serve human needs, etc., but all within the framework of institutions already set as solid as concrete. The frontiersmen's *"freedoms"* consisted in being turned loose with institutions *in their minds;* in a new relationship with their fellow men, with so-called society in a fluid state so that it may take the mold of their thinking and experience before it "sets."

At least this is what I got out of your paper and your answers to the comments.

Yours,
Bedi

Austin, Texas
Sunday, January 21, 1951

Dear Bedi:

Thank you for your letter, and for at least one man who got the rounded and balanced meaning of what I tried to say, and am trying to put down on paper in the toughest job I have ever undertaken. It helps to be understood because if one reasonably intelligent person understands, he is a sample of many others. My thesis is disturbing to a lot of people because it upsets their complacency and makes a certain class feel that they may have to revise their lecture notes. It is curious that in a supposedly intelligent audience so few will look at the major idea, namely that the abundance and impassive nature of the frontier acted as a new ingredient in history and compelled men to make the adaptations that characterize modern civilization. They tend to pick at some detail, usually one tangent to their own specialty. Of course this inertia is a good thing in that it *stabalizes* [sic] society and gives that continuity to history of which we historians are so proud. It perhaps explains why conditions must be very tough and imperative before they can compel society to move over and make room for new ideas and institutions.

The work is moving forward, a little each day, and occasionally a new vista opens up, and new depths of understanding are reached. It is such moments that reward the longer intervals of groping, fumbling with facts and ideas as one in a nightmare fumbles with an insoluble problem. Some time ago I wrote a 50-page chapter on the recrystallization of institutions around the frontiersman at his chosen task of work. It was a sort of haystack chapter which represented the best I could do at the time; it did express the idea I wanted to pin down. Recently I took it out, and saw it would not do. It wouldn't outline except in an arbitrary manner. Suddenly it *did* outline in a most logical and revealing manner, the subject, not what was written. There was nothing to do but rewrite the whole thing, five days on twenty pages, but now it is right for me and will be intelligible to a literate reader. Fortunately the last half is reasonably satisfactory in outline and logic, though it must be gone over to bring it in complete harmony with the predicate laid down in the first part. This is what may perhaps be described in terms that only the writer or other creative workers will understand as heartbreaking satisfaction.

I have gone too far with this thing now to turn back, even if I were inclined to, which I am not. If it has no other value, it has served to renovate me and to tap subconscious sources with results sometimes quite satisfactory.

At last I am putting in an orchard at Friday Mountain; should have done it years ago so that I could have enjoyed the fruit for a longer period. Five Mexicans spent four days digging the holes and filling them with compost and topsoil. The planting will have to await rain, but the ground is ready. Mr. Garrett supervised the work, and of course decided that the Mexicans were not worth a damn. By the way, your martin box is ready and must be returned. Watch for it on the west side by the fig trees. Mr. G. repaired it, cleaned out the old nests and repainted it. He made me one just like it, the materials for which cost $17.00! When do martins come?

As a nature student you may be interested in the habits of a creek. The long drouth caused Bear Creek to go drier in the fall than it has been since I owned the place. Only the Archer pool spring kept going, and then only a trickle; elsewhere stagnant pools. About a month ago the water began to rise, the pools have refilled, and the Archer pool spring is flowing the creek for a considerable distance. All this without a drop of rain. Is this water that came from some rainy season far to the west many years ago and now just arriving here? There have been no rains at all on the watersheds of Bear Creek. Also a large family of wild ducks seem to be more or less permanent guests on the Archer pool. When they are disturbed, they circle and return when things quiet down, lighting meanwhile on Roland Crystal's side of Friday Mountain. A 12-foot dam butting against Friday Mountain with a dirt wing extending northwest into the Archer field should, according to Mr. Garrett's engineering calculations, create a permanent lake of four or five acres, and if the dam is correctly made, one of 15 or 20 acres in floodtime, a body of water which would be payed out slowly until the lake recedes to normal. A twelve-foot lake lying along the west base of Friday Mountain ought to make a mallard's heart swell with joy, and cause no grief among bullfrogs and little fishes. The lake is not an immediate prospect, but a sort of dream whose realization depends on the growth of some "wool."

Mr. Rippetoe still does not remember you! A friend of yours whose native language is Chinese made solicitous inquiry about Mr. Butterchek of Kidd and me the other day. In spite of the bad report we gave, this individual insists that your presence makes the whole day bright. As between the two persons, I leave it to you as to which you will pay your respects. In such matters I trust your judgment implicitly!

Yours,
W. P. Webb

February 1, 1951

Dear Bedi:

When Allen Maxwell[23] asked me for a review of *Karankaway Country* I mutilated and added to what I had written for newspapers. It would be new to Dallas readers anyhow, as the Dallas *News* ceased taking my column long ago. I think this review may have the distinction of being the most scratched-up that you have seen. Therefore I send it to you.

This is fine weather for a fireplace but not enough moisture out of it to sprout an old onion. I am predicting generally dry weather until next August or September, though drouth could break in July. (It could break any time; local rains will not break it.)

I work on my book all the time and make about as much progress as a horse trotting all day in the shade of one tree. Let's have some conversation. With affection,

Dobie

Austin, Texas
February 3, 1951

Dear Dobie:

While we were talking over the phone yesterday, my wife was bringing in the mail with your letter of February 1 in it along with ms. of review you have furnished Allen Maxwell[24] for the *Southwest Review.*

I had rather read the scratched-up ms. of a real writer than his work in the most faultless print and after the severest editing. It is much more revealing, really tells more of what is in his mind, and certainly gives valuable insight into his method of composition. So I value this ms. highly. Thanks very much.

You give me credit for originality in the spelling of "Karankaway" when I really just follow that of the maps issued by the U. S. Geodetic Survey.

You are a master quoter. Saul, thou hast me almost persuaded that I am a writer.

I am greatly relieved to note that you have abandoned two precautions you used in the syndicated article (perhaps unintentionally) and so lay yourself open to future "criticism" as a "critic."

In the newspaper article you warned the reader that you were not undertaking to write a *review,* intimating that you are presenting an appreciation, pure and simple. Next, somewhere near the beginning, you further warn your readers that the author of *Karankaway Country* is your friend (read between the lines "faithful and just to me"). So, if some censorious critic of the future pointed out that Dobie was no critic —"Look! he swallowed that stuff Bedichek wrote as if it were really spiritual chow of a high order." If Dobie were thus accused, Dobie's defender could reply that Dobie specifically disclaimed reviewing the book, "and besides," your advocate would continue, "you son of a bitch,* he assures the public in advance that the author of *Karankaway Country* is his friend. Thus your insolent attack upon a name all Texans revere discloses that you are unaware of the difference between an *appreciation* and a *review,* or between friendship and pederasty. Indeed, you have written yourself down as one having neither the capacity for 'friendship' nor the ability to acquire 'sound learning,' the two things a human being must have in order to be 'pleasing to the gods,' truth of which was so generally accepted by the great Greeks that it passed as an unchallenged maxim among them for five hundred years: *'Friendship and sound learning so as to be pleasing to the gods.'* "

So I hope that your critic of 1975 bases his criticisms on your syndicated article rather than upon the piece in the *Southwest Review,* so that your defender may have a crushing rejoinder.

It is the kind of tantalizing review which makes one want to read the book, and I wish the *Southwest Review* had two million instead of two thousand subscribers.

Perhaps if you came up and sat around the wood stove with me in my study, you wouldn't be "trotting all day in the shade of one tree," but would make haste faster. Nothing like conversational churning to bring up the butter.

Yours, as ever,

Bedi

---

* This epithet escaped the whorehouses about 1920 and, along with cigarettes, was generally adopted around 1930 by the "smarter" women in respectable society. Epicene fiction-writers (1935–50) larded their pages with this or other whorish vernacularisms, hoping to veil the ambiguity of their own genitals with this ragged jock-strap of masculinity.

I am supposing that by 1975, year in which your review is thus caustically reviewed, literary criticism will have adopted the term, maybe for the same reason.

Austin, Texas
February 10, 1951

Dear Bedi:

On inquiry I learn that you "snuck out," but I am bound to suppose that you will eventually return. The chief reason for this letter is to tell you that the book is beginning to shape up, and now when I add something that is acceptable, I can feel that an advance has been made, I mean one that is visible. For some time I have been writing chapters, or, what is really heartbreaking, rewriting them, and tucking them away in unneat folders without regard to order. My original outline couldn't hold the horses, and so the chapters were not the ones I originally visualized. Some of them broke in two, one in three, and some evaporated completely. Last week I took them out, arranged them in the order in which they seemed to belong, and made a new outline of what I have and of what still remains to be done. It turned out that I shall have 11 chapters, besides an introduction, and that all but three are written. This was quite a lift, and under the impetus of it, I have the first more than half done, and have the stuff with which to complete it at hand. There is no question in my mind now that I have it made, provided I don't get hit by an automobile or one of the many maladies now lopping off branches of our age.

By the way, I have through the book often used the first person. This is not quite in keeping with conventional historical writing, but I have justified it on the ground that in order to present a new and complex idea clearly I am entitled to use all devices which will contribute to my purpose. For example, the chapter on "Windfalls" begins with an observation I made in Christ Church Gardens where I walked in the early winter mornings to produce heat which could not be had from rationed fires. One night a great storm came to whip the trees and knock off all the weak limbs, and there in the early morning were women, children, and old men gathering the fallen twigs and limbs to make brighter their puny fires. I recalled Woodrow Wilson's definition of a windfall, saying it had its origin in Europe when the poor people were given permission to pick up the wood that fell from the lord's trees. Well, there it was, the age-old rite being enacted under my very eyes.

Then I go on to say that the frontier was like a great tree that was constantly casting its windfalls down on humanity to make life a little richer and the fires brighter on their hearths. How can I use this symbol except by relating the incident in the first person? How can I find a symbol which illustrates so dramatically the part that the frontier played in the lives of modern people? Should history be written prosaically when life has been so dramatic, brimming with comedy and tragedy?

I am enclosing a copy of the outline which you need not return.

Sincerely yours,
W. P. Webb

THE GOLDEN DOOR
THE FRONTIER AND WESTERN CIVILIZATION

By Walter Prescott Webb

Chapter Outline

* I. Introduction
** II. The Boom Hypothesis of Modern History
III. Institutional Disintegration and the Individual
IV. The Recrystalization of Society
V. The Frontier as a Modifier
VI. The Genesis of Modern Dynamism
VII. Frontier Windfalls
VIII. Three Unwise Bubbles

IX. The Parabola of Individualism
* X. The Frontier Impact on Culture
XI. The Fallacy of New Frontiers
* XII. Prospects of a Frontierless Society

* Not written as of this date
** More than half written

February 10, 1951

What do you think of title?

February 15, 1951

Dear Webb:

Practicing what *you* preached a few years ago, I have just had a remarkable week of camping out in the deep woods in winter, returning greatly refreshed, but aghast at what I saw them doing to trees. Sawmills are chewing up what little is left, and now *Big Business* Wilson,[25] in charge of our mobilization, and more powerful than any other ten men in our government so far as acting on hunches and whims is concerned, is pressing the administration to let the lumber barons loose in our national forests. He will be successful in this malign business without a doubt, and will next open the gates to the cattlemen and sheepmen into the same areas. So, instead of reserving the "scorched earth policy" for our enemies, we are applying it to our own country in mere anticipation of attack. It is damned cowardly. This country has the worst case of hysterics of any country since ancient Greek cities abandoned everything and fled to the hills on approach of marauding bands of Spartans.

I don't like your title. *The Golden Door* is too sentimental, too romantic, and it raises false hopes, and is not descriptive of the work. I am purely a destructive critic: Call on someone else for a constructive suggestion. I have made such a mess of naming my own books that I can hardly be trusted.

The chapter headings are wonderful. "The Parabola of Individualism" is a stroke of genius. "Frontier Windfalls," and your explanation of "windfalls" is another. That's the kind of thing which will set you apart with the immortal historians— that is, the historians *who can write*. I have been reading Xenophon and I ought to be sensitive on this point.

"The Fallacy of New Frontiers" is a little misleading, but I like the alliteration. I would prefer not the sound but the sense of "The Fallacy of Technological Frontiers." I can't pass on "Three Unwise Bubbles." It doesn't give me a hint of what it is about. Crystallization has two l's. "Institutional Disintegration and the Individual" is certainly a mouth-filling title, tongue-tiring.

I am delighted that you have at last heaved within sight of the goal. Do you anywhere take up in some detail the interaction of the frontier and the Industrial Revolution? There should be no hesitation about using the personal pronoun. It consists of one letter, is the center and axle of the whole universe, everybody knows it, and it is an affectation to avoid it. I hope the book is full of personal observations from which conclusions germane to the text are drawn. Nothing else so humanizes writing, and certainly historical writing needs humanizing. Well, let's get together and communicate painlessly—that is, without the typewriter.

Yours,
Bedi

Austin, Texas
March 1, 1951

Dear Bedi:

You knocked out at one critical blow *The Golden Door.*
Let me try this

THE GREAT FRONTIER;

A STUDY IN WESTERN CIVILIZATION

W. P. Webb

Dear Webb:

Enjoyed your two letters. Hope you write oftener. Your
second letter about spelling moves me to enclose a note to Mrs.
Krey with stamped envelope for sending it to her. Please
address envelope properly and mail.

I never pay any attention to spelling in a letter. One can
hire for little money a stenographer who will correct his spelling. But since it seems to be eating on you a little, I call
your attention to the misspelling of "stabilize" in first paragraph of your letter of Jan. 21.

If you don't mind I shall keep the enclosures a little longer.
Maybe I shall want to copy out portions here and there, for
I have a notion that sometime or other I shall attempt an
essay on style.

You are going to have a great book and I am anxious
to see it in print. One who has tasted as you have the excitement of creative writing will never be satisfied doing anything
else—not even building air castles with Garrett.

The flushing up of the springs along Bear Creek was likely
due to some *local* rain. You know such rains have occurred
here and there during the present drouth. For instance, four
inches was recorded at Bergstrom field or near there when
there was no rain at all here. Then the activity of the springs

may be due to the percolating down of the rains we had in September—something around 5 inches.

But hell, I'm no hydrographer. Maybe it's buffalo piss just arriving from the Great Plains.

I confess I was a little puzzled by the reactions of the social science club to your paper. It seemed to me that the ones who spoke up about it failed to get the point, or to realize what you mean by the word "frontier." I suppose in your book you will have that word adequately defined, explained, and amply illustrated.

The sleet is falling, my wood fire is burning, and I am enjoying the luxury of arising intermittently from my seat at this typewriter to back my buttocks up to the genial heat.

Yours,

Bedi

P.S. I have found the martin box. What do I owe Garrett? Martins come anywhere from February 15 to March 10.

R.B.

Growl issued from a den in the hot end of an overheated garage at 800 East 22nd Street towards the sizzling close of a day temporarily set apart in the Christian calendar from other days just like it, as August 16, 1951

Dear Webb:

"We used to have something to say and wrote letters. Lately the well seems to be failing in an intellectual drought."

Quite so! my dear friend—if anyone may call an author or any artist a "friend" in any but the most trivial and conventional sense, since the whole tribe of suchlike persons has always an alien and completely dominating loyalty above and beyond any call of friendship.

So, to take an example from the above generalization, you have been faithful for the last year to *your public*—that fiction which the artist creates, empty of any content, but invested with a spurious personality by the "stargazer" mind, "fixed on vacancy," a mind always and forever beleaguered with hallucinations and miserably in the toils of self-spun cobwebs, unable to disentangle "seeming" from the little gleams and glimpses of reality which mortal mind in its few sane moments apprehends beyond the veil.

Hence, the superiority of the man of action over the man of thought, truly "sicklied o'er" (and, at that, *thickly* o'er), always doubting, lost in his phantasmagoric world.

It is therefore the fate of the artist to enjoy friendship only vicariously, as a dyspeptic poet enjoys eating only creating the illusion of some gusty individual sitting down in ravenous hunger, with the odor of a delayed and bloody beefsteak in his dilating nostrils.

These reflections, as you will suspect, are the legitimate children of your plaintive little note of August 11. Be assured that the "intellectual drought" is only the arid wind of your public's breath, and that the "dried-up well" has been exhausted in your vain attempt to satisfy your public's simulated thirst.

I like the clipping enclosed. The man has sense, sense of proportion, sense of relative values, style, and a point of view, true as a compass. I had the same view of Donald Culross Peattie that he has, until Peattie flattered the hell out of me with a sweetly tolerant review in the New York *Times* of my last book, and in a quite ingratiating note offered me collaboration with him on a section of his forthcoming book.

This easy palliation reminds me of another failing of the "artist mind"—it laps up flattery like a starved cat, stooped over a bowl of cream, with each individual whisker angled back, tail tip waving in unison with each thrilling pulse of the gratified gullet—lapping and licking until he becomes wobbly on his feet and weary in his mind with surfeiting an appetite whose only limit is the tensile strength of the belly tissues.

This, in short, is what I think of the artist, the author, preoccupied with his "public," the moony man threading his uncertain way in an endless forest peopled with shades and ghosts and shadows of ghosts, all of his own creation.

Ay, me, how true it is that "Complete sanity marks the philosopher"—or words more effective to that effect. I'm far too hot to look up a quotation.

With more sincerity than your present preoccupation with your public will permit you to see in this diatribe, I am nevertheless,

Yours sincerely,

Bedi

August 18, 1951

Dear Bedi:

When some dull graduate student paws over your literary remains and finds your letters to me, which I am keeping, he is going to decide either that you were a most inconsistent person or that you had a friend named Webb who combined within himself the most contradictory qualities. Out of one side of your mouth you have accused me of being materialistic, bent on gain, almost capitalistic in mentality; and out of the other side of your mouth you have said that I am something of a mystic (this orally) and that I have the artistic malady of being devoted to my public, concentrated on the thin shadows cast by the imagination in such form as to make them seem important to me, and real. How can I be all these things you charge me with being? Or are you like Gillespies Stacy's goose, who woke up every morning to a brand-new world? Are your impressions of the day your realities? And do they change with the temperature so that you have a winter mind and a summer mind, like a cat's coat?

I suspect the truth is that your conscience is hurting you, and that you are the one who is becoming more and more bottled up. Naturally I am a social being and am always wagging my tail in a friendly manner to those who exude a pleasant odor. It is true, however, that I have been something of a recluse this summer because I am trying to finish up a job before the fall drudgery begins. It is my conviction that for at least five months of the year this climate is the most unsocial factor in society. One sweats out all social impulses along with his energy and has just enough gumption left to know that misery is more bearable when not compounded with that of another.

I am convinced that winter is the right season here; and when it returns, if it ever does, we shall discover whether we are completely lost to each other. I daresay that by dint of economy we should be able by winter to buy one more steak and then burn it up over a wood fire à la Dobie.

This has been the worst summer that I remember in Austin, and the only way I have managed to keep going is to spend the hot hours from 2 to 5:30 or 6:00 in bed. It is no fun to go to the country because it is more desolate than the town. There have been times when I almost wished that I could drink whiskey in order that I could get lordly drunk and thus be able to skip at least one of these beastly days.

Finally, as to books. It does require a mild form of insanity to do all the things that are necessary to write one. Why one goes through it when he does not have to is hard to understand. I suspect that those who do it have some sort of inner restlessness that gives no peace until the job is done. When the work is in progress there is, despite the pain and misery of it, a sort of spiritual satisfaction, a sort of pleasure tinged with bitter. Also when I shirk the job, finding excuses for not getting on with it, I am more miserable than my lack of self-respect would seem to warrant. The main thing in writing a book is to keep yourself deceived into thinking what you have to say is important.

Sincerely yours,
Webb

Austin, Texas
August 22, 1951

Dear Webb:

No, my characterization of you is not necessarily contradictory. You may be a many-faceted personality, or, like a woman, you may have your periods. Anyway, if I am inconsistent, I can quote my favorite poet: "Do I contradict myself? Very well, I contradict myself; I am large; I contain multitudes."

You are right in saying my conscience hurts. It has never quit hurting since I unfortunately became conscious of a conscience. I fall so short of every undertaking, from entertaining my grandchildren, three of whom are now with me, to making lima beans produce in July and August. Two rows now on exhibit at 801 E. 23rd are bloomful but beanless, and have been for two solid months.

Only point I can find in yours of Aug. 18 with which I am in hearty agreement is your heated and eloquent condemnation of the weather. Well, on rereading your closing paragraph on the burden of books, I take that back. Swinburne should have added the sense of this paragraph to his melodious "Ballad of Burdens."

The only really heartening experience I have had this summer lies in my association with two charming young architects—both male. These two boys are intelligent, highly educated, forward-looking, hopeful, ambitious to do good, and gentlemen in the best sense of the word.

They dropped in on me out of a clear and beneficent sky.

Each one charmed me but each one with an individual charm, all his own. They differ widely in character and outlook, but they are bosom friends. I have been cruising around central Texas with them while they discuss and sketch examples of pioneer architecture, tools and crude mechanisms of the pioneer home. They are franklloydwrightists with emphasis. They are disciples of Gropius and the late Harvard school of architecture, and I find it easeful to listen to their enthusiastic discussions of a subject about which I know so little that I have no impulse to butt in. This is the only really notable experience of the summer. And in mitigation of the futility of writing books, I must tell you that these boys were brought to me by my books.

Have no fears on score of the reputation my letters will fix upon you in the minds of posterity. From all I can see, our posterity will be short-lived. Nothing of the world as we know it, that is, the human world, will long endure. And if I am a false prophet, still my letters taken in quantity soon reveal when I am in earnest, as at present, and when I choose to burlesque a personality or situation, as in my last. This alternation of seriousness and travesty explains itself. But you exaggerate the importance of my letters. I doubt if any "dull graduate student ever paws over my literary remains."

Speaking of conscience-pricking: slow progress on the great, definitive work on the Interscholastic League has become a positive torture. One false start after another, side issues, and interference of other interests have brought me almost to a condition of loss of confidence in myself, which is perhaps the most hideous torture of all. The sands are running out . . . well, well, enough!

Yours,

Bedi

February 15, 1952

Dear Webb:

Delighted to have this provocative chapter for inspection, and to make acquaintance of Kouvenhoven[26] (hereinafter identified as "K"), of whom I had never heard before. The chapter stirs my antagonism, and makes me feel like writing, or rather like talking, since there is a certain menial activity connected with writing.

But you are in a hurry (witness postage enclosed!) and want quick reaction or none at all. Hence, I am giving you in a paragraph or two the main things I think are the matter with this chapter which may easily be remedied. Then, if I hold out and can spare the hours from the great work now gestating on Interschool Contests, I shall indulge some speculations concerning the "Machine," adapted from a chapter entitled "The Machine" elided from the ms. of *Karankaway Country* because I found that to get it in I should have to invent its germaneness and lug it in by the ears, which I refused to do, although it is better writing than most of the chapters included in that work.

So to remedial suggestions, at once:

1. Begin the chapter with definition of what you mean by the "arts" and "art." "Vernacular art" is a good phrase when it is understood as you explain it, especially in this connection, since it suggests provincialism. Let the reader know before he gets half through what you are talking about by transferring material explaining "vernacular art," especially word derivation, to the beginning or near there. Then the first line of chapter should read "the emergence of the 'vernacular arts'" instead of "modern arts."

2. Make it clear that you do not claim "functionalism" as a necessary element in art, but only in the art of articles of use.

Look to the blowing rose about us—"Lo
Laughing," she says, "into the world I blow
At once the silken tassel of my Purse
Tear, and its Treasure on the Garden throw.[27]

Much of art, Beauty's slave, is like that.

3. To oppose "conventional" to "vernacular" is a false antithesis. K's[28] argument, so far as quoted, really boils to opposition to "bastard" art, always and forever an abomination. Witness the ancient feud over the caryatid. The 1900 rebellion, too, against overornamentation of Victorianism, the Victorian parlor, for instance, that afflicted your boyhood and mine, as it still afflicts three fourths of the residences in this city built before 1920.

4. I should think that in any reference to "functionalism" in architecture, Gropius should be mentioned, a German-born, German-educated, and German-and-English-practicing architect, and imported to this country by Harvard University after he was fifty years old. Also, Frank Lloyd Wright, the premier American functionalist, who was discovered by Europe and handed back to America on a silver platter loaded with European decorations. Also, S. Giedion, a Swiss architect, who has written the definitive work on the very "vernacular art" K is talking about, published by the Oxford University Press. Familiarity shown in chapter with these authorities will take kick out of criticism sure to be leveled at it as a piece of special pleading *for* American and *against* the older culture, reflecting the very inferiority complex of which you complain. (By the way, I think you could well substitute "culture" for "civilization" throughout.)

5. I regret that you must join in the chorus of 100 per cent Americans against Henry James, a genuine artist but an expatriate, which naturally arouses the prejudices of a patriot. They put poor old Ezra Pound in the pen or in an insane asylum when he returned. James doesn't see "art as something

apart from life," but sees art as you and I do, that is, with a readier appreciation as a part of the particular life he happens to like and to be most familiar with.

6. You make too deep an obeisance to K, I fear. I have not read his book, but all you quote from him is rather shelf-worn or slightly used with a musty odor.

7. I heartily disagree with what he says and you endorse about jazz. It's not an expression of individualism at all, has nothing to do with either the virtues or the vices of the frontier. But that's too long a story.

This is dashed off (literally) and I may be taking snap judgment on the whole chapter. Perhaps without the urgency of a stamped and addressed envelope before me, I would have read it twice before recording a judgment. This is not a judgment but an impression on first reading.

Wish I weren't so busy. I would come by and see you. I am working like hell every morning in (of all places!) the Education Library. And now it's time to go.

Much thanks for giving me this peep at the book.

Yours,

Bedi

February 23, 1952

Dear Bedi:

Did I not have a good deal of confidence in my own views, I would have, upon the receipt of your last letter, chucked the whole section on art into the wastepaper basket. Certainly you were never in a more devastating mood than when you wrote your criticism. Fortunately, I found a ray of hope in your preliminary statement that the view set forth aroused all your animosity, and knowing that enabled me to revise the manuscript, profiting I hope from your objective criticism and ignoring the rest. I have long held that all criticism is valid, useful to the author as representing the objection of one reader and all others like him, useful provided the author reserves to himself the right to profit from the critic and not try to please him. I have noted that you can give a manuscript to three or more readers, and that each reader will make an entirely different set of suggestions. In final analysis it is up to the author to preserve the unity of his work, stick to his purpose, and if possible save his sanity.

I reduced my tribute to K.,[29] clarified my use of vernacular, and did a number of other chores of like character. That I have done a pretty good job is indicated by a manuscript that is reduced in length.

My subject is not functionalism as represented by Wright and others, but it is the possibility that out of functionalism may emerge something that may be classed as art. In making this claim, there is no charge against the traditional art which had its center in the metropolis of Europe and which has perhaps been more at home there than in a raw frontier where, as James so ably pointed out, the points of reference to it did not exist. To deny that additions cannot be made to art is to concede that it is finished and dead. If it is not finished and dead, then it is reasonable to assume that the American people in their devotion to work have improved tools and made machines which may be classed as contributions to art, if not the old art, then the new one. There may be in this argument too much function for those who hold that art is something apart from life, with fixed laws of its own. I admit that there is a great deal of function in these tools and machines. I may point out that in their time, the Greek temple and the Roman forum and the medieval cathedral were highly practical things, closely related to the ideals of the society that sponsored them.

It was not my intention to join a chorus against Henry James, but the fact that he is your friend does not alter the fact that he was an artist who understood or sympathized with the European or traditional ideals without comprehending his own country. He happens to be very useful to me in bringing out the fact that there was little basis in raw America on which to rear the ideals of the metropolitan arts. Personally, I prefer to throw in with Walt Whitman and Mark Twain, though I admit that Mark was a little rude in referring to the images in European cathedrals and cemeteries as "trade-marked angels." The gap between Whitman and Twain on the one hand and Henry James on the other is a gap in ideals, and what I am trying to do is to bridge it with a little understanding. I realize that I am going to catch hell from several quarters, but I have made up my mind to take that risk for the reason that I think I have something to say that may be important. At any rate, I am having a good deal of fun in saying it, and whatever you and I at this time on the clock can find fun in is worth our doing. If you have any ideas of what we may do together comes spring, let's have them.

Sincerely yours,
W. P. Webb

February 26, 1952

Dear Webb:

In my "criticism" I didn't tell you how much I enjoy your general style of writing—especially the *ease,* or that quality which Aldous Huxley calls "dynamic relaxation," which keeps one pleasantly alert but not to the point of tension, and still avoids somnolent passages which puts the lazy reader such as I to sleep.

Yours,
Bedi

July 24, 1952

Dear Bedi:

I am sending you a copy of the *New Zealand Listener* because I think the article on American sports on p. 6 may be useful, and the page on the octopus on p. 8 may interest you as a nature observer. Also, I am struck with the clarity with which these New Zealanders write. I know of few publications with articles as easy to read as most anything these boys write about. Their touch is light, their lines of thinking are straight, and the result is a smooth clarity. For example, read "Corridors in the Sky" as an example on a subject that you and I are not too familiar with. The general style in this seemingly ephemeral magazine-newssheet is better than that in the *Saturday Review of Literature* and almost on a par with *The New Yorker,* the best in the country.

This matter of style always interests me, and the manner in which the English, and even the benighted New Zealanders, bring it off irritates me and makes me envious. It seems to me that they have the ability to *see* exactly what they are talking about, or writing about, and that they are able to shut out all extraneous material, which seems constantly to get in our way. They write as if what they are writing about is the only thing in the world and therefore something to which they can give their whole attention. Also they make no effort to be sensational, to shock the senses. You will find on p. 16 another piece from this Sundowner who must be a most unusual person, even in New Zealand.

What would you say is the secret of the N.Z. style? Or am I imagining things? I only know that I can read this rather specialized paper devoted to something that is no hobby of mine—radio—with a great deal of interest. Why?

Yours,
Webb

December 1, 1952

Dear Bedi:

I was relieved to have your letter this morning and to learn that your reason for absence was mere forgetfulness, something I can well understand. It kept coming back to me that in a considerable crowd there was no Bedi, and I began to run over my sins of omission and commission to see if I could figure out why you were remaining in your tent. I could not blame anyone for doing it because such occasions are often a little difficult for all concerned. This one was characterized by very brief talks and was not too sticky, owing to the character of the performers, who are not noted for sentimentalism.

This morning I received my shipment of the books, and soon I'll be getting a copy to you. Of course it would have been a fine thing if the book had been out and especially if every person present could have been pressured into purchasing a copy, or maybe two. The result is that this morning I have more books and more friends, which on the face of it, seems to make me a double gain.

I think you can chalk one up for Joe Frantz,[30] who presided. Joe is a young member of this department, and if you don't recall him I will remind you that he wrote *Gail Borden*. Dr. Rainey[31] was in the audience, and on his own hook, Joe asked him to say something, which he did. I think that shows a rare courage for a young man.

Your talk about your wood problem reminded me of what my friend Frank Spiller[32] said, namely, that the insurance companies and the termites are taking the country. As to your problems collateral to your wood problems, I can give you no comfort, but I damn sure can extend you my sympathy.

Yours,
Webb

MORNING REFLECTION OF MAN WRITING BOOK

I turn on light. I make fire in stove. I sharpen pencils—six nice soft pencils. I lay out scratch pad. I uncover typewriter and brush out type. Everything all set. All I need now is brains. God, have you done your part?

R.B.

February 4, 1954
4:15 A.M.

Austin, Texas
10/28/55

Dear Bedi:

I am writing a book on the West. I have a paragraph on the line of cleavage between Eastern birds and Western birds.

I make the point that since Texas bridges from east to west, and provides a funnel to the south, it is a natural flyway. I also state that as a consequence bird watchers can observe more species and more varieties in Texas than in any other state in the Union (or maybe in a large group of states). To illustrate my point, I want to list birds that can be seen in Texas. I would like species and varieties separated, and I would like for some of both to carry as their common designation the modifier "Eastern" or "Western."

Also, could you tell me how many birds Oberholser found in Texas? Would you also give me the correct name of Dr. O., and the correct title of his manuscript, so that I can make reference to him. I have the necessary data on you. I have looked in your *Naturalists,* but find it has no index, and no chapter suggests such prosaic facts. You evidently wrote the book to be enjoyed, and not to be used by another author out on a thieving expedition.

Don't give me all the birds, but give me some with character. Five or six varieties and as many species will be ample. Trusting that your coporostic congaciates as usual, I now put myself under obligations for a short cut—to what?

Yours,

Webb

June 23, 1956

Dear Dobie:

As I have told you, I am tinkering with a kind of auto-biography, titled *Memories, Chiefly of Animals*. I have only about 10,000 words written, but a lot of notes, scribbled here and there and stuffed away in places where I know I shall eventually run across them. I find in my earliest memories a cow; then a dog, bees, a boar, horse—the same species recurring in different individuals. Along down the line, only about fifty years ago, I find a note of the longhorn cow lifting her newborn calf to suckage with curved tip of horn, circa 1898–1903 on either D-cross or Sherrod Ranch. If and when this autobiography is ever published, I should like it to come as fresh as possible, and hence I would prefer that you not use the longhorn-cow-and-calf story until I have definitely given up my project.

I find another note which I should like to submit to you for your judgment:

"An Autobiography of Relationships. Under this head one could tell as much or as little of his life as he chooses, and still make a clean breast of it, as:

With medical profession	With newspapers
" legal "	" ranchmen
" teaching "	" boosters
" dogs	" hogs
	" domestic animals
	" wild animals

as a peddler salesman   etc., etc.

Really, every man's life is a series of relationships. No man's life is an island."

For illustration, I think I have told you a few of my experiences with doctors—all that could be included; so with newspapers, teaching and teachers, and so on.

Yours,
R.B.

Austin, Texas
October 20, 1956

Dear Bedi:

Don't postpone writing Lee Barker.[33] Get those plates if his publishing firm is not going to reprint. A man's "lifeblood" can be dried up by a publisher as well as by a censor. I got plates to *Tongues of the Monte* from Doubleday when they cut down on the book.

Dobie

XI. Westward Slopes

In their later years, as their letters frequently show, all three were concerned with problems of death and immortality, or lack of it. All three had been brought up in Christian surroundings, but had long since forsaken any formal religion. All three preferred a Sunday morning in the woods to a Sunday morning in church.

In February 1952, Dobie, in response to a request from Edward R. Murrow of the Columbia Broadcasting system, stated:

I believe in a Supreme Power, Unknowable and Impersonal, whose handiwork the soul-enlarging firmament declares—and the more science illuminates the universe, the more enlarging to contemplators does it become. My belief in this Supreme Power, however, has no effect on my conduct so far as hope for reward or fear of punishment hereafter is concerned. What we believe, so I think, makes no difference to this Power, although it makes all difference to the believers and to society.

I believe in questionings, doubtings, searchings, skepticism more than I believe in credulity or blind faith. The progress of man is based on disbelief of the commonly accepted. The noblest minds and natures of human history have thought and sung, lived and died, trying to budge the *status quo* towards a larger and fuller status. I am sustained by a belief in evolution—the "increasing purpose" of life in which the rational is with geological slowness evolving out of the irrational, beyond the prejudiced, and above the merely instinctive. To believe that goodness and wisdom and righteousness in Garden of Eden perfection lie somewhere far ahead instead of farther and farther behind gives me hope and somewhat explains existence. This is a long view. I do not pretend that it is always present in me. It raises me when I have it, however, and I remember Emerson's cry: "Patience, patience, with the shades of all the good and great for company."

Bedichek talked about his own belief in an interview:

I don't have what's commonly called religion. I think I must have a kind of a nature religion. I feel sometimes that the whole of life is—God is the whole—life in every manifestation is a manifestation of a part of God. Some kind of nature religion. It's very hazy in my mind. I wouldn't know how to write it but even less talk it. Never tried to write it out. I never could sit down and say what I believe. Of course, I have no thought that there is anything after a person dies; that is, any individual what Walt Whitman calls identity after death.

The last time I saw Bedichek, a year before he died, he had not changed his mind. He had come to New York for a visit and stayed overnight at my house for a bird walk on Tallman Mountain and along the Hudson. It was an unusually cold day in April and we talked by the fire more than we walked, though we walked enough to suit me, with him striding ahead of me up and down mountain trails and along the edge of a marsh, making abrupt and noiseless stops at the flight of a wing or the sound of a call.

That afternoon I took him to the 125th Street station in Manhattan. I never saw him again. May 20, 1959, he wrote me a chiding but forgiving letter. May 21 he died at noon.

As Mrs. Bedichek told me the story, he had planned to go to Dobie's Paisano Ranch for an outing and picnic with Dobie and Wilson Hudson. She was baking corn bread for lunch and it was not quite ready. She asked if he wanted to wait. "Yes, I'll wait," he said. "I want corn bread. I need corn bread." He died sitting in a chair and without another word. Dobie wired me: "Bedi died today without having been out of life five minutes."

At the funeral, I am told, Dobie, one of the pallbearers, sat on the aisle. Every time the minister spoke of everlasting life Dobie said, "No, no," in a voice loud enough to be heard all around him.

On March 8, 1963, I went to see Dobie at his home on Waller Creek in Austin. He inscribed a book to me as the editor of Bedichek's letters, and again affirmed his affection for Bedichek. Over a drink, he asked me if Bedichek ever talked about religion, if he talked about what he believed. He became explicit. Did Bedichek believe in life after death? I told him what I remembered from the tapes and he seemed satisfied.

Our talk turned to other things. I told him how much I had been influenced by *The Purple Land* and *Far Away and Long Ago*. He wanted to show me his collection of books by W. H. Hudson. I did not have time, nor did he, as he was going out to dinner. There would be time the next week. I had made a date to meet Webb for lunch on Monday and would call Dobie in the afternoon.

I never saw Dobie again, nor Webb. While Dobie and I were talking, Webb had died on the Austin-San Antonio highway, in an automobile accident.

Dobie died in his sleep September 23, 1964.

A short while before his death Bedichek said to Mrs. Bedichek, "Is this all there is to life?" She told me her reply: "That's all there is. There ain't no more."

All of life, perhaps, but not all of living. Webb had written years before:

What do words mean? The subject has always fascinated me, since I was a kid. There they lie, all of them in the dictionary, and yet in most hands they are dead, inanimate. Yet others have a photoelectric cell, a brain which when stimulated causes these words to leap to life and come in trains, in a million formations, creating all the glory and misery that man has known.

Their work was to pick the words that would leave a living record of a way of life that will not repeat itself.

> Austin, Texas
> December 16, 1944

Dear Webb:

I choose to remind you again (apropos of nothing) of the wisdom of a resolution we made on return from that nightmare land of the Big Bend a few years ago—that resolution to do something every so often utterly illogical, do it on whim or fancy, as for instance, striking out afoot to San Marcos, bedding up for the night anywhere along the road where accommodations were available—or taking plane to Brownsville—or camping a few days on Walnut Creek in worst days of winter. You'll recall we figured out a dozen irrational things to do just because they were irrational. But we've never done a one. In Thomas Mann's *Magic Mountain,* the author insists on divisions of time, occasions (as Christmas), routine, discomforts (as holding thermometer in mouth seven minutes—seems an hour)—all this continued insistence throughout the book on *divisions* of time is, in my opinion, for the purpose of emphasizing the *essential emptiness of the time concept.* It is the *content* of time that matters—all else is mere illusion. Artificial markings, as clocks, calendars, etc., have no significance. Poets often enlarge on this—cf. Browning's *Last Ride Together.* In short, my dear sir, slipping into a featureless routine is really slipping into death. And are we not, as Paul said, really "dying daily"?

Selah.
Bedichek

December 6, 1945

Dear Webb:

The lines you quote are impressive:

> But at my back I always hear
> Time's winged chariot drawing near.[1]

Your comment is deeply philosophic. Instead of being an historian, you should have been a philosopher. You have genuine philosophic insight, but not a professionally cultivated one. But maybe the professional philosophers would have sealed up the outlets of your intuitive wisdom. I have always contended that you are somewhat of a psychic.

The couplet you quote started me digging into my capacious memory for a couplet or two from a poem by some early American rhymester, maybe Bret Harte, maybe John Hay, maybe someone else—no matter. My digging, as usual, exhumed only the concluding lines, which run

> A few swift years and who can show
> Which dust was Bill and which was Joe.[2]

A few more days of digging and the digger brought up another fragment:

> . . . Ah, pensive scholar, what is fame?

This, you see, is a query and must have an answer. So searching the cubbyholes of deposits jumbled and overlaid with dust, I uncovered the title of a poem,

Lines to a Dying Athlete

but nothing came of it for a day or two, and then while I was taking a bath and thinking of what a mess of a winter garden I have, this couplet popped up uncalled:

Silence sounds no worse than cheers
After the earth has stopped his ears.

Do you notice that the rhyme of this is almost identical with the rhyme of your couplet? What strange alchemy goes on in the memory.

Still I knew this was a wrong scent—true it is in the same vein, but I knew that it didn't answer, except by indirection, the query, "Ah, pensive scholar, what is fame?"

Then I decided to give it up and write to the "memory" column of the NY *Times* and get the answer. But I was busy and put off writing. It kept ding-donging in my memory, "What is the rhyme for fame?" Finally "flame" came. It must be flame, but get the line I could not, so I decided to build up a line of my own, but with the figure the poet used clearly before me, that is, a comparison of "fame" to "flame." I got this poor line: "A sudden lift of leaping flame" and I repeated it aloud with dissatisfaction:

Ah, pensive scholar, what is fame?
A sudden lift of leaping flame.

Mighty sorry! No poet of any tunefulness would use it, but I knew the comparison was right. Then since the last couplet of the poem first dug up mentions "dust," another comparison of fame to dust must be next, and it came without much trouble:

> A giddy whirlwind's fickle gust
> That lifts a pinch of mortal dust.

So I think I have it, that is, the concluding three couplets. There is leading up to these three couplets a short life history of Bill and Joe! One a "pensive scholar" and the other a hail fellow well-met who takes life and life's joys and sorrows in his healthy stride.

> Ah, pensive scholar, what is fame?
> A slender tongue of leaping flame,
>
> A giddy whirlwind's fickle gust
> That lifts a pinch of mortal dust—
>
> A few swift years and who can show
> Which dust was Bill and which was Joe.

You can see what a burden and what superhuman exertion your suggestion put upon me that we are no longer friendly in the mails, or even neighborly, because

> Always at our backs we hear
> Time's winged chariot hurrying near.

I am afraid Toynbee[3] is too much for me. I have read your review in the Dallas *News*. It makes a stimulating introduction to the great man's work, but I hear "Time's winged chariot." I must stick to my humble knitting, and try to understand simpler things than the reasons for the fall, rise, endurances, and diseases of twenty-five or thirty civilizations since they began recording themselves in enduring and legible form. What does Toynbee say of the Minoan civilization, whose record recently discovered has not yet been deciphered?

Don't give yourself any more concern over my arrogance. It is definitely on its way out.

As ever, affectionately,
Bedi

Austin, Texas
December 1, 1952

Dear Webb:

A certain old man with whom I was not-by-choice closely associated for some years became a victim of a brain cancer. He gradually got to forgetting little things. He explained to me this failing memory on the ground that he was now able in his maturer years to concentrate on important problems and so was fortunately losing the power of recalling where he had put his hat, how long he had been talking to a class after the bell, or when the class was supposed to begin, or whether or not his bowels had moved that morning. The mind, he said, couldn't be burdened with such details along with a genuine concentration of which he was now capable after years of rigorous mental discipline. He often confided to me that, as a consequence, several world problems were now on the verge of solution. But the cancer, slowly encroaching upon brain areas, gradually rendered him incapable of remembering the great problems as well as the trivia of everyday life with which little minds busy themselves.

The doctors tried an operation, which only prolonged and intensified the agony until death took over.

When I found that I had clean forgot the reception honoring you the other day (Wed. Nov. 26), I immediately derived comfort from the old man's theory, but without remembering whence I had derived the theory or its gruesome finale.

I said to myself this lacuna in the memory doubtless comes of thinking too hard upon something really important, of "concentrating on the immediate purpose of all action," as Plutarch puts it.

Truth is, the termite man had told my wife that if she didn't get rid of all that old stovewood, rotten lumber, and kindling lying about, termites would eat our house down, and he couldn't be responsible any longer. She passed the word on to me with her usual exaggerations and with unusual emphasis, which is saying a good deal. I thereupon began to busy myself with the problem, not having the money with which to employ some half-witted yardman. The problem, as I tackled it, was not simply to dispose of waste material. I am a pioneer and can't stand to see wood of any kind carted off or burned up. The termite man had said that if this stuff were lifted off the ground and rested on a stone or metal foundation the wood-hungry insects would be completely frustrated. But no piece of wood, he warned, must be left in touch with the earth. One inch of contact ruins the whole pile and spreads the pest to every wooden building round about, like the proverbial rotten apple in a barrel of good ones.

This was a problem in construction which I was not qualified by training, experience, or physical prowess to solve, and still I didn't want the house converted into fecal matter from a horde of pestiferous insects. So I set myself with my accustomed courage to consider and meet the terrific challenge. All this commotion occurred in the early part of last week.

First, I took an inventory of all the material on the place which might be used in defense of my home and fireside. Having gotten this inventory thoroughly in mind, I set my imagination to work building up before my mind's eye an adequate structure. After hours of mental effort, "burningly it came upon me all at once." I was as one possessed; indeed, I was possessed. I had an engagement in Ft. Worth on Nov. 28, and the two days preceding I worked, materializing my brain child—thinking, measuring, nailing, wheelbarrowing, and in other activities mental and physical too numerous to mention. At last it was done. All the wooden waste on the old home place was stored on a stone foundation where, according to the termite man, the termites, try as they may, cannot get at it.

Although (doubtless due to a clerical error) I had received *two* invitations, I worked on through the afternoon hours of the 26th, sublimely unconscious of what was going on over at the Eugene Barker Texas History Center.

I remembered it on the bus en route to Ft. Worth some 18 hours after it had occurred, my memory even then aided by the account on an inside page of the *Austin-American*. Not much of an account, either—just a cub reporter's report, written, as I used to write up such affairs, entirely from the data in a previously published announcement of what was *going* to occur. Still it was enough to remind me of what had happened, and to set me congratulating myself on finally mastering the art of concentration, on how at last I could bring all my powers of mind, body, emotion, and will to bear upon the important things of life. This set me to speculating rather pleasantly upon how, even at my advanced age, I would still become a great man. And what a disappointment that would be to the evil people who don't like me! I licked this newborn thought over in my mind with relish. Honestly, it was more flavorsome than the cognate thought of how much pleasure it would be to my family and friends. It was only as these two satisfactions were fading out that I thought with the chill of terror of the old man who was, a short time before his demise, congratulating himself on the same identical ability and indulging the same dreams, when the brutal fact was that a rather lively cancer was mutilating the brain cells responsible for those mental images we call memory. Not of fire and brimstone but of such humiliating disillusionments is the hell set apart for the wishful thinkers.

If it ain't cancer, it's certainly senile degeneracy of some sort.

Yours,

Bedi

P.S. Had I been arranging that function, I think I should have delayed it until the book was on the stands.

R.B.

Austin, Texas
December 11, 1953

Dear Webb:

I like your Dr. Horton[4] very much. He has a large, generous nature, like his handwriting, with clear ideas and a sense of humor. The sop he submits I shall duly memorize.

Old age is a vast subject for an old man to undertake, and yet who but an old man knows old age experientially? A young poet may write,

> And so God evens age with youth
> Tormenting Youth with lies and
> Age with truth.[5]

Sounds good, but it's not so. Youth is often wiser than Age, and Age is often tormented with lies, too. Every age from the womb to the tomb or from erection to resurrection is tormented with lies. The ancient Greek, I know now how old she was when she wrote it, was nearer the tempo of old age, more objective, more witty, certainly more incontrovertible:

> Age is an ill: at least the gods think so
> Or else themselves had withered long ago.[6]

I had a secondhand contact with old age a while back that froze my liver and caused each particular hair to stand on end. A little child led us into this ghastly spectacle, a little girl, with wide, blue innocent eyes, blue like our sky in a clearing norther. She lives nearby and never intrudes but insinuates herself into my company now and then. She is interested in me, God knows why—in fact God *only* knows what sweet innocent thoughts harbor and nestle under that spread of molasses-colored curls.

I was spading up a little garden plot when Susie insinuated herself, this time with two dogs, Boxer and Sheba.

"Haven't seen you lately. Where have you been, Susie?"

"At my grandmother's and Pete is still there."

"How long is Pete to stay away?"

"He's comin' back Saturday, 'cause Grandma has to go to Red Rock and bathe her father."

"Can't her father bathe himself?"

"Oh, no, he can't even turn over in bed."

"My, too bad."

"Yes, it is. The woman who nurses him has to be gone Saturday, and Grandma has to go and bathe him."

"How old is your grandma's father?"

"Eighty-nine."

"My! that's pretty old."

"Yes, and two years ago he fell in the bathtub and broke his hip, and he's been in bed ever since."

"What does he do?"

"Nothing."

"Doesn't he read?"

"No, he can't see."

"Guess he has a radio?"

"No, he can't hear, either."

"Well, that is too bad."

"Yes, it is."

I started spading again, for the matter seemed to be getting worse and my poor attempts at consolation were frustrated every time.

But Susie hadn't told me all. As soon as I stopped to get my breath again, she resumed:

"I was down there last Saturday and saw him."

"You did?"

"Yes; and he began to talk all at once."

"What did he say?"

"I couldn't understand what he said."

"Could anyone understand him?"

"Yes, Grandma could. When we got away, I said, 'Grandma,

what did Great-grandpa say?' She said he began talking about
a convention."

"What convention?"

"I don't know. Just a convention."

I resumed spading, but Susie was full of her subject.

"He has something awful the matter with his knee."

"What is it?"

"Well, they pulled the cover back when I was right at the
bed, and all his knee was bleeding awful."

"What made it bleed?"

"It was all over full of pimples and they itch, and he
scratches the pimples and they bleed—and bleed."

"Susie, your great-grandpa is mighty bad off, I'm afraid."

"And he can't eat either."

"Why not?"

"All his teeth are gone, and if they feed him meat, which
he begs for all the time, it gets stuck in his throat and it
won't come up or go down, either. Just stays there."

"Well, Susie, what on earth does he do without anything to
eat?"

"He just lays there and scratches; they feed him baby food.
You know," she went on after petting her two dogs, very
affectionately, "they have him on one of them beds you can
tilt up and down, so they can make him sit up or lay down,
just by turning a crank."

I spaded on for some little time. Presently Susie, with her
pups struggling in her arms, said, "Mr. Bedichek, what is
'sans'?"

"Sans?"

"Yes, *sans*—you said 'sans' over and over."

"Oh, did I? That's just a byword, Susie, I use when I get
tired."

I must have vocalized unconsciously the lines that were
flowing in the grand meter through my head:

. . . Last scene of all,
What ends this strange, eventful history
Is second childishness and mere oblivion;
Sans teeth, sans eyes, sans taste, sans—everything.[7]

I told Bill Owens this story when he was here and he made me talk it into his tape recorder. And here I have seized upon you, my usual victim, to unload it via typewriter. Please return it, for I want an extra copy besides the carbon I have kept. I want it to be ready to shoot to the next Dr. Pangloss who comes along prating about this being the best of all possible worlds.

Yours,

Bedi

Austin, Texas
November 1, 1956

Dear Webb:

Here's the Maxwell[8] letter.

Activity is not an escape but perhaps a deferment. At any rate, all is lost when activity is lost. I try to keep busy even after any intelligent direction of the business has ceased. I wrote this morning until I became utterly inarticulate. Had I been articulate I doubt much if what I was trying to articulate was worth articulating. But it was busyness.

Albert Gore[9] last night literally lifted me out of my seat. What a handsome, young cavalier he is with a golden voice and a smile as sweet as a girl's!

Wonder what you think of Heinsohn's[10] sermon on Barker.[11] I think it's almost worth dying to have Heinsohn obscure your faults and magnify your virtues with that smooth, caressing language he seems to be master of.

Well, I'll be seeing you tonite.

Bedi

Austin, Texas
February 25, 1957

Dear, dear Dobie:

After I had been about an hour at work this morning, I glanced up and saw the volume *Socrates* you gave me yesterday. I remembered that I had seen some writing on the flyleaf which I didn't take time to read while you were here. I had dismissed it momentarily as a "good wishes" inscription and so had let it escape my attention.

I reached up and got the volume in my hand "just to see." I was affected to tears, and I don't mean metaphorical tears but a real secretion from the lachrymose glands. One got loose from the inner corner of my left eye and it felt wet and warm, so I know they were real.

The old Greeks (bless them) were not ashamed of tears. That shame was a part of the sentimentalism and masculine assumption of superiority of that romanticism which assigned tears to women. I am profoundly affected (stirred emotionally in that nervous plexus situated in the abdomen) by your placing me in a unique position in your affections. Truly, I have felt towards you a friendship I never felt for anyone else except for Harry Steger, who died 44 years ago.

Bless you for recording this where I can turn to it when sometimes: "the world is dark and I a wanderer who has lost his way."

Yours,
Bedi

Austin, Texas
October 10, 1957

Dear Dobie:

I believe that you and I reached our conclusion concerning helpless old age independently of each other and perhaps independently of our reading, or of our listening to the wise. Anyway, it takes a Greek to put it into words that seem to me to leave nothing unsaid:

> Only the base will long for length of life
> that never turns another way from evil.
> What joy is there in day that follows day,
> now swift, now slow, and death the only goal.
> I count as nothing him who feels within
> the glow of empty hopes.[12]

Yours for a long life as long as it is a merry one, or as you say, as long as one can stay "lit up with life."

R.B.

Austin, Texas
June 10, 1958

Dear Bedi:

I am cleaning house, preparatory to entering the new life of retirement. In cleaning up I come upon many dead or dormant memories, things I once thought worth laying aside. The one I send you seems to me to express the philosophy some of us live by, or should.

> Do what thy manhood bids you do;
> From none but self expect applause.
> The noblest lives, and noblest dies,
> Who makes, and keeps, his self-made laws.[13]
>
> Sir Richard Francis

It is really good fun to start over again, to burn some bridges, to be rid of some deadly routine—and the necessity of making decisions affecting others. I have never wanted power, any power other than that of persuasion by the written word. That I have wanted, and the exercise of it I enjoy more than any experience I have ever had.

Yours,
W. P. Webb

Dobie, on the road between Deming and Lordsburg, New Mexico, wrote on a postcard to Bedichek words that can stand for us all when we think of the three friends:

At 6 o'clock in the morning, when the dew, such as there is of it, is on the greasewood—and a dewy memory is in my heart for Bedi—

XII. Acknowledgments; Bibliographies; Notes

This book has been developing since Bedichek presented his correspondence to the University of Texas and the three friends tape-recorded related memoirs. Many have helped me along the way, so many that I am unable to acknowledge all their names. To a few, however, I must express my gratitude.

The three wives—Lillian Greer Bedichek, Bertha McKee Dobie, and Terrell Maverick Webb—have been especially generous in allowing me to present the letters together in order that the continuity of their friendship might be demonstrated by their correspondence. They have also been generous with their time when I have called on them for additional information about their husbands.

Rodney J. (Cap'n.) Kidd was Athletic Director of the Interscholastic League during the time I worked in Bedichek's office. He succeeded Bedichek as Director. He bought Friday Mountain Ranch from Webb and turned it into a summer camp for boys. Out of his associations with the three friends he has a valuable store of information, which he generously shared with me.

My special thanks go also to Ronnie Dugger, who in special editions of *The Texas Observer* brought together the record of the three men as seen by their friends. Ronnie Dugger has now printed these records in a handsome book entitled *Three Men in Texas.* This book was essential to me. It remains a valuable aid to those who want to know how Bedichek, Dobie, and Webb were regarded by those whose lives they touched.

Professor Wilson M. Hudson of the University of Texas was waiting to go to the country for the afternoon with Bedichek and Dobie when he got word that Bedichek was dead. Out of the richness of his knowledge of the three friends he has given valuable advice and suggestions for this book.

Dr. Llerena Friend, historian, editor, and Librarian in the Eugene C. Barker Texas History Center Library at the University of Texas, gave generously of her time and of her remarkable knowledge of Texas history. Her close association with the three friends made her contribution unique.

Miss Kathleen Blow, Chief Reference Librarian of the University of Texas library, who often helped Bedichek in his research, located many of the quotations for me, a generous contribution.

Dr. Chester V. Kielman, Archivist for the University of Texas, assisted me greatly by organizing the letters that appear in this volume and by providing photocopies of material as I needed them. In addition, he was of considerable help in identifying many of the persons whose names appear in the letters.

I wish to thank my wife, Ann, for helpful editorial suggestions, and my daughter, Jessie Ann, for helping prepare the manuscript.

My editor, Miss Margaret Cousins, is a graduate of the University of Texas, where she studied under Dobie and Webb. Her knowledge of the men and their work was extremely helpful both in the organization of the material and the tone of the introductory essays. The title is hers, and, for me, a happy one.

BIBLIOGRAPHIES

Space does not permit listing the many works of these men. It is essential, however, to list their books.

BEDICHEK

Adventures with a Texas Naturalist, 1947
Karankaway Country, 1950
Educational Competition, 1956
The Sense of Smell, 1960

DOBIE

A Vaquero of the Brush Country, 1929
Coronado's Children, 1931
On the Open Range, 1931
Tongues of the Monte, 1935
Tales of the Mustangs, 1936
The Flavor of Texas, 1936
Apache Gold and Yaqui Silver, 1939
John C. Duval: First Texas Man of Letters, 1939
The Longhorns, 1941
Guide to Life and Literature of the Southwest, 1943
A Texan in England, 1945
The Voice of the Coyote, 1949
The Ben Lilly Legend, 1959
The Mustangs, 1952

WEBB

The Texas Rangers: A Century of Frontier Defense, 1935
Divided We Stand, 1937

The Great Frontier, 1952
More Water for Texas, 1954
The Story of the Texas Rangers, 1957

NOTES

I.   A TRUCKLOAD OF LIVING

1. No other identification of X.
2. J. Frank Dobie, "For Years We Three Sat To-
    gether," in *Three Men in Texas,* edited by Ronnie
    Dugger, p. 99.
3. Tom Lea, Texas writer and painter.

II. PIONEERS OF BRUSH AND PLAIN

1. I am indebted to J. Frank Dobie's *Some Part of
    Myself* for much of the information in this passage.
2. Dobie, *Some Part of Myself,* p. 13.
3. Walter Prescott Webb, "The Search for William
    E. Hinds," *Harper's* magazine, July 1961, p. 62.
4. Ibid.
5. Interview with Bedichek and Webb taped August
    18, 1953. Webb later used the material in this
    interview for "The Search for William E. Hinds."
6. Webb, "The Search for William E. Hinds," p. 63.

III. SCHOOL BELLS AND THE VARMINT'S CRY

1. Mrs. Anna J. Pennybacker, *A New History of
    Texas for Schools.*

2. Dobie, *Some Part of Myself,* p. 26.
3. Ibid., p. 29.

IV. UP TO THE UNIVERSITY

1. James Francis Greer, Professor of Latin Language and Literature; later Bedichek's father-in-law.
2. James E. Ferguson, a former Governor of Texas.
3. Dobie, *Some Part of Myself,* p. 141.
4. Ibid., p. 236.
5. Webb married Jane Elizabeth Oliphant September 16, 1916. She died June 27, 1960. He married Mrs. Maury Maverick, Sr., December 14, 1961.

V. MAVERICKS ROAM THE FORTY ACRES

1. Pompeo Coppini, sculptor of the Littlefield Fountain at the University of Texas and the Alamo Cenotaph, both of which drew Dobie's ire.
2. Dobie, *A Texan in England,* p. 19.
3. Eugene C. Barker, Professor of History, University of Texas.
4. Interview taped August 18, 1953.
5. Mody C. Boatright, "A Mustang in the Groves of Academe," in *Three Men in Texas,* edited by Ronnie Dugger, p. 192.
6. Augustus Delafield Zanzig, Associate Professor of Music, University of Texas.
7. William M. (Tudey) Thornton, Austin correspondent of the Dallas *Morning News.*
8. Orville Bullington, member of the University of Texas Board of Regents.
9. Ashbel Smith, first chairman of the University of Texas Board of Regents.

10. Thomas J. Devine, member of the University of Texas Board of Regents.

11. Smith Ragsdale, member of the University of Texas Board of Regents.

12. Coke Stevenson, a former Governor of Texas.

13. Homer Price Rainey, President of the University of Texas, 1939–44.

14. Frederic Duncalf, Professor of History, University of Texas.

15. Theophilus Schickel Painter, Acting President of the University of Texas, 1944; President, 1946.

16. Robert Weldon Stayton, Professor of Law, University of Texas.

17. James R. Parten, former chairman of the University of Texas Board of Regents.

18. Robert Lee Bobbitt, former attorney general of the state of Texas.

19. Benjamin Floyd Pittenger, former Dean of the University of Texas College of Education.

20. John William Calhoun, comptroller of the University of Texas and president *ad interim* 1937–39.

21. Eugene C. Barker, see V., 3.

22. William James Battle, Professor of Greek, University of Texas.

23. James Anderson Fitzgerald, Dean of the University of Texas School of Business Administration.

24. James C. Dolley, Vice-President of the University of Texas, 1947.

25. J. Alton Burdine, a former Vice-President of the University of Texas.

26. Dudley K. Woodward, member of the University of Texas Board of Regents.

27. James Pinckney Hart, Chancellor of the University of Texas.

28. Milton R. Gutsch, Professor of History, University of Texas.

VI. FRIDAY MOUNTAIN BOYS

1. Leon Green, Professor of Law, University of Texas.
2. Rodney J. Kidd, athletic director of the Inter-scholastic League and successor to Bedichek as director. He entered into a partnership with Webb to run a boys' camp at Friday Mountain Ranch and eventually bought the ranch from Webb.
3. Thomas H. Shelby, Dean of Extension, University of Texas.
4. Ed Seyers, Austin newspaperman and publicity director.
5. Theophilus Schickel Painter, see V., 15.
6. Mrs. H. Y. Benedict, widow of a former President of the University of Texas.
7. Odie Minatra, assistant director, Texas State Department of Public Welfare; a resident of Cedar Valley.
8. George William Curtis, *The Howadji in Syria,* p. 227.
9. H. Bailey Carroll, director of the Texas Historical Association. This letter was included because Webb meant it also for Bedichek.
10. Lewis J. Ireland, a wholesale dealer in oils in Austin.
11. Sarah Bedichek Pipkin, Bedichek's daughter. Bedichek had two other children: a daughter, Mary, and a son, Bachman.
12. Alton Parker (Tony) Thomason, poet and instructor in English at the University of Texas.

VII. TALK SWAPPING

1. James Edwin Pearce, Professor of Anthropology and director of the Memorial Museum at the University of Texas.
2. Otha Frank Dent, one of the commissioners of the Texas Water Rights Commission.
3. Ruth Dodson, Mathis, Texas.
4. Dana Brackenridge Casteel, Professor of Zoology, University of Texas.
5. Osmond P. Breland, Professor of Zoology, University of Texas.
6. Ellen D. Schulz, author of *Texas Wild Flowers*.
7. Jesse Jones, Houston financier and former Secretary of Commerce.
8. Drew Pearson, newspaper columnist.
9. Bob Snow, a Texas game warden.
10. Sam Rayburn, U.S. congressman from Texas.
11. Woodward, see V., 26.
12. Charles Tilford McCormick, Dean of the University of Texas Law School.

VIII. TEXANS ABROAD

1. Burdine, see V., 25.
2. Freddy Duncalf, see V., 14.
3. G. W. Stumberg, Professor of History, University of Texas.
4. Dr. R., see V., 13.
5. Robert D. Mason, official with Dun & Bradstreet.
6. Melvin Joseph Maas, U.S. congressman from Minnesota; colonel in the U. S. Marine Corps in the South Pacific.
7. Cordell Hull, Secretary of State.

8. François Darlan, Ministre de la Marine, France.
9. Dorothy Thompson, writer and newspaper columnist.
10. Kenneth Crawford, writer.
11. Wendell Willkie, Republican presidential candidate, 1940.
12. Winston Churchill, Prime Minister of Great Britain.
13. Franklin Delano Roosevelt, President of the United States.
14. Joseph Stalin, Premier of the Soviet Union.
15. Edward R. Murrow, radio commentator.
16. Harry Steger, friend of Bedichek; *The Letters of Harry Payton Steger 1899–1912,* published by the Ex-Students' Association of the University of Texas, 1915.
17. Jack Wise, land supervisor and tourist camp owner along the Santa Helena Canyon.
18. Harry Steger, see VIII., 16.
19. Calhoun, see V., 20; papers referred to are "The Privy Papers of Sitting Bull."
20. Sarah Bedichek Pipkin, see VI., 11.
21. George B. Dealey, publisher of the Dallas *Morning News.*
22. John Henry Faulk, writer and radio performer from Austin, Texas.
23. Harry Steger, see VIII., 16.
24. George B. Dealey, see VIII., 21.
25. Mrs. Connie Hagar, Rockport, Texas.
26. Barker, see V., 3.
27. M. H. Crockett, Austin real estate dealer.
28. Lloyd Gregory, Houston newspaper columnist.
29. Wilbur Lee O'Daniel, former Governor of Texas.
30. John Avery Lomax, folklorist and writer.

31. Edgar Witt, former lieutenant governor of Texas, and chairman of the Indian Claims Commission.
32. Ruth Johnson Kyle, social secretary in a women's dormitory, University of Texas.
33. Barker, see V., 3.
34. Bernard De Voto, writer.
35. Maco Stewart, member of the University of Texas Board of Regents.
36. Lewis Valentine Ulrey, secretary to Maco Stewart.
37. Dolley, see V., 24.
38. Leonidas W. Payne, Professor of English, University of Texas.
39. Paul Boner, Professor of Physics, University of Texas.
40. H. Y. Benedict, a former President of the University of Texas.
41. Rainey, see V., 13.
42. W. W. M. Splawn, a former President of the University of Texas.
43. Edgar Kincaid, ornithologist and nephew of Bertha McKee Dobie.
44. Rainey, see V., 13.
45. William Wordsworth, "Peter Bell," Part I, stanza 15.
46. Lomax, see VIII., 30.

IX. A BOOK CORRALLED

1. Walter Prescott, "Dear Bedi:," *Three Men in Texas,* edited by Ronnie Dugger, pp. 84–85.
2. Lorena Drummond, News and Information Service, University of Texas.
3. A. C. Krey, Professor of History, University of Texas and husband of Laura Krey, the novelist.
4. Pictor, perhaps Theophilus Schickel Painter.

5. Barker, see V., 3.
6. Dr. M. F. Kreisle, Sr., an Austin physician.
7. Paul Boner, see VIII., 39.
8. John Henry Faulk, see VIII., 22.
9. Alan Lomax, folklorist and writer; son of John Avery Lomax.
10. Tom Gooch, editor, the Dallas *Times-Herald*.
11. Wallace Garrett, Webb's employee at Friday Mountain Ranch.
12. H. Bailey Carroll, see VI., 9.
13. John Hugh Hill, instructor in history, University of Texas.
14. Duncalf, see V., 14.
15. Frederick Simpich, a writer for the *National Geographic*.
16. Lynn Landrum, columnist for the Dallas *Morning News*.
17. L. J. Struhall, tax consultant in Austin.
18. George Jean Nathan, writer and drama critic.
19. H. L. Mencken, writer and critic.
20. Théophile Gautier, "L'Art," stanzas 1 and 14.
21. The *Spectator,* 1945–48; precursor of *The Texas Observer*.
22. Rodney J. Kidd, see VI., 2.
23. Rainey, Coral M., see V., 13.
24. Mrs. Tullis, Texas Historical Association.
25. Lee Barker, editor at Doubleday.
26. Lomax, see VIII., 30.

X. BOOKS, BOOKS, BOOKS

1. Leonidas W. Payne, Professor of English, University of Texas.
2. Calhoun, see V., 20.

3. Dorothy Thompson, see VIII., 9.
4. Harry Church Oberholser, U. S. Biological Survey.
5. Bachman Bedichek, Bedichek's son.
6. Curtis Walker.
7. Bach, see X., 5.
8. John William Rogers, newspaper writer and critic.
9. Lomax, see VIII., 30.
10. Lomax, see VIII., 30.
11. Charles Wilson Hackett, Professor of Latin-American History, University of Texas.
12. Kidd, see VI., 2.
13. Tom Lea, see I., 3.
14. George Fuermann, columnist for the Houston *Post*.
15. Allen Maxwell, editor of the Southern Methodist University Press.
16. Earl Butler.
17. John Thomas Paterson, Professor of Biology, University of Texas.
18. Angus Cameron, Dobie's editor at Little, Brown Company.
19. Tom Lea, see I., 3.
20. Dudley Dobie, Dobie's cousin.
21. Edward Crane, Professor of Law, University of Texas.
22. Lon Tinkle, book editor of the Dallas *Morning News* and Professor of French, Southern Methodist University.
23. Allen Maxwell, see X., 15.
24. Allen Maxwell, see X., 15.
25. Charles E. Wilson, Detroit financier and former Secretary of Commerce.
26. John A. Kouvenhoven, author of *Made in America: The Arts in Modern Civilization*.
27. *The Rubáiyát* of Omar Khayyam, translated by Edward FitzGerald, stanza 15, 1868 version.

28. K, see X., 26.
29. K, see X., 26.
30. Joe B. Frantz, Professor of History, University of Texas.
31. Dr. Rainey, see V., 13.
32. Frank Spiller, Austin businessman.
33. Lee Barker, see IX., 25.

XI. WESTWARD SLOPES

1. Andrew Marvell, "To His Coy Mistress."
2. Oliver Wendell Holmes, "Bill and Joe."
3. Arnold J. Toynbee, historian; wrote introduction to *The Great Frontier.*
4. Dr. J. J. Horton, Buda, Texas.
5. Unidentified poem.
6. Sappho.
7. Shakespeare, *As You Like It,* Act II, Scene VII.
8. Maxwell, see X., 13.
9. Albert Gore, U.S. senator from Tennessee.
10. Edmond Heinsohn, pastor of the University Methodist Church, Austin.
11. Barker, see V., 3.
12. Sophocles, *Oedipus at Kolonus.*
13. Quotation incorrectly identified by Webb. Sir Richard Burton, *The Kasîdah,* Part ix, stanza 28.